THE
SAN FRANCISCO
EARTHQUAKE

The order was "shoot to kill" all suspected looters (*Moshe Cohen*)

THE
SAN FRANCISCO
EARTHQUAKE

Gordon Thomas and

Max Morgan Witts

STEIN AND DAY/*Publishers*/New York

With great respect, we would like to dedicate this book to all those who were kind enough to grant us an interview, to tell us about themselves and their experiences, and in general to give us the sort of welcome that San Franciscans are famous for.

Without the help and cooperation of all those that follow, this book could not have been written.

1906 Eyewitnesses

Mrs. William Wood Adams
Gwendolyn Applegarth (née Powers)
Jack Applegarth
Robert S. Babin
Marjorie Brown
Bettina Bruckman
Moshe Cohen
George H. Cabannis
Major General James Code (Ret.)
John Conlon, Jr.
Margaret Edith Dawson (née Robertson)
Captain William Figari
Edgar Gleeson
Roy Graves

Ethel Grubb
Hanson Grubb
Harry Hilp
Chingwah Lee
Larry Lewis
Peter Michelson
Geneve Shaffer Parsons
Celia Poitrier
Augusta Politzer
Paul Redenger
William Roddy
Louise Schlaich
Karl Schlaich
Marjorie Shinkel
Frank Sprenger

Today

Mayor Joseph L. Alioto
Disaster Corps Director Edward P. Joyce

Fire Chief William F. Murray
Mac Slee

Contents

List of Illustrations

TODAY

San Francisco today (*San Francisco Convention and Visitors Bureau*)

San Francisco has violated all underwriting traditions and precedents by not burning up.
　　　　—NATIONAL BOARD OF FIRE
　　　　　　UNDERWRITERS, October 1905

The further you are from the last big earthquake, the nearer you are to the next.
　　　　—PERRY BYERLY, Department of
　　　　　　Seismology, University of California

San Francisco, serene, indifferent to Fate.
　　　　—BRET HARTE

IT WILL happen again.

Yet, with a disregard for reality almost beyond comprehension, San Francisco ignores the sentence nature has passed on it. At any given moment, probably with one great convulsive opening of the earth's crust, much of the forty-seven square miles the city occupies will crumble in an avalanche of reinforced concrete, iron, steel, and plate glass. The destruction of San Francisco will be just one of the by-products of a major earthquake somewhere along the San Andreas Fault.

Depending on its strength, duration, and epicenter, San Francisco and its hinterland will be either leveled or raised.

When the moment comes, the earthquake will show no prejudice. It will mete out death equally to white and black, Chinese and Indian. It will level brothels and luxury hotels. Supermarkets, department stores, and banks will be treated as one. Desks, filing cabinets, shelves, and other free-standing items will go first. Then the plate-glass windows will shatter. Even reinforced concrete and steel will be forced to yield. It could be over in a matter of seconds.

Some of the more modern buildings meet present-day building codes. But no building code so far devised can guarantee total protection against even a minor earthquake.

Neither size nor beauty will offer protection against the tremor. The Golden Gate Bridge will be on equal terms with billboards and neon signs urging people to fly Trans World Airlines. San Francisco International Airport can expect to fare no better than the shrimp sellers on Fisherman's Wharf. Churches and synagogues, cocktail

11

lounges and massage parlors, will all be treated on the same basis.

Some experts say the earthquake is overdue. Others, more cautious, calculate it will happen any time during the next hundred years. Most scientists refuse to make a positive prediction. If they did, they contend, it could cause immediate panic. They say that panic can wait.

Perhaps not for long. No one who has made a study of earthquakes will be surprised if it occurs before you finish reading this book.

It will happen in one of three ways: the earth will be displaced either horizontally, or vertically, or—more likely—in a combination of both. The shifting forces, which will course upward twenty or thirty miles through the earth's crust, will, at the breaching point, produce enough destructive power to collapse whole areas of the city.

Over the years several attempts have been made to estimate the energy likely to be generated. In the fifties scientists speculated that the quake would produce enough energy to power the entire U.S. Sixth Fleet at full speed for five hundred years. In the mid-sixties it was compared to the explosive force of ten thousand atomic bombs. A more meaningful comparison might be: if the entire energy force were concentrated on the one-square-mile business section of the city, the whole area would be lifted six thousand feet into the air.

The San Andreas Fault passes within eight miles of the center of San Francisco. It is one of the great fractures of the world, a scar that runs most of the length of California. For years now, pressure has been steadily mounting along the fault. Whole areas of California have been slowly moving as a result of the strain.

Three times the bedrock found the pressure too great to withstand. Then, when the three major earthquakes occurred, the area was sparsely populated. Most of the rupture ran through beaches, fields, valleys, and hillsides. Today these areas are thickly populated. On the average, one thousand people settle on or near the San Andreas Fault each day. Nowhere in the United States is the density of population greater than in San Francisco and its environs. Nowhere is disregard of the danger more apparent.

For more than ten years, the experts—the seismologists, the geologists, the structural and civil engineers—have warned the city of the impending disaster. They have recommended that the height of buildings be limited and the locating of new housing developments be carefully planned. The advice is usually politely received, but all too often it is rejected under the influence of the profit motive.

To cope now with the experts' predictions, San Francisco has a Disaster Corps Director. He is the man the experts can talk to, while the rest of the city gets on with the real business of living.

His office is located in the downtown area, where the greatest effect of the earthquake will undoubtedly be felt. His salary is $1400 a month, little more than a topless waitress in one of the city's bars makes in tips. He has a staff of fifteen, a budget of $160,000, and an Emergency Operations Plan to meet the aftermath of a major earthquake. He is a reasonable, sincere, and practical man. When the tremor comes, he says, he will face a number of rather bizarre problems—for example, the conversion of local buses into motorized morgues and ambulances to carry away the dead and the dying. He estimates that casualties could total up to 350,000.

If San Francisco is worried about such grim predictions, it hides its fears well as it expands. Every year the city pushes deeper into the great Bay. Tower blocks of offices and apartments rise from foundations of dumped rubble. Thirty years ago San Francisco Bay occupied over seven hundred square miles of sea; today it takes up less than four hundred.

By late 1970, San Francisco was experiencing an unprecedented building boom; fourteen new hotels, three new motels, and major additions to five existing hotels and motels were under construction. Developers had built or were planning model suburbs, schools, parking lots, and cemeteries beside and even across the San Andreas Fault. Giant corporations build on shaky bases downtown (witness the Bank of America's fifty-two-story world headquarters building and the Trans America Corporation 840-foot skyscraper), while the more modest build on hillsides on either side of the fault. Frequently the developers level out the slopes with imported earth, compounding the danger of slippage.

The high-rise buildings, hillside apartments, and Bay Shore homes all have one thing in common: they are inhabited by people who demand the best possible view. To satisfy them, the developers have enclosed as much of the structures as possible in plate glass. Nobody has yet found a way to make even thirty-two-ounce glass earthquake-proof.

When the big shake comes, the Disaster Corps Director expects that the "glass fallout" from the Bank of America building alone could spread over a quarter of a square mile of densely populated streets, offices, hotels, restaurants, and bars.

Theoretically, no architect, builder, or contractor may build without complying with the California Uniform Building Code on "earthquake-stressing buildings." The code explains what the stresses are, but it gives little guidance in the matter of overcoming them. Many believe the standards—such as they are—are too low.

How unrealistic the standards may be was demonstrated in Caracas, Venezuela, in 1967. An earthquake killed two hundred and seventy-five people in the city; two hundred of them died when the new high-rise apartments they occupied collapsed. Geologists from California discovered that the Caracas apartments were similar in foundation, design, and construction to those built in San Francisco. Even more frightening, they were adjacent to a fault almost identical in behavior to the San Andreas. The Caracas buildings were thought to be earthquakeproof.

Seismologists rated the Venezuela tremor as one of moderate intensity. Some say it was about half the intensity they expect when the San Andreas rips.

When it does there may be a warning. Seagulls along the Bay Shore will probably fly away from the land; the city's dogs and cats may howl and bristle. Such behavior has been noted in previous earthquakes, and while the phenomenon has not been substantiated, scientists cautiously accept the hypothesis that animals frequently sense an approaching earthquake. Then there is the further warning of earthquake "sound": something between a low moan and the distant rumble of a freight train. Evidence from previous earthquakes indicates that these warning signs may occur only seconds before the tremor strikes.

In San Francisco, it is unlikely that many will stand around to count. The warning signs will go unseen and unheard. They will be lost in the clatter of the cable cars; the foghorns on the Golden Gate Bridge; the clamor in Jack's Restaurant; the tooting along North Beach; the wail of fire and police wagons; the tension of black Fillmore Street; the babble of dialects—Russian, Armenian, Jewish, Italian, Greek, Chinese, French, German; the roar of the freeways; the thunder of steam shovels burrowing out a subway system; the mindless commercials on any of the eight television or fifty-nine radio stations; the finger-snapping in the gay bars off Broadway; the murmur of fashionable gossip in the Mark, Fairmont, and Sheraton-Palace Hotels.

The voices of reason—among them Disaster Corps Director Edward Joyce, seismologist Dr. Charles F. Richter, the geologists at the National Center for Earthquake Research at Menlo Park, and structural engineer Karl Steinbrugge—will all have spoken in vain. For San Francisco—incredibly beautiful, corrupt, tolerant, prejudiced—has become dangerously blasé. It has turned a singularly deaf ear to those who predict that when it comes, it will come as it did in April 1906—unexpectedly, rushing up from the Pacific seabed, ripping south at over seven thousand miles an hour, preceded by an uncommonly warm day . . .

TUESDAY
APRIL 17, 1906

Noon to 6 P.M.

Snapshot of Caruso taken on a San Francisco hill hours after he was believed to have fled (*Margaret Dawson*)

A 1906 publicity photograph of Enrico Caruso (*New York Public Library*)

1. Tension Backstage

ENRICO CARUSO WAS angry, but not because of the heat. The anger had been there since the previous night, when he stalked out of the Grand Opera House before the final curtain rang down on *The Queen of Sheba.*

Caruso's anger had in fact been rising and falling for many months, almost as if orchestrated. It rose when he found he was to lead the Metropolitan Opera of New York on tour across America. It fell when the Metropolitan's management agreed to pay him a record $1350 for each performance. But at the end of the winter season, his anger returned. He was exhausted; the manners of his audience infuriated him. "They are bored with everything except themselves, and they talk animatedly to each other right to the final curtain," he confided to fellow singer Antonio Scotti.

He feared that on tour the audiences would be even more callow, even more unappreciative of the subtleties of "Questa o quella" and "La donna è mobile." To Caruso, anything west of New York was "wild"—a gun was still more than a stage prop. When he asked the Metropolitan management to release him from the tour, or at least to shorten it, they firmly refused. Feeling himself trapped, Caruso decided he would need more protection than the insurance policy the opera company had taken out on his life. He bought himself a revolver and fifty rounds of ammunition shortly before the Pullman train carrying the company had rumbled out of New York.

Only as the train sped westward did the tenor realize that he did not even know how to load the weapon. He showed the gun to

Scotti, who for three years had been the Jester to Caruso's Duke of Mantua in Verdi's *Rigoletto*. Scotti recalled that the two men spent their first night on the Pullman together, practicing loading and drawing. By the time the train reached San Francisco, Caruso had become a passable gun handler.

Caruso's relationship with many of his colleagues, never warm, grew positively icy as the train carried them across the prairies of the Middle West, and down through central Nevada, Reno, and Sacramento, and finally to Oakland Pier. There, the inevitable group of reporters waited to accompany Caruso on the last stage of his journey, the short ferry trip across the Bay of San Francisco to the city itself. They seemed to have only one question for the singer: what could he tell them about Vesuvius, in whose shadow he had been born.

The volcano had just erupted. Reports said that the death toll was already over two thousand; thousands more were homeless. In San Francisco itself, the powerful Italian community had organized a relief committee. Caruso, "emotional and patriotic," according to one reporter, offered his services for a charity concert. Turning to the waiting newspapermen Caruso said, "I cannot tell you what Vesuvius is really like. No man can. It is the most frightening experience of all."

Even worse, asked a reporter, than an earthquake? Caruso shrugged. He had never experienced an earthquake, but he doubted that it held more terror than an erupting volcano.

On the ferry trip across the Bay, the tenor confided a somber thought to his conductor, Alfred Hertz. If he had not made the tour, he would be in Naples now, and Naples, according to the afternoon edition of the San Francisco *Examiner,* was threatened with extinction from lava flow. "Maybe it was God's will after all that I should come this far," he said to Hertz.

As the ferry boat docked, Caruso asked the reporters if they knew any place in town that served roast beef and macaroni as an entrée. The newspapermen smiled happily. The thirty-four-year-old Italian looked as if he would provide colorful copy in the days to come.

They had in fact not long to wait. At the Palace Hotel, Caruso was shown to Suite 622. He took one look at the redwood-paneled walls and heavy tan drapes and dismissed it as resembling a funeral parlor. An assistant manager pointed out that General William T. Sherman had once occupied the rooms. Caruso retorted that after marching through Georgia, Sherman would no doubt have been well satisfied with this sort of accommodation.

Caruso was finally installed in Suite 580, once occupied by another American folk hero, General Ulysses S. Grant. The suite consisted of two parlors, furnished in California laurel overlaid with maroon satin. With its French chandeliers, English marble fireplace surrounds, Persian bedspread, and Turkish carpets, the overall effect was something approaching a set for *The Queen of Sheba.*

The hotel staff watched in awe as the seemingly endless shuttle of trunks went up to the Caruso suite. Martino, his valet, spent Monday evening unpacking them. One contained forty pairs of boots; another held fifty self-portraits of Caruso; a third, nothing but dressing gowns; a fourth, silk shirts.

When everything was in place, Caruso, fortified by a bottle of Californian red wine, sang the tenor role of *Carmen.*

In the early hours of the morning, he retired beneath his Persian bedspread, with instructions for Martino to awaken him with the morning papers.

Nine hours later, shortly after midday on Tuesday, those newspapers rekindled Caruso's anger. All three of the city's major newspapers had panned *The Queen of Sheba.* Caruso had not performed on opening night; what hurt him most was that he agreed with the critics—he knew the responsibility would fall on him to redress the balance tonight, when he took the stage in Bizet's *Carmen.*

The thought provoked him to order yet another bottle of wine to be brought up from the hotel's cellar.

From its very conception, the Palace Hotel had been designed to meet the two great natural hazards native to San Francisco: earthquake and fire. To guard against the former, the hotel had been built on massive pillar foundations twelve feet deep. Its outer walls of brick were two feet thick. To give them even greater solidity, they had been reinforced every four feet by double strips of iron bolted together, forming continuous bands. In the end three thousand tons of this reinforcing iron had been woven into the walls. Fire precautions were equally thorough. In addition to the basement tank, seven more, with a firefighting capacity of another 130,000 gallons, had been placed on the roof. Even if the city's reservoirs ran dry, the Palace would be able to protect itself. To distribute this volume of water, five miles of piping had been built into the hotel, quite independent of the normal domestic plumbing system. The piping was connected to three hundred and fifty outlets, to which in turn twenty thousand feet of fire hose were attached.

In the basement were three high-pressure pumps capable of maintaining water pressure at one hundred pounds per square inch. Each of the hotel's eight hundred rooms was fitted with a sensitive automatic fire detector which triggered an alarm in the duty manager's office at the first sign of excessive heat. Finally, a team of watchmen patrolled every floor at thirty-minute intervals. On their rounds they had to touch an electrical impulse button sited at any of the seventy-nine points. If they forgot one, their omission automatically registered in the office.

In its thirty-one years, the hotel had successfully and quickly stifled a number of fires as a result of these precautions.

It was said in San Francisco that if the Palace ever burned down, the city itself would also be gutted.

Police Officer Leonard Ingham had dreamed yet again that the Palace, along with much of the city, had been destroyed by such a fire.

Officer Ingham was a solid and unimaginative man of forty, the sort of policeman who would end his career where it had started—pounding a beat. He and his wife Bess lived on Dolores Street, six blocks from the Mission Police Station, to which he was attached.

For two months, since the nightmares had begun, he had dreaded going on patrol in the Mission district, a cramped cluster of wooden frame houses, factories, and railroad yards. In his dreams they were the first to be gutted. His imaginary fire swept up Market Street, the city's main thoroughfare, and then across it, taking with it not only the Palace Hotel but also most of San Francisco's principal buildings. Finally, totally out of control, it engulfed the city, driving its inhabitants into the sea.

At this point Patrolman Ingham always awakened. Each time he told Bess of his dreams; each time she tried to soothe him. And as the nightmares became increasingly vivid, it took longer for him to fall asleep again.

So real had the dream been on Monday night that he had finally decided to act upon it. He would report his fears to Chief of Police Jeremiah Dinan. Earlier on Tuesday he had been given an appointment to see Chief Dinan at 9:00 Wednesday morning.

He also decided to obtain personal protection for his home, destroyed though it would be according to his dream. He went to the Hartford Fire Insurance Company's office on California Street. There the company's Pacific agent, Adam Gilliland, drew up a two-thousand-dollar fire insurance policy on the Ingham home.

With the policy safely signed and tucked away in his uniform pocket, Patrolman Ingham returned to duty with a new purpose. He viewed buildings not just for their crime potential, but as fire risks. In the interview with Chief Dinan the following morning he planned to reveal his findings.

He did not have to look far. Every district in the city contained a high percentage of wooden buildings. Russian, Nob, and Telegraph Hills, and the predominantly Italian area of North Beach, were built almost entirely of wood. So was the expensive residential quarter between Powell and Van Ness Avenue. The alleys of Chinatown, where forty thousand people lived in appalling squalor, and the streets above—Pacific, Vallejo, Jackson, and Washington—were lined with wooden buildings.

Downtown—south of the Slot—the situation was even more critical for anyone concerned about fire hazard. The Slot was exactly that—a slot in the street between the cablecar tracks which ran along Market Street. The area beyond was a conglomeration of warehouses, factories, small hotels, rooming houses, all crammed together —a pyromaniac's dream. Six times in three years—between December 1849 and June 1851—fire had raged through the district. And each time it had been rebuilt, largely from clapboard. Now one sixth of the city's population lived in the area. Few had insured themselves against the risk of another conflagration.

Ingham found some comfort as he patrolled. The era of the brick-built high-rise building had arrived, crowding the skyline, offering visible proof of San Francisco's claim to be the metropolis of the West.

Yet this afternoon as he patrolled, Leonard Ingham again had the feeling that he was walking through a giant tinderbox—that the flames, when they came, would engulf these splendid structures as well.

Though Ingham did not know it, his fears were shared by the

man primarily responsible for defending the city against such a
holocaust: Dennis Sullivan, Chief of the San Francisco Fire
Department.

In his quarters on the third floor of the Bush Street fire station,
Dennis Sullivan waited, brooding on the progress of a meeting being
held a few blocks away.

The meeting was taking place in the courtroom of Judge W. W.
Morrow in the Hall of Justice—the building where tomorrow morning
Patrolman Ingham planned to relate his nightmare to the Chief of
Police.

Judge Morrow had convened the meeting to prepare for any
future emergency which might arise in San Francisco. At the suggestion of the Mayor, Eugene Schmitz, the Judge had gathered
together a cross section of civic-minded citizens specifically to discuss a report which had haunted Sullivan since he had first seen a
copy of it seven months before.

He had received the report in October 1905, the month it had
been made public by the National Board of Fire Underwriters. It
contained this startling statement: "San Francisco has violated all
underwriting traditions and precedents by not burning up. That it
has not already done so is largely due to the vigilance of the Fire
Department, which cannot be relied upon indefinitely to stave off
the inevitable."

It was the inevitable—the destruction of a city he would be
helpless to save—that Sullivan had fought so bitterly to avoid in
the thirteen years and thirteen days he had been Fire Chief.

This battle had brought him into headlong conflict with Mayor
Schmitz and the city's supervisors. The battle revolved around one
commodity which was plentiful in San Francisco—money.

As soon as he assumed office, twelve years of hard-won firefighting experience behind him, Sullivan began the struggle to wrest
money out of City Hall to provide the firefighting facilities he
deemed essential. He wanted money to build a supplementary salt-
water system; money to reactivate scores of long-neglected cisterns
which had been laid beneath the downtown streets a generation
before; money to buy high explosives and train his men how to use
them to check a major fire.

The War Department in Washington "consented to furnish a

competent corps of engineers and sappers, with the necessary explosives, to be always in readiness at the Presidio," the Army's Pacific garrison on the outskirts of the city. But once more the Mayor and his supervisors thwarted Sullivan. The War Department asked the city to provide one thousand dollars to build a brick vault in the Presidio grounds to house the explosives. City Hall refused to provide the money. Sullivan's plan to have a dynamite squad trained and on hand to meet any emergency was squelched.

The Fire Underwriters report underscored the risk. After a careful and exhaustive survey, the board's engineers found a vital flaw in the firefighting water supply for the city: "Its distributing pipe system is inadequate to meet the demands for water flow necessary to fight a conflagration." But the board could not enforce changes, only inform of the danger.

Armed with the report, Sullivan resumed his assault on City Hall. Seven months later, Mayor Schmitz ordered Judge Morrow to convene his citizens' committee. Sullivan was not scheduled to testify before them until the following day.

Sullivan was not the only man City Hall angered. Brigadier General Frederick Funston, acting commander at the Presidio garrison, was equally furious at the behavior of the civil administration. For he had put pressure on the War Department to accept the Fire Chief's scheme for a dynamite squad, only to have it rejected by Mayor Eugene Schmitz.

That rejection virtually severed further contact between soldier and politician.

Funston had come to San Francisco in 1901, shortly after Schmitz was installed in City Hall. From their first meeting, Funston distrusted the Mayor. "He's too sure, he smiles too quickly and turns away." All his life Funston had judged men by a simple set of rules: they had to be quietly confident and level-headed, and have a firm handshake. Eugene Schmitz failed on all counts.

On the other hand, Fire Chief Sullivan passed muster. Over the years a bond had grown between the two men, based on their desire to further improve the city's fire defenses. Funston admired the qualities of leadership Sullivan brought to the Fire Department; he respected, too, the efficiency of the firemen. Like Sullivan, he was aware of the implications of the Fire Underwriters report. Funston brought his brilliant tactical mind to bear on the problems of defending a city against a future conflagration. But his strategy was voided by the refusal of City Hall to approve Sullivan's dynamite squad. The Fire Chief urged Funston to bring personal pressure on the Mayor. Funston refused; he wanted no contact with Schmitz.

"Yet I love the city and will do anything for it," he confided to Sullivan. "I would take any action if San Francisco was in danger."

He said that in January 1906, when he had last called on the Fire Chief. Since then the Brigadier General had not gone downtown. To his staff officers at the Presidio he stated bluntly that he could not trust himself "not to march into City Hall and throw all those boodlers out!"

It was a reaction typical of Frederick Funston. National hero, Medal of Honor winner, a living legend who had proved himself under fire, he saw things with simple directness. "A problem is black or white," he was fond of saying. The problem at City Hall was black in his eyes.

Having failed the entrance examination to West Point in 1890, Frederick Funston had temporarily abandoned what he believed to be his destiny—becoming an Army officer—to seek adventure as a newspaperman.

The trouble with that job, he told a friend, was "all the reading and listening you have to do." It was adventure he wanted, the more full-blooded and outlandish the better. He joined an expedition to Death Valley. He tramped Alaska five years before the great Gold Rush, and sailed down the Yukon River single-handed.

In between he was building a reputation as somebody not to trifle with. It was not entirely undeserved.

In Kansas he frog-marched the town bully through the streets at gunpoint when the man threatened him with a razor. In front of a crowd outside the sheriff's office. Funston, a mere 120 pounds, thrashed the man in a fistfight. While working as a passenger-train conductor on the Santa Fe Line, he bodily threw off a cowboy he thought was too drunk to travel. When the ranchhand retaliated by hurling a rock through a coach window, Funston chased him on foot across country while the train waited.

But Funston found that a railwayman's uniform did not invest him with the sort of authority he wanted. His yearning to wear military uniform—any military uniform—returned, stronger than ever. Rejected by his own Army, he turned to Cuba, where an insurrection had begun against the Spanish occupiers. Funston hurried to the island and joined the insurgent cause. There he rose to the rank of Lieutenant Colonel in the Artillery.

Twenty-three battles later he returned to America, having survived capture and sentence of death. Almost immediately he was given command of the 20th Kansas Regiment. He led it to the Philippines, where rebels had declared war on the United States.

A series of personal acts of bravery earned him the nickname "Fearless Freddie." His proudest moment came during the great battle of Calumpit on the Rio Grande. Funston's troops were on one bank; the enemy—Filipino revolutionaries—were on the other. There were no bridges. Funston had a raft built and crossed the river under heavy fire, establishing a rope ferry, across which his troops scrambled. It was here that he earned his Medal of Honor and promotion to brigadier general.

In 1901, at the age of thirty-five, with no more wars to fight, and having survived a bullet wound received in the Philippines, he was assigned by the War Department to command the Department of California.

It was a mistake. Funston was ill equipped for the social demands made on one in his position. Small talk, a prerequisite of San Francisco society, consisted for Funston in stories more suitable for an Army barrack. He disliked dancing, high fashion, and fancy manners, all of which the city offered in profusion. He was not an impressive-looking officer; he was little more than five feet tall. His shock of red hair hinted at the explosive temper concealed by his dapper outward appearance.

In spite of all these drawbacks, he was able to capture the heart of one of the West Coast's outstanding society belles. Eda Blankart met Funston in 1898 as he was passing through Oakland on his way to the Philippine war, and in a world gone mad, theirs was a classic love story. They met over afternoon tea at the home of a mutual friend. By evening Funston was madly in love with the gay, blue-eyed Eda. She in turn was captivated by his shyness and old-fashioned courtesy. Within hours he proposed—and she accepted. Just two days after they were married, Funston sailed for Manila; his wife followed twelve days later on a troop ship.

By the time she returned to San Francisco with her husband,

she had become the perfect Army wife. She held tea parties for the wives of senior officers, made regular calls on the families of junior officers, and was always ready to offer advice to the wives of enlisted men on almost any problem.

Her social life revolved around the Presidio garrison. She soon established a reputation as a matchmaker: more than one young subaltern owed a romance with a local belle to an introduction by Eda Funston. An excellent cook, she became famous for her blueberry pie. When her husband was brusque and sharp-tongued to his colleagues and subordinates, Eda would frequently follow with soothing words and a sympathetic ear. Here, too, she showed a degree of skill far beyond her age: although she was understanding, she would never utter, or allow to be said, one word of criticism of anything her husband said or did.

She had made their house on Nob Hill a place of comfortable refuge from the outside world. Like Frederick Funston, his wife had come to detest the wheeling and dealing of City Hall.

"If Freddie ran the city," she often said, "things would be different."

Adam Gilliland, some of his colleagues would have said, spent part of his day behaving illogically for an insurance agent. Since writing up the fire-protection policy for Patrolman Ingham, Gilliland had become fascinated with the policeman's recurring dream.

By late afternoon the nightmare of a devastated city was no longer preposterous to Gilliland.

After a few hours of research, he discovered that the city lay on the great San Andreas Fault, whose existence had been brought to light only thirteen years earlier. The distinguished geologist Andrew Lawson had noted that the Santa Clara, San Benito, and San Francisco Bay valleys were remarkably linear and that the general topography "was marked by tilting and movements that may yet be active." Lawson had named the fault after the San Andreas Lake on the San Francisco Peninsula.

Gilliland discovered that in 1857 the fault had pulled the earth apart, making a gap twenty feet wide and forty miles long before clamping shut again. In 1865, San Francisco, already caught up in the Gold Rush, was rocked to its plank sidewalks. Two tremors cracked open the City Hall and the area along Market Street. Lampposts and water and gas pipes were broken. But there were no deaths. Three years later an even worse earthquake, more directly associated with the other active fault that spells trouble for San Francisco—the Hayward Fault, eighteen miles east of the San Andreas Fault—claimed its first victims in the city. Five persons were killed by falling bricks and glass. Twice more, in 1890 and 1898, the city had been shaken.

Gilliland learned for certain that San Francisco was not the most comfortable place to gamble on the insurance potential of a building—or a life.

For a very different reason, Mayor Eugene Schmitz would have endorsed the sentiment about gambling at the close of this particular working day. For over five years he had gambled that he and Abe Ruef, the local attorney who had plucked him out of the orchestra pit and placed him in City Hall, would never be unmasked in their wholesale grafting.

But now Schmitz sensed that his halcyon days as the political figurehead of the city were numbered. That afternoon he had at last learned that millionaire Rudolph Spreckels, one of San Francisco's most powerful citizens, had, two months ago, made a decisive move. Spreckels had promised one hundred thousand dollars to finance an investigation of City Hall. The money had been instrumental in persuading President Roosevelt to loan a brilliant Secret Service agent, William J. Burns, to gather evidence against Schmitz and Ruef. Already San Francisco's District Attorney, William Langdon—whom Schmitz had personally appointed—had begun collating evidence of bribery and corruption by the two men.

One of the most extraordinary and bizarre chapters in the colorful history of the city's political life was moving toward a climax.

It had begun six years earlier when Abe Ruef—wily, accommodating, ambitious—the product of a middle-class French-Jewish upbringing, had finally made his bid for total political power over the city.

Ruef had bided his time for fourteen years. In that time he had eased himself up the Republican ladder; he had learned the harsh facts of San Francisco's political life—that wheedling, bartering, bribing, and physical violence were the keys to political success. But he had no stomach for rough-housing; for him graft was a delicate, smooth operation, where tracks were always carefully covered. Relying on this blend of well-mannered villainy, Ruef gradually manipulated himself into an impregnable position.

In 1901 he seized his opportunity. The city had become entangled in a bitter labor dispute. Both the Republican and the Democratic Party split within their ranks on how to handle the militant workers. Then the workers themselves made an unprecedented move. They demanded a say in their own affairs, insisting on the formation of their own political party. Ruef swiftly organized a clique of local precinct workers to provide the nucleus for San Francisco's newest political force, the Union Labor Party. Now all Ruef needed was a suitable candidate to front that party, somebody whom he could control completely.

He found him in Eugene Schmitz, the epitome of a Western folk hero. He had the right background: an Irish mother and a German father, guaranteed to have a decisive influence on the intensely patriotic Irish-German community in the city. He was a staunch Catholic, again an important vote-catching factor with the religious working classes. He was married, had two daughters, and lived a scandal-free life. He didn't drink or smoke, dressed well, laughed easily; above all, he was indisputably working class. For years Schmitz had played the violin and then conducted the orchestra at the fashionable Columbia Theatre on Powell Street for forty dollars a week. He even had a local reputation as a promising composer.

After their first meeting, Ruef had shrewdly assessed the potential of his man: "He was a commanding figure. He had natural ability, good intelligence, keen perception. He possessed a tenacious memory and insuperable nerve. He could assume a pretense which covered up all deficiencies. His face completely masked his real feelings."

Schmitz was quite clear about what those feelings were: "From boyhood I had ever heard: make money, no matter how. People will never ask how you made it, only get it. I had no money, no influence, no prestige. He [Ruef] had all these, and they were at my service. I readily agreed to the proposition. There was no financial risk, and to think of being Mayor of my native city was inspiring."

Ruef also made it clear that it would be highly profitable. An alliance was formed. A king-maker had found his pawn, a Svengali his Trilby. Between them they would rob not only the coffers of City Hall, but the city itself. They would develop a new, sophisticated kind of grafting: not a coarse version of Tammany Hall in New York, or the crude banditry that passed for municipal till-dipping in Philadelphia. The Ruef-Schmitz axis would be plunder by politeness.

During the five years since the alliance had been formed, Schmitz had developed an easy, familiar relationship with Governor George C. Pardee of California. He had dined with the President of the United States. He maintained a smooth control over the city, with two noticeable exceptions: the Fire Chief, Sullivan, had frequently proved himself a nuisance with his demands, and Brigadier General Frederick Funston, acting commander of all Army troops in the city, was not captivated by the Mayor.

Funston believed that the whole notorious Barbary Coast a mile below him was a blot on the city he loved, and he blamed the city administration for not doing anything about it. More than once Funston had said to colleagues that the city's reputation would always remain tarnished as long as the tawdry cesspool which spread from the foot of Telegraph Hill to the shoreline—taking in Chinatown and part of the business section on the way—was allowed to remain.

He had a simple solution: move the whole vice quarter down the Peninsula, certainly far enough away to be out of sight of his quarters at 1310 Washington Street, almost the highest point on Nob Hill.

The move, Funston believed, would also alleviate another pressing issue in San Francisco: the question of Chinese and Japanese immigration. The issue had steadily grown over the years, particularly among the white working class, to become a matter of serious contention in the city. The orientals were blamed for much they were not responsible for, for instance the Barbary Coast: three solid blocks of dance halls, blaring forth music from orchestras, steam pianos, and Gramophones.

To Funston, the blight on the city was also a personal thing: the previous night carousing sailors, too drunk to know where they were going, had staggered up Washington Street and awakened him with their singing. Later Funston vowed to staff officers at the Presidio garrison that if it happened again he would place sentries outside his house to forcibly keep the peace. He would not allow a handful of drunks to violate his rest.

In any other city, the commander of the Army's local forces would probably have had a word with City Hall over the incident. But this was impossible for Funston so long as Schmitz and Ruef were in power.

At about the time that the General was preparing to dine with his wife, Enrico Caruso was fulfilling perfectly the role of the capricious opera singer. The staff of the Palace Hotel were being fully stretched to meet his demands. In rapid succession, he ordered coffee, cocktails, roast beef rare and macaroni, and the latest editions of the afternoon newspapers. There, his interest veered between the continuing crushing reviews for last night's *Queen of Sheba* and the latest news on the eruption of Mount Vesuvius.

The volcano, according to the *Examiner,* was presenting such a threat to the city of Naples that readers should support Mayor Schmitz's relief committee to raise funds to aid that distressed city. Calling for money, the *Examiner* said that "men who suffer when humanity suffers and are glad when other hearts are gladdened hasten to place their names on the subscription list." It was clear from the way money was being donated that San Franciscans were eager to help the unfortunate Italians, though many of the newspaper's readers could not help wondering what prompted people to live practically on top of an active volcano.

To discover the answer, the newspaper sent a reporter to interview Caruso, a Neapolitan. The tenor refused to receive him because of the paper's review of *The Queen of Sheba.*

But Caruso made his own feelings quite clear to the cast about the previous night's performance. He had gone from room to room castigating them in turn, and threatening that if there was a repeat performance in *Carmen* he would return immediately to New York.

More than a hundred thousand dollars' worth of tickets—ten dollars each for the best seats—had been sold in advance. To Caruso this only confirmed his standing as the world's leading opera singer; but for Olive Fremstad, the Wagnerian soprano who was to take the title role in *Carmen* that night, the tenor's overbearing attitude only increased the tension she felt.

"It was not just 'first night nerves.' It was an accumulation of his behavior since we had left New York," she said, looking back on the evening years later.

By early evening, Madame Fremstad, attending the final dress rehearsal for *Carmen* at the Grand Opera House, had decided that she, too, could be temperamental. The moment Caruso arrived backstage she planned to create a scene. And she had found the perfect excuse—the behavior of one of the local extras hired by the Opera House for walk-on roles.

Just over a mile away, in a rear cubicle of the Pup Restaurant, Abe Ruef and his confidential law clerk, George B. Keane, were deep in discussion. Ruef, who used the booth nightly as a political consulting room from which he dispensed favors of one kind or another, left strict instructions with the Pup's owner that he was not to be disturbed. The discussion he was having with Keane marked a turning point in the career of Ruef. At the end of it he had come to a momentous decision: the time had come to move in on the Southern Pacific Railroad.

The railroad *was* California. It had controlled the state for over forty years with subvention, pressure, and massive corruption of public authority. Its power was felt everywhere: newspapers, banks, insurance companies, lean-to stores, bars—nothing and nobody was too great or too small to be exploited in the cause of greater railway profits. Opposition, when it became too tiresome, was either bought off or eliminated. The railroad improvised its own legal code. The California legislature and the courts implemented that code.

There had been one outstanding opponent to the Southern Pacific —the San Francisco *Examiner*. The railroad was being steadily wounded by the relentless campaign of exposures, mockery, and jeering insult that the newspaper directed against it. It was a war of words that not even all the railroad's money could stem. Indeed, any attempt to buy off the paper with advertising revenue was rewarded with a fresh stream of invective from the editorial columns.

The clash between the railroad and newspaper was a longstanding feud. It had been started by William Randolph Hearst as a simple yet highly effective way to boost the circulation of the *Examiner,* while indulging his belief that "journalism is an enchanted playground in which giants and dragons were to be slain simply for the fun of the thing."

The trains, according to the newspaper, were always so late that "the passengers were exposed to the perils of senility." When the Southern Pacific suffered a derailment, however small, the *Examiner* sent a large team of reporters and quick-sketch artists to the scene. Between them they filled the newspaper with horrific sketches of destruction and interviews with "survivors." All of it was laced together with harsh editorial comment about "murderous railroad laxity." By sheer repetition, the sustained campaign had started a groundswell of public opinion against the railroad.

It was this swell that Abe Ruef had detected and hoped to ride in on. The time, he felt, had come when the Southern Pacific could well benefit from his advice. To Ruef the situation was the classic one he loved: both sides against the middle, with him acting as the fulcrum of this seesaw. The *Examiner* had supported Eugene Schmitz for office, and had continued to do so during his tenure at City Hall. The railroad, indirectly and discreetly, had provided funds for the Mayor's three successful election campaigns. Yet the crusading Hearst and his newspaper found little cause for concern at the way the city was being administered.

To Abe Ruef the situation was ripe for exploiting. He asked Keane to set up a meeting with the Southern Pacific. Then he turned his attention to other business; this night there was to be only one favor seeker: a man who wanted a building permit to open yet another "French Restaurant" on Jackson Street.

The French Restaurants on Jackson were all part of the commercialized web of vice that sustained San Francisco's reputation as a roaring, randy city. The restaurants were strictly respectable on the ground floor, offering superb food and wine at high prices. The upper floors were divided into private rooms, each furnished with a dining table, a bed, and an inside door lock. The upper floors were reached by a separate entrance, ensuring discretion for a price.

Granting French Restaurant franchises was another means Ruef had of augmenting his income.

The first part of the day, the working half, was at an end for most of the city. Now the second half, the pleasure-seeking half, was beginning.

Queues were forming outside the Mechanics Pavilion, where the annual Mardi Gras masked carnival on roller skates was being held.

The Orpheum Theatre had a strong vaudeville bill: Charles Sweet, Armstrong and Hall, Solomon's Dogs, Jimmy Wall, and Artie Hall "with his astonishing motion pictures." At the Tivoli *Miss Timidity* was playing; the Columbia on Powell Street offered Victor Herbert's *Babes in Toyland,* which was drawing huge crowds. The young John Barrymore was in town, having just ended a short run in *The Dictator.* Walter Perkins had opened at the Majestic in his own farce, *Who Goes There?* The answer, judging by box office returns, seemed to be not that many. Perkins had found the bitter truth of that old show business maxim: "If they like you in San Francisco, you're all right."

In the pantry at the rear of the Palace Hotel kitchen, Fred Mergenthaler, the master chef, was coming to the end of his ideal form of relaxation: clipping interesting items from the newspapers. The current editions had provided him with a particularly rich haul.

The *Call* reported that Geronimo, the chief of the Apaches, had taken his eighth wife at the age of seventy-six. There was a report of two men at Oakland who were "engaged in a friendly wrestling bout." One partner threw his opponent, "causing him to fall on his whisky bottle." The fallen man promptly pumped three bullets into the other man. Police had booked him on a drunk and disorderly charge. The *Examiner*'s readers were dubious about any suggestion that cars would replace the horse. Up in the gold fields two hundred angry miners were hunting claim jumpers in the Sierra Hills.

These stories all found a place in Mergenthaler's collection, joining paragraphs about Suffragettes being arrested for picketing No. 10 Downing Street in London, Kaiser Wilhelm saber rattling, and the American Bison Society appealing for funds to save the vanishing buffalo.

All told, it was a good time for news. A revolution had been crushed by Czar Nicholas of Russia; France was in national mourning for a mine disaster that had killed one thousand in Calais; an earthquake had taken fifty lives in Formosa.

Talbot Williams, a kitchen porter, was trying to work out how he could meet gambling debts of nearly five hundred dollars. He had just found a possible solution to his problem in an advertisement in the *Call.* It was an invitation to visit Ismar, a fortune teller: "The list of those whom I have benefited would fill a page of small type. If you have any problems of love, investment, sickness, or if you would like to know anything about the future it will profit you to pay me a visit."

Talbot Williams decided he would do just that on his next day off, this coming Thursday.

Patrolman Ingham had finished duty for the day, and was explaining to his wife the meaning of the clauses in the fire insurance policy he had purchased. Adam Gilliland, the insurance agent who had sold it to him, was preparing to attend a lecture at the Academy of Sciences. Professor Clarence Edwards was lecturing on "California Industries," and illustrating it with "magnificent stereopticon views and moving pictures."

Brigadier General Frederick Funston was also discussing his plans for the evening with his wife. Over dinner, he admitted he was excited by the prospect of the "war games" he was to command at the end of the month. However, the prospect of writing a "presentation" in advance of the games was not exciting.

Eda Funston gently reminded her husband that the "games" would make him forget the paperwork; even if it was not real action, it was the next best thing. It would also temporarily remove the temptation to pay a call on the Mayor and have a showdown with him over corruption in the city. It was not just Eugene Schmitz, Mrs. Funston suggested, but his entire administration, that "needed a clean sweep."

The couple looked at each other, both aware of the deeper meaning behind the statement.

In his quarters above the fire station on Bush Street, Dennis Sullivan, the Fire Chief, heard that the gossip at City Hall was that the Mayor was "in some sort of trouble."

Eugene Schmitz had left City Hall, and was attending a cocktail party at the St. Francis Hotel. He would stay only long enough to sip his standard orange juice and discuss with other guests the latest attack President Teddy Roosevelt had launched, this time against the insurance trust. Hardly a day passed now without Roosevelt claiming the headlines. A couple of days earlier he had blasted away at the newspapers—the "muckraking" writers who exposed the evils of such diverse institutions as John D. Rockefeller and the meat-canning industry.

Hearst's *Examiner* earned approval from some of the cocktail-party guests with its demanding: "Whom did Mr. Roosevelt expect to please by delivering his disquisition? Either he meant to give aid and comfort at some quarter or else in his swollen vanity he was guilty of gratuitous impudence in lecturing writers and publishers who to say the very least are his equals in patriotic purpose and much his superiors in brains."

It was the sort of vitriolic attack that one of the guests at the party hoped soon to print about the Mayor of San Francisco, exploiting the tension that Eugene Schmitz was living under.

6 P.M. to Midnight

San Francisco's Chinatown before the earthquake
(*Southern Pacific Railroad*)

2. Personal Grounds

TENSION, WHETHER CAUSED by anger, fear, resentment, or even excitement, was something that Amadeo Peter Giannini had long learned to control in his thirty-six years. Like everything else about him, this particular control had taken years of careful practice to achieve. It was the same with the way he moved. Every movement was easy and comfortable, designed to minimize the massiveness of his six-foot-two-inch body. The head too was huge, blue-jowled, with a jaw that was square and hard like pumice stone. The eyes were hooded, the irises a clear hazel—appraising and shrewdly speculative. The voice, deep and steady, revealed the same control.

Tonight, on the ground floor of a wood-frame building at the corner of Columbus and Washington Avenues, Giannini's voice could well be forgiven for assuming a contented note. His dream had been realized.

Within two years he had successfully launched a bank, a feat that nobody had really believed possible. Yet the success story was neatly laid out in the Bank of Italy's ledgers. After nearly two years of trading, deposits had reached almost one million dollars. To provide more money for expansion, the directors planned to increase the bank's capital by two hundred thousand dollars. In three days' time, two thousand paid-up shares would be distributed.

To mark this step forward, the bank's board also voted to pay Giannini, founder and first vice-president, a salary of two hundred dollars a month.

If the gesture gave him pleasure, Giannini was not exuberant. That was an emotion which did not fit his concept of a banker.

Tonight, as with every other night for the last eighteen months, he was concerned only that the daily books were balanced in time for him to get home for an early supper. He lived with his wife Clorinda in their two-story frame house in San Mateo, a few miles down from the Peninsula. There, after supper, he could enjoy one of his favorite pastimes: wandering about the garden, learning about the land and what could be done with the soil.

Years before, in another career, it had helped him learn about people and their needs. Then a produce buyer, he had found that a good farmer, given the right soil and the willingness to work hard, would prosper. But frequently he needed what so many other people in San Francisco also needed: money to get started.

San Francisco had a philosophy of "big banks for big people." In spite of being the financial capital of the West, it provided mainly banking services for wealthy upstate ranchers, mines, lumber mills, and city developments. A bank would loan a million dollars to buy a ranch or extend a railroad, but would refuse fifty dollars to improve a home. Bank chronicler Paul Rink records that "these humbler, smaller citizens, no matter how deserving, were invariably drawn into the arms of the loan sharks, who charged them exorbitant interest, unless they could pull off the improbable feat of finding a wealthy friend to lend them the money."

A. P. Giannini founded his bank to change this situation. From the outset he made sure that the Bank of Italy would be a "people's bank," not a financial colossus for wealthy men to grow wealthier on. Three thousand shares of stock were issued. No stockholder, including Giannini, could hold more than one hundred shares. Over half the shares were in fact in the hands of 1620 stockholders; among them were a fish dealer, a grocer, a teamster, a druggist. Many held no more than two or three shares.

The Bank of Italy opened in October 1904, conducting business according to the strict policy that Giannini had laid down. No loan was too small, no customer too humble. At the end of the first day, twenty-eight people had deposited eight thousand dollars with the bank. Not having a proper safe, Giannini persuaded the nearby Crocker National Bank to keep the deposits in its vaults. Each evening a buggy would carry the pouches of gold and silver to the Crocker Bank, and collect them in the morning.

Soon the president of the other bank, William H. Crocker, felt confident enough to buy fifty shares of Bank of Italy stock—never dreaming that one day the "baby bank," as some called it, would be rich enough to buy many of the city's banks over and again.

In the eighteen months of its existence, the Bank of Italy had established a completely new concept of banking. It openly solicited accounts. Every day Giannini tramped the Italian district of North Beach, where he had grown up, touting for business. The outcome was a stream of small investors, men and women who were persuaded that it was safer to put their money in the care of the Bank of Italy, where it earned 3½ percent interest, than to leave it in a tin on a shelf in the back parlor.

The bank also loaned money and, observes Paul Rink, "for the first time in the history of San Francisco, a working man in an emergency had a place he could go to for a small loan without falling into the clutches of the extortionate money lenders."

Over the months the bank's image and status changed among the city's bankers from indifference to bleak rejection of Giannini's methods. When the bank opened, all the other bankers except Crocker had ignored him—the aristocratic Crocker could afford to be magnanimous and extend his hospitality and protection to the money of the little one-room establishment down the street.

But as the Bank of Italy prospered, the other bankers—men raised and nurtured in the remote, lofty tradition of the Rothschilds of London and Lazard Frères of Paris—looked with disdain at Giannini scrabbling after business. To some it was no better than they expected of an Italian who had once sold farm produce, and was now treating the serious business of banking as if it were an operation similar to selling grapefruit, which Giannini had introduced to San Francisco.

To them he was the "Dago Banker," somebody to be watched, possibly, but never to be admitted to that intimate circle dominated by the American National Bank and the men of Wells Fargo.

Now, shortly after half-past six, the day's books safely balanced, Giannini let himself out of the Bank of Italy and set off on the jogging buggy ride home to his wife and supper.

At the Grand Opera House on Mission Street, at least two members of the cast of *Carmen* were making the painful discovery that they needed more than enthusiasm to realize their yearnings for public acclaim.

It was they who had played a part in providing Madame Olive Fremstad, the statuesque Wagnerian soprano, with the justification for the outburst that threatened to wreck Bizet's opera even before the curtain rose.

Never an easy time in any production, the dress rehearsal for *Carmen* had been marred by tension and bickering. Caruso himself was not there, but the private lashing he had meted out to some members of the company, coupled with the public drubbing *The Queen of Sheba* had received at the hands of the critics, had affected the members of the touring company deeply. There was an air of tension backstage that had not been there in St. Louis or Kansas. Antonio Scotti, the company's long-accepted peacemaker, found it "a tricky situation; everybody seemed to be spoiling for a fight. Dressers were blamed for costumes that had fit in St. Louis, but did not fit now."

The situation had not been improved by some clumsy scene changing. During one, a vase was knocked from its plinth, with the result that Madame Fremstad screeched the top notes of her aria.

At this moment Caruso chose to arrive backstage.

To him the dying echo of Madame Fremstad's off-key voice must have sounded like a repetition of the lifeless performance the company's other leading lady, Edith Walker, had given in *The Queen of Sheba*.

"Caruso made it be known to anybody near enough to listen that he would not share the stage with such a performance," Scotti recalled years later.

Madame Fremstad bore down in full fury on Caruso. Their meeting in the wings had an air of farce about it. Caruso, cloaked, a silk top hat magnifying his five feet eight inches, looked like a caricature of a stage lover in a comedy of manners. Madame Fremstad seemed to have taken on the guise of a figurine on a Grecian man-o'-war. The impression was heightened by the way she propelled herself across stage; two hundred pounds of what appeared to be mostly bosom and buttock thrusting against silk.

Stage lover and figurine faced up to each other in one of the most magnificent backstage encounters the Grand Opera House had ever seen in its twenty-six-year history.

In a voice filled with vehemence, with "the furious aspect of a wounded lioness," she roared that *anybody's* voice would have broken under the conditions that existed at the Opera House: how could *anybody* give even an adequate performance in the chaos backstage —all of which had been created by the touring company's reliance on local labor to shift props and augment crowd scenes.

"It was clear what lay behind her argument—the point that we all knew: that to pay Caruso his great salary there had to be economies. Local players had been recruited to help the production. This had also played a part in the tensions," recalled Scotti.

The matter of Caruso's salary attracted keen interest in newspapers: his recent four-thousand-dollar fee for one special concert in New York drew almost as much attention as his singing. The Metropolitan Opera of New York maintained the position that no matter how much they paid the tenor, he always turned out to be the least expensive of singers when it came to box-office returns. It was an attitude that did not exactly endear the Italian to his often equally temperamental colleagues.

Now Madame Fremstad had obliquely raised again the matter of money. Caruso ignored the issue and mounted a frontal assault on the soprano. He asked her how she would solve the problem.

Madame Fremstad, her voice vibrating through the wings, violent and irresistible, demanded that the local extras be fired, otherwise she would walk out.

Caruso had other ideas. Possibly sensing that Madame Fremstad could unchain a situation that would damage his own reputation, possibly angry at the allusion to his income, the tenor braced himself to deliver a verbal lashing which equaled any of his stage performances in its inflamed emotion and passion.

"He made it plain that if anybody was dismissed without his approval, there would be no opera, and no Olive Fremstad," Scotti later recalled. "He would personally see to it that she would never again even enter the same theatre he would play in."

Out front the unsuspecting audience of three thousand were settling themselves in their seats. There were row after row of jeweled ladies in décolletage and their escorts in stiff white shirts and black frock coats or dinner jackets.

The barnlike opera house, and the audience, were a source of inspiration to Laura Bride Powers, the society reporter of the *Call*. From her seat in the stalls she observed that "the house was a terraced garden of orchids and narcissus and nodding roses, with fruit blossoms scattered between. And the odor of roses from the pit assailed the senses like the breath that blows from the flowery orchids of Santa Clara."

On the other hand she felt that many of the women were overdressed. More to her liking was the comparative simplicity of Mrs. James Flood, who had limited herself to "a tiara, a dog collar, shoulder straps, a stomacher and corsage decorations of diamonds and pearls." Mrs. Frederick Kohl, sitting in her usual box, had also restricted herself to a tiara, "a two-inch-wide dog collar of pearls and diamonds, with matching assorted shimmering things on the corsage line, topped with a brilliant American Beauty rose."

Another box was occupied by Chief of Police Jeremiah Dinan and his wife. The rear of the auditorium was lined with his officers. They were there to quell any repetition of a scene the previous night at the Alhambra Theatre. Then the audience had rioted over the standard of acting being offered. When a policeman had tried to break up the pandemonium, the audience had turned on him with cries of "mob him" and "kill the cop."

Dinan had dismissed the incident as all being part of the everyday lot of a policeman in a city where many people still liked to settle a grievance the way it had always been done in San Francisco— man to man, with either fists or a handy weapon.

Jeremiah Dinan had been appointed Chief barely a year before, the third in six years. One of his first acts had been to introduce the police car to the city at the beginning of 1906. It had given added mobility to a police force frequently stretched to its limit. In the weeks the car had been operating, it had proved itself an effective crime deterrent in a city with an appalling record of lawlessness.

Life was cheap in San Francisco. In the Tenderloin and Barbary Coast districts a man could be murdered for the price of a bottle of whiskey. Shanghai-ing was still commonplace. Only that morning Dinan's officers had rescued a fifteen-year-old boy from being snatched in Dupont Street. The *Examiner* commented that "force, fraud and trickery were resorted to by the masters of vessels to complete their crews."

Vice, too, was a serious blight: one not made easier for Dinan by the "municipal crib" in which Mayor Eugene Schmitz and Abe Ruef had a financial stake. Dinan knew it would be more than his job was worth to raid the three-floor brothel on Jackson Street. He would not change his mind, even in the face of a protest which a group of Methodist ministers had delivered to him that afternoon, demanding a cleanup in the city.

If this demand troubled Dinan as he sat in his box, he gave no sign of it. He could always draw comfort from precedent. Demands for a cleanup were noted—and forgotten.

To have curbed vice would have meant throttling the image of a city in which flesh and alcohol were for sale in unrestricted quantities. Protection rackets abounded. Sexual satisfaction was available round the clock. Opium clubs—many offering good-quality gum and pills at exorbitant prices—flourished. The city seemed to have long found in sex and drugs a quivering personal uniqueness, perhaps a calming hope for some different experience. San Francisco, far removed from the puritanism of New England, had long shown a tolerance of strumpeting; it was as if the city had reached back to Middle Ages Europe and adopted as its motto Aquinas's remark in *Summa Theologica* that "prostitution in the town is like a cesspool in the palace. Do away with the cesspool, and the palace will become an unclean place."

Jeremiah Dinan, on all the evidence available, learned to live easily enough under the rakish mantle San Francisco wore. Yet as Chief of Police he was better than many of his predecessors. He increased the force to seven hundred, and showed interest in the use of photography in crime detection, an idea first introduced to America by the city's police department forty years earlier. Police patrols were strengthened, and the number of street boxes from which officers could summon help increased. He had probably done as much as anybody could do under the circumstances, for like most of the city's officials, the Chief of Police was frequently under pressure from either the Mayor or Abe Ruef.

Tonight, Dinan could see, neither was at the opera. At least he would have a few hours away from law enforcement.

Abe Ruef decided to do something he now rarely had the time to do: spend a quiet evening at home with his family in their modest house near Telegraph Hill.

In many ways the house reflected his personal tastes; moderation was the key to everything in his private life. He abhorred smoking and gambling. His clothes were conservative; his attendance to the religious side of his life was strict. The son of a French-Jewish mercantile family, he could, at forty-two, get real pleasure from seeing the family name still listed in the *Jewish Elite Directory and Social List of San Francisco.*

The man who so rapaciously looted a city for his own purposes was, as one biographer stated, "contentedly middle-class." His plunder, augmented by honestly earned legal fees, was all invested in real estate.

Eugene Schmitz, too, had decided to spend a quiet evening at home. He and his family lived in a gingerbread house at the select end of Fillmore Street. It was a home, observed Ruef's confidential law clerk, George B. Keane, that "everyone knew could not have been erected out of the proceeds of a Mayor's salary."

Tonight Schmitz dined early, and then retired to the basement room he had fitted up as a den, to ponder the intervention of Rudolph Spreckels and the real threat it posed.

Rudolph Spreckels, whose fortune came from sugar, had acted against City Hall policy, which called for a sweetener with every franchise and contract. A few days before, Schmitz had snubbed Spreckels by refusing him an appointment to discuss a franchise to take over the streetcar system in the city. The Spreckels company to operate the cars had been incorporated with capital of fourteen million dollars. One unique stipulation in the company's charter was that the city might take over the system at any time, purchasing it for the exact amount of money invested, plus any interest. It was a major step toward publically owned transportation; to Schmitz and Ruef it offered nothing.

In refusing to see Rudolph Spreckels, the Mayor of San Francisco made a major blunder. He also made the decision without consulting Abe Ruef.

The behavior of the Mayor since he had learned of the case being mounted against him and Abe Ruef is not easily explained. He made no attempt to contact Ruef. Instead, he attended that cocktail party at the St. Francis, where he gave no indication that anything was amiss. On his return home he said nothing to his wife; later, his family recalled that he had behaved perfectly normally.

When Ruef put Schmitz into City Hall, the personal relationship between the two men had been good: they had a common ground in graft. But after he had been returned to office a third time, in November 1905, the friendship cooled. Schmitz was becoming increasingly obsessed with his social standing.

Eugene Schmitz, well aware that for a seemingly limitless supply of money all he had to do was give mayoral endorsement to Ruef's wily schemes, assumed the part of a man bred to high living. In playing the very negation of "the people's man for the people"—which had sustained him through three elections—he moved in a circle Abe Ruef despised: the newly rich with all their vagaries, the social climbers, who regarded socializing with the Mayor of San Francisco as a steppingstone to hobnobbing with the Governor of California and the potentates above him.

Money, which had bound Schmitz and Ruef together for so long, finally drove a wedge between them.

The signs had been there for some months. On more than one occasion, Schmitz granted a franchise without a bribe to some wealthy and socially acceptable man, a gesture that alarmed Ruef. One who benefited was Downey Harvey, a major shareholder in the Ocean Shore Railway: the franchise was to construct an interurban rail line to Santa Cruz. A warm friendship grew between Harvey and Schmitz, a relationship, Ruef noted, that provided "the social nectar that Eugene craves."

On this night Eugene Schmitz decided he would seek help to meet the threat that Rudolph Spreckels posed. He telephoned Downey Harvey. The maid who took the call informed the Mayor that her Mr. Harvey was at the opera.

In their home on Nob Hill, the Funstons dined alone, then retired to the drawing room, where a maid served coffee.

During the evening they had heard clearly the sound of gunshots from the Barbary Coast district below. It was not unusual, but it reminded Brigadier General Frederick Funston of the problem which preoccupied him nowadays: the need for a purge of City Hall.

Eda Funston volunteered a suggestion she had heard others voice recently: Why didn't her husband resign his commission and run for office at the next election?

Frederick Funston looked at his wife in astonishment. "Good God, woman, the Army's my career."

But San Francisco, Eda Funston pointed out, was their home. If civic events were left to follow their present course, the city would not be safe for anyone. A strong man was needed to fight the corruption in City Hall.

"It needs you," she said.

Backstage at the Grand Opera House, a peace of a kind was achieved by the intervention of the company's conductor, Alfred Hertz.

He persuaded Caruso and Madame Fremstad to discuss their differences in his dressing room. There a formula was talked out in which neither tenor nor soprano lost face. Hertz soothed away their tantrums as being caused by the rigors of the tour. In the meantime, the show must go on; the question of dispensing with the services of any of the locally hired extras would be dealt with the following day.

Caruso and Madame Fremstad accepted the point. But Hertz failed in his attempt to get the volatile star to hand over his gun. Caruso insisted on wearing it under his stage cummerbund.

The critics in the audience, jotting down their comments on the pageant unfolding on stage, were not long in coming to certain unanimous conclusions. Blanche Partington, music critic of the *Call*, decided by the end of the first act that Madame Fremstad was "a Teuton of the Teutons, temperamentally at war with the role." The *Examiner*'s critic agreed: "Fremstad was inclined to be dutchy." Caruso, on the other hand, was giving a towering performance. Ashton Stevens, the august critic of that newspaper, felt that the tenor had already "lifted the large audience to an enthusiasm that was denied the unfortunate *Queen of Sheba*."

Nine times the curtain rose and fell as Caruso took his curtain calls.

Exultant, exhausted, he made his way to his dressing room. As he reached it, the tower bell in Old St. Mary's Church chimed midnight.

WEDNESDAY
APRIL 18, 1906

Midnight to 5 A.M.

A. P. Giannini, the founder of the Bank of America (*Bank of America Archives*)

The horse team that Giannini used to transport his bank's money to his brother's home during the earthquake (*Bank of America Archives*)

3. An Excited Horse

SHORTLY AFTER MIDNIGHT the Fire Department received its first call of a new day. It was a three-alarm summons to a warehouse fire near Market Street. A four-wheeled steamer, a hose wagon, and a chemical company, all horse-drawn, soon had the blaze under control.

To Dennis Sullivan, who arrived at the scene in his buggy, the sight of his firemen moving with disciplined speed was again positive proof of his claim to be chief of the finest fire department in the West. He had nearly seven hundred men under his command, manning eighty fire stations around the city, but the twelve square blocks of Chinatown's ghetto—a gigantic tinderbox of slat-board—did not have a fire station: the city's combined firefighting force would be hard put to contain a major fire in this warren, especially if blustering winds from the Pacific fanned the flames.

Sullivan and his firemen had noticed a change in the weather that boded ill if there were any further fire calls in the coming hours. The wind had veered. Now it was gusting off the Pacific, through the Golden Gate, around the island of Alcatraz, to blow on to the city.

It would not affect the fire off Market Street. But fighting new blazes would be a different matter if the wind continued to blow from the same direction. The six times that the heart of San Francisco had been burnt out, the wind had come from the sea.

The fire that Sullivan and his men doused would get no coverage in the editions of the morning newspapers now being prepared for press. The *Call,* the *Chronicle,* indeed all of the city's newspapers, were going to need every column inch to do justice to the night at the opera.

Laura Bride Powers had written a story with the characteristic grasp for detail and acute observation which had made her the doyenne of the city's reporters. By 2 A.M. she was in bed, asleep beside her husband.

James Hopper was still turning out his copy for the *Call.* In the end it would be a brilliantly detailed piece of writing that captured perfectly the mood of the opera audience.

Now, shortly after two o'clock, Hopper was on his way home, gratified to know that his story would be by-lined. As he walked up Post Street to his hotel, the Neptune, six blocks away, the reporter noticed that the sea breeze was losing some of its force.

James Hopper had nobody waiting for him in his room. He could look forward to eight hours of uninterrupted sleep before he was due to return to the office. As he walked home his journalist's eye was observing "the dark loom of the big buildings, the bay beyond with the red and green lights and the long silhouettes of ships at anchor, and still further the familiar hearthlike glow of the mainland towns. The night struck me as particularly peaceful."

As he passed a livery stable between Powell and Mason Streets, a horse "screamed with a sudden, shrill cry. I asked a stableman lolling in the darkened doorway what was the matter. 'Restless tonight! Don't know why!' he answered. And then, with my head poked in, I heard the thunder of a score of hoofs crashing in tattoo against the stalls."

Hopper, continuing his uphill walk, mused on what had caused the animals to be restive.

A few blocks away, John Conlon Sr., second assistant chief of the city's fire department, was also awakened by the restlessness of the horses quartered below his bedroom. He could hear the muted voices of the duty firemen soothing the animals. In an adjoining room his son, John Jr., slept soundly.

The horses tethered at the rear of millionaire James Haggin's wooden mansion on Nob Hill had also started to snort and fret. To Haggin, giving a postopera supper for friends, the sound, he would later remember, "was a little puzzling. I put it down to the weather."

The weather would also be initially blamed by Father Charles Ramm for the barking of dogs which disturbed his sleep. The priest had retired to bed around midnight. From his bed, Father Ramm was able to isolate the barking. It was coming from the city dog pound in the Mission district.

Caruso and Antonio Scotti left the Palace Hotel soon after 1 A.M.

They had stayed at the hotel only long enough to have a drink with other members of the cast. The leading ladies—Edith Walker and Olive Fremstad—had retired to their suites. Caruso had sipped a pony of cognac with Alfred Hertz. The brandy reinforced the warm glow of satisfaction the tenor felt. The tension and brittleness that had filled him before *Carmen* had been washed away by the tumultuous applause his performance had drawn: he *knew* that he had given a superb rendering of Don José, and that whatever the critics said of the rest of the opera tomorrow, they would not fault him.

So sure was he of the justifiable acclaim due to him that he said he would "not even wait for the first editions with the reviews to arrive," Scotti recalled.

As he, Hertz, and Caruso drank, members of the cast slipped away to sample something of the social life the city still offered. They made their way to Coppa's, Delmonico's, and the Poodle Dog, to round off their night of triumph.

Caruso also wanted to make a night of it. Hertz, who was to conduct *Lohengrin* at the Grand Opera House's next gala offering, declined the tenor's suggestion to go "hunt some spaghetti and fun." In the end Caruso and Scotti left by a side entrance, climbed into a hack, and made their way to Zinkand's Restaurant. There, over steaming plates of spaghetti, they listened tolerantly to a stout young girl pounding out operatic airs on a piano in their honor; Elsa Maxwell had yet to find her real vocation as a society hostess.

At 3 A.M. Caruso decided he wanted something more exciting than a plump pianist to amuse him.

For actor John Barrymore, the question of his night's amusement had been settled some hours earlier when he had briefly attended the party James Haggin was giving. Barrymore, according to the staff of the St. Francis Hotel, where he was staying, met a young woman and persuaded her to share a bottle of champagne with him back in his room at the hotel. Now, he and the girl were safely into the second bottle. Barrymore was to be quoted later as saying: "I still didn't even know her surname."

A few blocks to the north, Brigadier General Frederick Funston was still awake in his study, working on a reply to a long memorandum from the War Department. In all the many guises he had taken on—newspaper editor, botanist, explorer, soldier of fortune, and military officer—the one he liked least was interpreter of the arid officialese of the War Department. The memorandum had arrived the previous afternoon at the Presidio. It contained still more detailed instructions for the "war games" Funston was to command later in the month. Now, after hours of studying it, he still was not clear what reply to give the War Department. He read until the type swam before his eyes.

At 4 A.M. he put the paperwork aside and made his way to bed.

Shortly before 5 A.M., Leonard Ingham, the visionary patrolman, awoke. His nightmare had not recurred to terrify him. It was nothing more sinister than the sound of a milk cart rattling down the street. It was some moments before Patrolman Ingham realized why this everyday sound had bothered him. The milkman was having trouble pacifying his excited horse. At that moment the city clocks struck 5 A.M.

5 A.M. to 5:12:59

Abe Ruef, Mayor Eugene Schmitz (*San Francisco Chronicle*)

General Funston (fourth from right) and some of the Committee of Fifty, including E. H. Harriman (fifth from left), and W. H. Crocker (second from right) (*Southern Pacific Railroad*)

4. Time Hung Poised

FROM THE TERRACE of his villa, Bailey Millard could clearly distinguish the five peals from the tower bell of Old St. Mary's Church on the edge of Chinatown. They had a clarity all of their own that the painter had come to recognize through the weeks he had sat before his easel and tried to capture on canvas the tints of an awakening city.

He had chosen an almost perfect site for his task. Below him, San Francisco spread itself over the hills and down to the great Bay.

From where he sat, at the very peak of Russian Hill, a summit reached only by a long winding path, Millard could look across the Bay to the little towns of Sausalito and Belvedere. Rising beyond them was Mount Tamalpais, its wooded slopes bringing the real forest closer to San Francisco than to any other American city: deer and coyote still roamed there.

Nearer was the Golden Gate itself, a huge funnel drawing in the winds and mists from the Pacific to cool off the great hot interior valleys of Sacramento and San Joaquin. The sea fog had a trick of painting every exposed object a sea gray tinged with dull green; the effect was gentle and infinitely attractive, dappling the hills with subtle hues that no paintbrush could quite reproduce.

Nearer still was the city itself, rising toward him in a sequence of hill terraces from the harbor. One terrace rose to Telegraph Hill, with its two-hundred-foot cliff sheering down to the sea; another led to Nob Hill, with the citadellike Mark Hopkins Mansion at its crown; a third rose up through Vallejo Street to Russian Hill, the highest point of the city.

Below Millard was the business district and the Chinese quarter. Built and rebuilt, Chinatown had an architecture all its own. It was a huddled irregularity of balconies, tiny pagodas on top. Below were the clothing and cigar factories, cribs, opium dens, and passageways running beneath dirty streets lined with tenement houses.

At this moment, a few minutes after 5:00, nothing seemed to stir at all in the entire city. It was this mood Millard hoped to reproduce on canvas, concentrating first on Telegraph Hill, on the homes the Italians had tumbled all over its slopes with Neapolitan abandonment. Later, when the sun was higher, his brushes would paint the eastern end of the city, which had been built up entirely on reclaimed land.

Here, over the years, real estate men had satisfied the demand for building land by filling in the sea bed the cheapest and quickest way possible: wagonloads of refuse, trash, garbage, rubble, packing cases, old beds, *anything,* had been dumped to fill in and reclaim the ground. Over it all was laid a thin skin of sand and earth. On this had risen the warehouses, factories, hotels, boardinghouses, and homes around Union and Battery Streets, south of Market and around Montgomery Street. The same policy was applied to the structures themselves: poor-quality materials were frequently used in their construction, materials that could never hope to resist the strain put upon them by the shifting of their treacherous foundations. But when they fell down, as the United States Bonded Warehouse had, the jerry-builders flattened the rubble and constructed an almost identical building in its place.

Nevertheless, from where he sat, the buildings looked solid enough. Millard started to paint.

In the hinterland beyond and across San Francisco Bay, the day's life was beginning.

In the telephone company office at Salinas, an operator chatted sleepily with her friend one hundred and eighty miles down the coast at the telephone exchange at San Luis Obispo.

At the State Insane Asylum at Agnews, near San Jose, a huge five-storied complex, the 1088 patients were being awakened in the dormitories and cells in which they were confined.

At San Raphael, fifteen miles north of San Francisco, United States Circuit Judge W. W. Morrow had been awakened by his bedroom clock striking 5 A.M. "The morning," he later recalled, "was bright and clear, and the air fragrant and balmy. The birds were unusually busy, and through the open window came the message of an early dawn promising a pleasant day."

Down the Peninsula, seventeen miles from San Francisco, A. P. Giannini was also preparing to face another long day. Sleep, luckily, was something he needed little of since those years earlier when his "day" had started at midnight as a buyer in the city's produce district. At the age of thirty-one, he had sold his half share in the business for one hundred thousand dollars. The money itself held little fascination for him. To his wife he confided: "I don't want to be rich. No man actually owns a fortune; it owns him."

He planned to adopt the same philosophy to banking. He would make a fortune, but never actually own one, and never be owned by it. Nothing, he would maintain all his life, could ever replace the simple things of life—such as the sunrise now coming up behind the curve of the continent.

Bailey Millard was working hard to capture the rise of the sun as it embraced the Bay and shoreline, sheening all it touched with gold. He already had a title for his picture: *When Altruria Awoke.*

The clock on the Ferry Building stood at 5:14 A.M.

It was, noted police sergeant Jesse Cook, on patrol in the produce district, two minutes faster than his timepiece. All around him was the babble of a dozen different languages; of lots being auctioned and haggled over; mounds of fruit and vegetables being dumped and lifted with bewildering speed. The air was full of sharp bargaining and shrewd judging by men reared with an inborn instinct for supply and demand.

As Jesse Cook watched, the seconds on his watch ticked by. Fifty-nine passed. Time hung poised at 5:12 A.M.

At that moment the earthquake came.

5:13 to 5:30 A.M.

In seconds the earthquake changed the shape of the city
(*Worden Collection, Wells Fargo Bank History Room*)

5. The Big Rip

ONE HUNDRED AND FIFTY MILES due west of the Golden Gate, the schooner *John A. Campbell* shuddered. Her bow rose in the water, exposing the waterline, remained there for a split second, then crashed back into the sea. The crew bolted out of their bunks in alarm, thinking that the boat had rammed a derelict, or even a whale. They ran to the rail and stared at the sea, but there was nothing to be seen. Baffled, they looked to the bridge for guidance. There, Captain Svenson was equally puzzled; the charts indicated no shipwrecks or reefs to steer clear of—nor had a whale ever been seen this far north. In the log the captain later entered: "Sudden motion, unexplained. The shock felt as if the vessel struck . . . and then appeared to drag over soft ground." But the sea bed was 2400 fathoms below.

The "sudden motion" was the result of stresses and strains which had accumulated miles below the ocean's surface, where the San Andreas Fault ran under the sea bed. The tremors had built up until in one tectonic jolt one wall of the Fault slipped in one direction, the other the opposite way, grinding and thrusting and wrenching until finally the earth split open like a great wound.

Unknown to the crew of the *John A. Campbell,* the wound had opened a few miles ahead of them; what they experienced was a kickback from the rip—one of the thousands of seismic shock waves which at that very instant were making seismographs quiver as far away as Cape Town, London, Tokyo, Berlin, and Moscow.

By then the tremor was well on course, traveling at a speed of two miles a second.

65

Ripping open the ocean bed, it passed only forty fathoms below the steamer *Argo*. The impact on the ship's hull was equivalent to a depth charge at point-blank range. Steel plate buckled; bolts flew out of their riveting. For "one mad moment," her captain recalled later, "the whole ship appeared to be breaking up—and in a perfectly calm sea!"

The "mad moment" was gone before anybody on the *Argo* could move. Then, almost simultaneously, the earthquake struck shore.

It came out of the sea at seven thousand miles an hour, almost directly beneath the lighthouse on Point Arena, ninety miles north of San Francisco. The 110-foot-high structure began swaying like a blade of grass. In a second, the beacon which had withstood thirty-six years of storms and gales was creaking and cracking, its lantern and lenses fragmenting and falling onto the iron floor in a shower of glass.

Relentlessly the rip raced south, veering when it met the resistance of the land, but keeping the same general direction, boring down toward San Francisco, shifting billions of tons of earth, sending masses of rock rising and falling to form cliffs where only a second before there had been flat land.

With an energy greater than all the explosives used in World War II, it had started its journey by smashing through the coastline of Humboldt County, two hundred miles north of San Francisco, demolishing whole forests of redwoods, bleak mountain spurs, and black shale bluffs.

As it dived back into the sea, its tail lashed the False Cape Cliffs; millions of tons of rock and shale collapsed into the ocean a thousand feet below to re-form the coastline.

As it furrowed through the sea bed, the rip sent out a shudder that wrecked the small town of Fort Bragg on the coast. It was the first of a string of towns to be wrecked within minutes.

After smashing ashore again by the lighthouse at Point Arena, it tore along the land, crushing the Russian Church at Fort Ross as if it were made of matchwood. Deep in the Coast Range canyons, five-hundred-year-old trees were uprooted and split asunder like saplings.

Then for a moment the rip returned to the sea again, plowing up beaches, starting landslides, sinking sandstone bluffs where they stood. Like a gigantic plowshare, it furrowed its way ashore by Bodega Head, demolishing a hotel and leaving a telltale crack eighty feet long and twenty feet wide.

It swept on toward Point Reyes Station, a handful of houses, a school, and a hardware store built around a tiny railway station. On the track, fireman Andy McNab was stoking the locomotive boiler in preparation for the commuter run into San Francisco. His engine and its four cars jackknifed into the air as the track buckled from the subterranean pressure. The train toppled on its side into the poppies growing along the right-of-way. McNab landed yards away, still clutching his shovel.

Pausing only to reduce a copse to kindling wood, the rip selected its next human target—the Skinner dairy farm at Olema.

Morning milking had just started in the farm's barnyard when the earthquake struck.

The Skinner farmhouse stood north of the cowshed. In front of it was a row of tall cypress trees that an early Skinner had planted to shade the path leading to the house. Behind the house was a granary. North of the trees was a rose garden. Farther north was a row of eucalyptus trees and a raspberry patch. Against the cowshed was a pile of manure.

In seconds the rip completely realigned the landscape. It moved the cypress trees fifteen feet south toward the cowshed. The rose garden was placed where the path had been. The eucalyptus trees and raspberry bushes slid into the space vacated by the rose garden. The farmhouse was shifted north, and the granary behind it moved south. The heap of manure and the cowshed were lifted and placed a full sixteen feet from where they had originally stood.

Stunned, the Skinner hands had an immediate problem. The rip caused the cows to stampede. It was several hours before they could be calmed, and days before the animals again gave milk.

A mile down the road, at the Shafter ranch, the earthquake cut straight through the corral. The ground opened directly beneath a cow. Its bellow of terror as it plunged head first into the gap was cut short as the ground closed again, leaving only its quivering tail still visible.

It was still twitching when the rip struck fifty miles farther on.

After falling upon the unsuspecting fishing village of Bolinas, where it snapped boats from their moorings and dropped the wharf into the water, the earthquake dived into the water again, burrowed briefly along the sea bed, and then reappeared, cutting into the cliffs at Mussel Rock.

Following the scarred trails of other ancient fault breaks, it swept over peninsula uplands and along the beds of valleys. In the process it wrecked the stone quadrangle of Stanford University at Palo Alto. Fourteen buildings crumbled to dust. In seconds the rip plowed through the university's botanical garden, three acres of rare plants from a dozen countries, leaving behind it a trail of damage estimated at over two million dollars. Miraculously, only two lives were lost; Easter vacation was still on.

Hills, valleys, and ridges were redefined as if by some demented Creator. Stands of giant redwoods, centuries old, many ten feet in girth, were snapped like matchsticks.

Villages and small towns, rough-and-ready places built around a church or schoolhouse, some with a main street lined with taverns, others with only a few bars, disintegrated with a shudder.

In San Luis Obispo, the telephone operator heard a scream, and the connection with Salinas broke off in midsentence. In Salinas, the exchange had been wrecked—along with Rudolph Spreckels' sugar factory, the Elks Hall, the Masonic Temple, and the Odd Fellows Building. In San Jose, twenty-one men, women, and children died from the effects of the lash.

Then, it moved on to strike terror in those who were locked up with their own fears. Agnews State Insane Asylum had stood for decades as a monument to society's attitude toward the mentally ill —lock them away behind bars.

The imposing edifice, a grim, rambling fortress of padded cells, restraint wings, and dormitories, stood in splendid isolation outside San Jose. The inmates spent most of their time locked away, guarded by attendants with little or no psychiatric nursing experience, men and women who for the most part considered themselves keepers rather than helpers.

The earthquake made no differentiation as it sheared under the asylum: the hopelessly mad tumbled to their death along with their guards as the buildings tottered and collapsed in a roar heard miles away. In that moment eighty-seven patients, eleven nurses, the superintendent, and his wife died. Hours passed before rescuers could dig out the many others trapped in the rubble; days elapsed before the last madman who had escaped into the countryside was captured.

Far to the south, the rip found another target: a sawmill at Hinckley Gulch. The gulch was a narrow gorge about a hundred feet deep with the mill at its far end. Effortlessly, the earthquake eased hundreds of thousands of tons of earth and rubble into the gorge in seconds, burying the mill and the nine men working inside it. As a final token, the earthquake deposited a hundred-foot-high redwood tree, erect, on the spot where the men were entombed.

The tremor slashed through San Juan, an old mission settlement, wrecking the hamlet's venerable Mission of San Juan Bautista with the same savage flick that had split the earth open for 270 miles.

In the process, the reserve water supply to San Francisco had been broken. In the marshy lowlands south of the city, the giant iron pipes running from the Peninsula reservoir buckled and snapped, twisting and telescoping into grotesque shapes. From them, great white spumes of water rose high into the air.

In San Francisco, two people actually *saw* the earthquake.

Jesse Cook, the police sergeant on duty in the produce market, saw it a moment after he became aware of panic among the horses all around him. Years later Cook recalled: "There was a deep rumble, deep and terrible, and then I could see it actually coming up Washington Street. The whole street was undulating. It was as if the waves of the ocean were coming towards me, billowing as they came."

Before Cook could move, the shock waves sent him reeling.

A few blocks away, John Barrett, the *Examiner*'s city desk news editor, also saw and heard its approach; a long, low, moaning sound that set buildings "dancing" on their foundations. Suddenly he and his colleagues found themselves staggering. "It was as though the earth was slipping quietly away from under our feet. There was a sickening sway, and we were all flat on our faces."

They seemed to be "glued to the ground," held there as if by some gigantic unseen vacuum.

From this position Barrett saw that the *Examiner* building and all the others around were caught up in a macabre jig of their own. They swayed out into the street, then rocked back, only to repeat the movement with even more determination.

Everywhere there was the roar of sound, caused by wood, masonry, and glass thrown out of kilter by the uncanny force of the quake. "Trolley tracks were twisted, their wires down, wriggling like serpents, flashing blue sparks all the time. The street was gashed in any number of places. From some of the holes water was spurting; from others, gas."

Barrett somehow staggered to his feet and turned toward the office.

"This is going to be a hell of a day," he said to his two reporter colleagues. "Let's start covering it." Despite the accuracy of his prediction, the *Examiner* was unable to publish one word of it during that day.

High up on Russian Hill, Bailey Millard lay stunned, his canvas ripped, his easel smashed, his paints scattered by the force of the jolt.

Below, the whole city seemed to be "rocking and rolling under the most fantastic motion."

It was as if San Francisco were being pushed into the sea. The sound accompanying the movement reminded some of whiplash: "Each crack would be the signal for more chimneys, more spires, more cornices to be snapped off."

The tower bell of Old St. Mary's Church in Chinatown, clanging senselessly, was joined at once by the city's other churchbells. To Millard and many others, Judgment Day was tolling for a city that deserved it.

From where he sprawled, held fast by fear, he had a panoramic view of the destruction below. Brick walls crashed to the ground as if they had been erected from a child's construction kit; wood-frame buildings splintered.

Then, slowly, the area south of Market began to move.

Earth waves, two to three feet high, undulated through the ground, trembling foundations, rocking buildings, toppling towers and cornices.

The whole skyline was dancing, and suddenly it seemed to Millard that City Hall was leading that dance.

At that moment seven million dollars' worth of stone and brickwork was shaken off the administrative headquarters of San Francisco, leaving its frame standing among the shattered columns like a monstrous birdcage.

Then the shaking stopped. Above the dust and rumble of falling masonry, the bell of Old St. Mary's Church still beat frantically—a harbinger of even worse devastation to come.

Ten whole seconds passed before the second phase of the tremor began.

It was just long enough for Britain's Consul General, Walter Courtney Bennett, to pull his wife and daughter from their beds in their rooms overlooking Union Square. All three stood in the doorway of one of their rooms; the frame would afford some protection.

From outside came a sound like nails being wrenched out of the lid of a packing crate—and then the front of a building across the street sprang outward and dropped to the ground.

The same thing was happening all over the city. Roofs were caving in, spreading their rafters. The rafters in turn kicked out the walls, collapsing buildings in a deafening roar.

"And everywhere," Bennett recalled, "there was the noise, like thousands of violins, all at a discord. The most harrowing sound one could imagine."

Thousands of brick chimneys crashed through ceilings, sometimes falling on occupants below before they could leap clear. Plaster showered everywhere, raising clouds of dust. And through everything, the church bells jangled.

6. A Fatal Fall

JAMES HOPPER, THE REPORTER on the *Call* who had written so evocatively about the scene at the Opera House the night before, gazed out from his third-floor bedroom with mounting disbelief.

He had slept badly, dreaming a confused dream in which Caruso's voice, screaming over Carmen's prostrate form, intermingled with the tattooing of the horses' hooves in the livery stable. The images mingled, rose, interwoven in a fiendish crescendo, "and then I awoke to the city's destruction. Right away it was incredible, the violence of the 'quake. It started with a determination that left no doubt of its purpose. It pounced upon the earth like a bulldog."

The earth was a rat, shaking, shaken. "The motion seemed to be vertical with a rotary twist, like a French cook tossing a fish in a frying pan."

He scrambled out of bed, shouting: "It's incredible, incredible." As he reached the window a fire escape outside crashed to the ground; with it went the glass in the frame he leaned against.

"I heard the roar of bricks coming down, and twisted girders, and at the same time saw a pale crescent moon in the green sky. The St. Francis Hotel was waving to and fro with a swing as violent and exaggerated as a tree in a tempest. Then the rear of my building, for three stories upward, fell. The mass struck a series of little wooden houses in the alley below. I saw them crash in like emptied eggs, the bricks passing through the roofs as though through tissue paper. I had this feeling of finality. This is death. Then curiosity took over. I had to see what had happened."

All over the city, reporters and photographers were having similar experiences.

At that moment, the second great tremor struck.

In his home, at 154 Seventh Street, Edgar Gleeson, who had worked as a reporter on the fledgling *Daily News* for two years, thought this second tremor "could have had its origin in our front parlor, lurched down the hallway and expended itself in my bedroom."

The first shock flung him across the bed. The second sent him skidding across the floor. Over the sound of the creaking wood, Gleeson could hear his mother and grandmother praying in the next bedroom.

Struggling to keep his footing, he reached their bedroom. The door was jammed. Using all his strength he forced it open, and found that a heavy dresser had tipped over; only the headboard of the bed had saved his grandmother from being crushed beneath it. Carefully Gleeson eased them to safety. By then he had the feeling that he would be reporting one of the great disasters of the world.

In his suite at the Palace Hotel, Alfred Hertz lay in bed on his stomach, gripping the mattress, while the frame leaped up and down as if it were alive. It took him a few seconds to grasp that everything else in the suite was also moving. His dressing table careened across the room and crashed into the wardrobe. An armchair waltzed in crazy tempo with a coffee table. From outside came a fresh shattering of glass, and the deep, ominous crunch of cracking masonry. Augmenting it all was the sound of timber creaking under strain.

Alfred Hertz, conductor, listened with professional interest to the medley of sound: "Even in this moment I was conscious of sound effects. In operas such elementary catastrophes are invariably orchestrated FFF, while musically speaking, the earthquake gave me the sensation of an uncanny *mezzo forte* effect; something comparable to the *mezzo forte* roll on a cymbal or gong."

As if cued by a celestial conductor the tremor rose to a crescendo of noise, held it there for a long, last second, and stopped.

The silence was complete.

In his bedroom, James Hopper found the silence more ominous

than the roaring which had preceded it. "Throughout the long quaking, I had not heard a cry, not a sound, not a sob, not a whisper. And now, when the roar of crumbling buildings was over, and only a brick fell here and there, this silence continued, and it was an awful thing. Then, in the alley below, someone began to groan. It was a woman's groan, soft and low."

In a moment, mingled with the groaning, came another new sound—the hiss of escaping gas.

Enrico Caruso had been weeping hysterically for some minutes when Alfred Hertz reached the tenor's suite. The two parlors looked as if they had been ransacked by inept burglars. Bureau drawers were open, their contents spilled everywhere. The earthquake had piled Caruso's forty pairs of boots alongside his silk shirts and dressing gowns, heaping the whole lot in a fireplace. One of the Turkish carpets had been rolled up; where it had lain, the remnants of a French chandelier were now scattered.

In the rear parlor, Caruso sat bolt upright in bed, clutching at his nightshirt with both hands. To Hertz, the singer was in many ways a figure as pitiable as any he had ever portrayed on stage. The earthquake seemed to have visibly shrunk Caruso, "as if the cataclysmic terror had singled him out to obliterate his glory of the previous night; as if Providence had evil designs on him personally."

The conductor asked Caruso if he was injured. Like a confused child, the singer first shook his head, then nodded, tears streaming down his cheeks. "He then embraced me hysterically, repeatedly insisting that we were doomed."

Disengaging himself, the conductor tried to ascertain just what injuries the singer had suffered. It was, wept Caruso, his voice: the shock, he feared, had damaged his vocal cords.

Hertz, understandably, found this rather baffling. Caruso could speak, even if his words came in sobbing gulps. But this reaction was typical: in spite of all the evidence around him, Caruso managed to take the earthquake personally. Hertz, experienced in dealing with the self-inflicted crises that many of his singers seemed to undergo periodically, knew how to deal with Caruso's fears.

Had the tenor tried his voice?

Caruso shook his head. Besides, how could a man sing when the world had collapsed on him?

"But the earthquake," coaxed Hertz gently, "is over." He moved to the window, beckoning Caruso to come and see for himself.

"The street presented an amazing series of grotesque sights. Most people had fled from their rooms without stopping to dress, many of them a little less than naked. But excitement was running so high that nobody noticed or cared."

As they watched, a woman in a nightgown ran down the street, carrying a baby by its legs—"as if it were a trussed turkey." Several men stood around with shaving lather on their faces. A couple were carrying a large painting out of a tenement block across the street. Everybody seemed to be talking, "as if it was all too much to take in, and hoping that by talking they could make some sense of what had happened."

Opening the window (one of the few in the Palace that were still intact), Hertz tapped imperiously on the sill and commanded Caruso to sing.

For a moment the tenor hesitated. Then, at the top of his voice:

> *La fanta mi salva*
> *L'immondo ritrova—*

In the street below, people stopped talking and stared up toward the window. To Horatio Hovey, a guest at the Palace, the sound of Caruso's voice was electrifying. He, like many others, maintained that it was the "bravest and best" performance the singer had ever given, an "attempt on the singer's part to show the world that at least he had not been scared."

Reassured that his voice had lost none of its potency, Caruso now used it to heap invective on those who had insisted that he make a tour he had never wanted to make. The man who only two days earlier had said that it was "God's will" that he should have come to San Francisco, so avoiding the catastrophe threatening Naples, now shouted that if he had followed his first instinct he would not have found himself in a situation where his splendid wardrobe of clothes and gallery of self-portraits had been ruined.

Alfred Hertz suggested that Caruso get dressed. With the help of his valet, the tenor selected a shirt, striped trousers, and jacket. Once dressed, he looked as if "he were off to pay a courtesy call on some Embassy, rather than escape from an earthquake." Hertz, who had dressed himself in the dark, now became aware that his clothes were anything but formal: he was wearing the trousers from an evening suit, a gray vest, and a brown coat; inexplicably, he had stuffed an empty bottle of eau de cologne into his pocket.

Caruso began rummaging through his collection of portraits, and eventually found what he was looking for: a photograph of a man with a belligerent expression and rather prominent teeth. It was inscribed: "To Enrico Caruso. From Theodore Roosevelt."

Hugh Brown was leaning protectively over his wife, Marjorie, repeating: "It's all right, dear! It's all right!"

Marjorie Brown nodded, smiling reassurance that the baby she carried was still alive. In the silence she had felt it kick.

Hugh had tried to salvage what he could while his wife dressed. For Marjorie "it wasn't easy to get into my clothes, but I did manage a maternity dress of black silk. Then I looked over my hats. I chose a black lace one, with feathers. It was utterly inappropriate, but it was the handsomest so I thought it ought to be saved. Then I wondered what I should carry."

Marjorie Brown soon found that she was not alone in her desire to save something personal, and preferably expensive, at this moment. Women insisted on taking their best ball gowns; men salvaged a silver-topped walking stick, a top hat, or a formal morning coat. The streets began to fill with incongruous sights—a woman pushing a pram filled with objets d'art and jewelry, a man rolling a desk along on its casters; people carried family portraits, heavy Bibles, remnants of a dowry, a favorite frying pan, candelabras.

In minutes, Marjorie Brown decided what she would save: a sewing machine, the layette for her baby, and her toothbrush: "It would have taken more than an earthquake for me to go anywhere without this toilet article."

From his home on Dolores Street, Officer Leonard Ingham saw black smoke drift languidly over roofs and cottage tops a dozen blocks away. Through the smoke came a fork of flame. To him it was a precursor of doom; his nightmare had come true. He calmly ordered his wife to pack what she could and then make her way to one of the ferries which would take her to safety across the Bay.

Then, kissing her goodbye, the patrolman hurried off to report for duty.

High up on Washington Street, Brigadier General Funston had been observing the city intently for some minutes. He could see flames coming from the other side of Market Street, the breeze carrying the smoke slowly toward Twin Peaks. From where he stood on Nob Hill, he was roughly in the center of the city's second great division, the area north of Market. Compact, closely built since pioneer days, it included the financial and shopping districts, most of the city's theaters and hotels, Chinatown, the waterfront warehouses and wharves, the steep streets leading up Nob, Russian, and Telegraph Hills, the dives, cribs, and ginmills of the Barbary Coast district, the North Beach shacks and tenements of the Mexican, Spanish, and Italian quarters, the piers of Fisherman's Wharf. The section north of Market extended on his left to the Bay, and behind him to Van Ness Avenue, a 125-foot-wide boulevard of expensive homes. Beyond Van Ness lay the Presidio garrison.

As he watched, Funston observed two things especially. The columns of smoke, still isolated from one another but multiplying all the time, were rising a thousand feet from the fires below. People watching with him from Washington Street "were shocked and white."

He knew enough about human reactions to realize that when that first stunned feeling passed, "these very same people, along with the city's entire population, would need firm handling." In sort, Brigadier General Funston saw the probability of panic taking control of the situation. For a military commander, this was intolerable.

He looked toward the Presidio. He had nearly two thousand men under arms there, "troops," he said later, "who would brook no nonsense, who would obey orders implicitly."

Though it was not confirmed for some hours, at that moment Brigadier General Funston assumed a new role for himself—that of self-appointed military governor of San Francisco. He did so without any presidential authority, without the blessing of Congress, and in direct violation of the Constitution. He did so solely because he believed he was the man God had ordained to save godless San Francisco.

Without waiting even for a cup of coffee, the forty-year-old soldier, like some latter-day Renaissance hero, started to run down Washington Street, startling neighbors because he was dressed in civilian clothes.

In the seventeen minutes following the earthquake, nearly fifty fires were reported in the downtown area of the city. Not one fire bell clanged. The Fire Department's central alarm system, housed in a building in Chinatown, had been wrecked. The first jarring shock of the earthquake broke 556 of the 600 wet-cell batteries that operated the system.

A mile away from where the system lay in shambles, the man who had installed it was dying.

The earthquake woke Dennis Sullivan, the city's Fire Chief, after less than an hour's sleep. His last conscious impression was the sound of avalanching brick as he ran to his wife's rescue in the rear bedroom of their home above the fire station on Bush Street.

The roar Sullivan heard came from the high ornamental tower of the adjoining California Hotel as it punched through the firehouse roof, carrying away part of Mrs. Sullivan's bedroom floor. Blinded by mortar dust, Sullivan fell through the opening, pitched three floors below and landed across a fire wagon. His skull was fractured, as were his ribs, legs, and arms.

In moments the firemen had lifted him clear, carried him outside, and gently laid him on a cart. Then they raced him through the debris-laden streets to the Southern Pacific Hospital.

The Fire Chief, mercifully unconscious, was the twenty-seventh emergency case the hospital had admitted in fifteen minutes.

The time of his admission was logged at exactly 5:30 A.M.

5:30 A.M. to 12:30 P.M.

Derailed train at Point Reyes Station (*Bruce A. Bolt, Director Seismographic Stations, Univ. of Calif., Berkeley*)

Kearney Street with the Hall of Justice on the right (*Metropolitan Life*)

7. Polishing Coffin Handles

BY HALF PAST FIVE, a few people in the outside world already knew that the West Coast of America had been hit by a major earthquake.

Within eleven and a half minutes of the rip, seismographs in Tokyo's Imperial University were busy recording the wave motions traversing the world from the rupture along the San Andreas Fault. Dr. F. Omori, Professor of Seismology and a member of the Imperial Earthquake Investigation Committee, had waited anxiously at his seismographs for exactly twenty-three minutes for the earthquake to strike. At 10 P.M. Japan Standard Time, the seismograph pendulums began recording preliminary tremors, small waves traveling through the crust of the earth at the rate of about six or seven miles a second.

Such waves give advance warning of impending disaster; they are inaudible to the human ear but are somehow recognized by animals as danger signals. It was these waves that had frightened the animals in San Francisco.

On the Tokyo seismographs these smaller tremors lasted nine minutes and forty-nine seconds. In Birmingham, England, where they had farther to travel, the tremors were recorded for twenty-five minutes.

In the Bay of San Francisco, the tide was dropping, and continued to drop until four inches of water had drained out through the Golden Gate. Moments later it re-formed in the Pacific and surged back into the Bay. Along the coastal edge of the San Andreas Fault, other phenomena were occurring. Near Santa Cruz a beach suddenly sank ten feet, as if it had taken the full weight of a giant footprint; below Monterey, a cliff face crumbled. At Castorville, a fresh row of mud geysers appeared, a line of punctures in the earth's surface spouting hot blue shale. In the Coast Range canyons, forests of redwoods that had withstood the initial impact of the rip now keeled over. All of this was caused by the aftershocks. These compounded the terror of thousands of people who lived along the Fault, as the early morning light revealed the full state of the destruction.

At the State Asylum of Agnews, Sheriff Ross and twenty deputies from San Jose surrounded the wrecked buildings and began to advance on a scene that Ross later testified "had never before been seen in an asylum. The moans of the dying were terrible. To add to the horror of the situation many lunatics had broken from the rubble and were trying to escape. They were wild and rushed to and fro, attacking everyone who came in their path. The question of what to do with them arose. There was no building nearby in which they could be confined, and as they were violent, it was necessary to restrain them in some way. A doctor suggested that they be tied to trees."

Ropes were procured and the acutely disturbed were bound hand and foot to the small trees which surrounded the hospital and miraculously remained standing.

Two thousand six hundred miles away in his extravagantly furnished New York apartment, William Randolph Hearst was awakened by a telephone call from the city desk of his New York *American* morning newspaper. The caller told him that San Francisco had been hit by an earthquake.

Hearst had built up a newspaper empire on a mixture of pious crusading, muckraking, and dubious advertising. His San Francisco *Examiner* had been labeled "The Whore's Daily Guide and Handy Compendium" because of the classified advertising it carried offering the services of young masseuses.

Hearst saw nothing wrong with this kind of reader service. Born and raised in San Francisco, he had assumed something of the city's own personality; he was sentimental, vigorous, stimulating, ruthless, and frequently eccentric.

The news that his city had been struck by a major earthquake produced an uncharacteristic response. Without even waiting to ascertain the severity of the shock, he issued orders to the city desk of the *American:* "Don't overplay it. They have earthquakes often in California."

He expanded on that theme in his editorial for the *American:* "The plain facts are that earthquakes in California, which occur at intervals of about twenty-year periods, kill far fewer people than the cyclones in the Middle West, the flood tornadoes in the South Coast states, and the lightning storms and heat waves along the Atlantic states kill every year. Californians don't wholly approve of earthquakes, but they prefer them to cyclones or tornadoes or floods or protracted heat or lightning storms. All of the earthquakes which have occurred in California since it was discovered nearly four hundred years ago have not killed so many people as one or two great cyclones of the Middle West."

The editorial appeared alongside a retouched photograph of the great Baltimore Fire of 1904—in keeping with the *American*'s claim to be always first with the news in words and pictures.

In San Francisco the reality was far grimmer than any faked photograph could portray.

Shortly after 5:30 A.M., James Hopper, the *Call* reporter, began the almost impossible task of trying to get an overall impression of the disaster.

The hiss of escaping gas which he had noticed from the hotel bedroom window had increased by the time he reached the street. But the groans from the woman trapped beneath the pile of rubble in the alley below had stopped.

Smoke was now billowing insolently beyond Market, that grim area of stockyards, lodging houses, saloons, schools, and modest homes, built for the most part from clapboard tinder.

All his life Hopper remembered those first minutes after the earthquake: "The streets were full of people, half-clad, dishevelled, but silent, absolutely silent, as if suddenly they had become speech-less idiots. It went down Post Street towards the center of town, and in the morning's garish light I saw many men and women with gray faces. No one spoke. All of them had a singular hurt expression —not one of physical pain, but rather one of injured sensibilities, as if some trusted friend had suddenly wronged them, or as if someone had been rude to them.

"Personally, I felt a strange elation. I was immensely proud of myself. I had gone through those hideous moments in full command of myself, and now I was calm, obviously calm. I threw my chest out and looked with amazement upon my dazed co-citizens. And yet, a few days later, when I saw a friend who had met me just at this time, he told me that I had been so excited I couldn't talk, that my arms shook, and that my eyes were an inch out of their sockets. As I walked slowly down the street, I was very busy taking notes for my paper. 'Such and such number, such and such street, cornice down; this building roof down; that building, crumbled.' And then I exclaimed 'Good Lord! I'm not going to take a list of *all* the buildings in the city.'

"I kept on going toward the paper. I thought I was observing very carefully, but I wasn't. I remember now, for instance, seeing the roof of the Hotel Savoy caved into the building; but I did not try to find out if many had been hurt or killed.

"It was rather unimportant detail that struck me. In Union Square I saw a man in pink pajamas and a pink bathrobe, carrying a pink comforter under his arms, walking barefooted upon the gravel. In the center of the Square an old man was, with great deliberation, trying to decipher the inscription of the Dewey monument through spectacles from which the lenses had fallen.

"I cut across through the Square and for the first time, heard someone speak. A man said to me 'Look!' I looked the way he was pointing, at a three-story wooden building called the Geary, which stood between an unfinished building at the corner of Stockton and Geary Streets and another tall building. The two skyscrapers had shaken off their side walls onto the wooden one nestling between them, and only the façade of the latter stood, like cardboard scenery.

"A man stood at one of the windows, trailing to the ground a long piece of cloth that looked no thicker than a ribbon, with the evident intention of sliding down it. I shouted to him to wait a moment, and ran to the door. I found the stairs still intact, stuck along the front wall as if with mucilage.

"I scrambled up to the third floor over piles of plaster and laths, and there forgot about the man. For I came to a piece of room in which I found a bed covered with debris. A slim white hand and wrist reached out of the debris, like an appeal."

The horror of the earthquake suddenly hit James Hopper with

full force. For a moment he stood there, frozen by the enormity of his realization. He moved toward the bed, beckoned by the curious twisting of the hand in relation to the wrist.

"I threw off the stuff, and found a woman underneath, still alive, a little, slender thing whom I had no trouble carrying down to the sidewalk, where someone put her in an express wagon. I went back with another man and we found a second woman, whom we took down on a door. There was another woman in another corner, covered by a pile of bricks. She was dead.

"By this time the ruins were fairly swarming with rescuers, and a policeman had to drive many of them away with his club. All the time, however, I could hear a mysterious wailing somewhere in the back. Finally I located it on the second floor. A strip of the hallway still remained along the right wall. I followed it till I came to a place where the whole hall was intact, and there, on a platform amid the ruins, a woman with long dishevelled hair was pacing to and fro, repeating in a long, drawn-out wail, over and over again, 'Oh, my husband is dead, and a young man is dead, and a woman is dead; oh, my husband is dead and a young man is dead and a woman is dead.'

" 'Where is your husband?' we roared in her ear, for she seemed unable to hear us. She pointed toward the back. We went toward the back and came to an abrupt end of the hall."

Below, sticking out of a mound of bricks, was a bedpost. Hopper and two other men looked at each other. Then, simultaneously, they jumped down onto the rubble and began throwing it clear.

"Above us the walls of the homicidal building towered. After a while a fireman joined us. He seemed stupefied, and like us began to pick up bricks one by one. Finally another fireman came and called him. 'Come on, Bill,' he said. 'There's fires.'

"They went off, and then, after we had worked a time longer, a red-headed youth who was digging with us said, 'What's de use of digging out those that's dead?'

"His remark struck us all as being so profoundly true that without another word, we all quit."

All over the city, rescue parties were experiencing the same helpless feeling.

At 6 A.M., a rescue team abandoned work at an apartment house on Ninth and Brannan Streets, leaving the dead in the wreckage. Some who were pinned down by wreckage were drowned in water from a broken main. That ruptured water pipe, and hundreds like it, decided the future of the city.

As far as Bill Marston, president of the city's Chamber of Commerce, was concerned, the future was being "decided there and then," in Mission Street.

On awakening, Marston, a sanguine, middle-aged man, had made a number of rapid calculations. The rocking his own home had undergone was a bad sign for the flimsy area south of Market. The risk of panic was high, especially since many of those living in the area were first-generation immigrants who had never experienced a Californian "shaker."

Dressed, he hurried down in his buggy to the Merchant's Exchange Building, where the Chamber of Commerce had a second-floor office. Satisfied that the structure appeared intact, he headed south, across the silent, twisted cablecar tracks, to Mission Street, toward the column of smoke Brigadier General Funston was observing from his home at about the same time.

Marston reached the site of the first fire, a restaurant, to find the No. 17 engine of the Fire Department, a Clapp and Jones steamer, standing idly by a hydrant. Surrounded by a group of stunned firemen, the pump operator kept on repeating. "I can't get any pressure. The main is busted!"

Marston's heart sank. He knew enough about the city's water system to realize that the fact that there was no pressure meant that the spiderwork of mains in the downtown area had been put out of action. One of the world's largest and finest fire departments had been rendered virtually helpless. The earthquake had shattered pipes leading from Crystal Springs Lake and the San Andreas Lake into the city.

Bill Marston quickly assessed the situation. The fire could not be stopped south of Market; at best all one could hope was that the area on the other side of the Slot could be protected.

As he mounted his buggy, a new column of light-colored smoke rose into the air. The produce district had caught fire.

And that, as Marston knew only too well, was situated north of Market Street.

In that first hour there were many who did not notice the fires. They were the victims of shock in one form or another. When they had recovered, the memories of what they *thought* they had seen or done remained with them, helping to create the mythology surrounding the disaster.

Leo Agoust, a guest at the Grand Hotel, believed he saw a lion and a prey of leopards "slinking through the ruins" as he fled to safety—twenty years before the city housed a zoo. Miss Margaret Underhill of Chicago maintained until her death forty years later that "sometime before 6 A.M," she saw a soldier "shoot a man hopelessly entombed" in the wreckage of a collapsed house, to "end his suffering"—ninety minutes before the first soldier entered the city. William Overton of Los Angeles, in San Francisco on a business trip, swore that he saw a blaze in Chinatown hours before that district caught fire.

Still others became unduly preoccupied with the trivia of life. Little Geneve Shaffer saw an old woman sitting on the sidewalk outside her home, intently toying with a pair of shoes. In another part of town, Susy Ponson watched an undertaker squatting outside his funeral parlor, completely absorbed in the task of polishing coffin handles.

8. A Tumult of Noise

To Dr. Howard D'Arcy Power, a London physician visiting the city, these would undoubtedly have been interpreted as reassuring signs that life in San Francisco was still normal. Dr. Power, a devoted student of "psychic effects," seized upon the earthquake as an opportunity to obtain some practical firsthand field experience of how these "effects" manifested themselves in a mass of people.

At 5:45 A.M., he had dressed and left the St. Francis Hotel— a tall, imposing figure in black frock coat and striped trousers— moving assuredly, with the air of a consultant off to pay a house call on a patient with unusual symptoms.

As he walked through the streets, he made a number of remarkable medical deductions: "Only a very few had come out minus clothing; this, I hold, is the best evidence of control."

By the time he had covered a few blocks, he believed he had the clinical answer to this "control." The earthquake "came at a time when the nervous system was rested by sleep."

To test the validity of his conclusion, Dr. Power decided, amid all the chaos and confusion, to take the pulse rate of those people who had shown "control" by fully dressing before leaving their endangered homes. He found, he later reported solemnly in the *Pacific Medicine Journal,* that "the pulse rates showed an acceleration of from ten to twenty beats above the average."

If Dr. Power thought it unusual that an eminent London physician should behave in this manner, he gave no sign of it as he moved from person to person, politely asking if he might measure pulse rates.

Soon he had held enough wrists to make an assessment that must rank as one of the most original in the history of medicine: "These people I have observed have fortunately been deprived of car service, alcohol and luxuries; they have nothing but simple food, and have been compelled to take physical exercise in the open air to obtain it. The men have found it possible to live without cigars or whisky, and the ladies, without candy—they have had the enforced benefits of a sanitorium, and good health is the result."

It would be charitable to think that the doctor was so preoccupied with pulse-taking that he, too, failed to notice the fires which were beginning to destroy property at the rate of one million dollars every ten minutes.

From where he stood at the corner of Sansome Street, the black column of smoke ahead was indeed like a dark precursor of destruction to Brigadier General Funston. The great retreat from south of the Slot was already well underway. What astonished Funston was the quantity people carried: bathtubs, rugs, furniture, bedding—all were being carried past where he stood in the doorway of a dress shop. He noticed, too, that the blankness—the shocked, stony faces he had seen up on Washington Street—had been replaced down on Sansome with looks of fear and terror; many of the evacuees were close to panic.

Funston felt justified in his decision to take over the city.

Later, he was asked if it had not troubled his conscience that he had acted so imperiously.

"Why?" he replied.

Frederick Funston never doubted any of his judgments all his life. Having made one, he seldom changed his mind, preferring to act on impulse and with speed to back up his instinct.

Perhaps it was this that finally decided him to plunge into a role which surrounded him with controversy until his death. Or perhaps he was no more than a man protecting his home.

Whatever the reason, shortly after 6:15 A.M., Brigadier General Frederick Funston decided he would act, alone and independently of any other agency; he would not even consult with Mayor Schmitz before placing San Francisco under military control.

Thirty-five years earlier, another general—Sheridan—had faced the same problem in another city—Chicago—during the great fire there. He had ordered in his soldiers to maintain order, only to be forced to withdraw them under pressure from the outraged civil administration.

Even if Funston had recalled that incident, he said later, it would not have influenced the course he was about to take.

Forcing his way through the crowds fleeing from the fires, he cut across Sansome Street, breaking into a run.

Ever since that fateful morning, argument has surrounded the first, vital moves Funston made. Some reports place him at the Hall of Justice, briefing Police Chief Jeremiah Dinan on what he intended to do; others have Funston meeting Schmitz outside the wrecked City Hall, deciding "between them" to call in soldiers to "assist" the police force in maintaining law and order. Even William Bronson, in his excellent pictorial study of the San Francisco disaster, maintains that Funston acted at all times with civic blessing.

He did not.

The evidence lies today in the files of the Presidio archives. Dr. William O'Brien, the archivist, has no doubt at all that in those first moments, decisions were made entirely by Funston. What he was doing, Dr. O'Brien has said, was "putting the city in effect under martial law, and assuming total initial responsibility for that act."

Later, Secretary of War William Howard Taft told Congress that it "would take an Act of Congress to relieve him of the responsibility for the violence the Army did to the Constitution in San Francisco."

Funston's own carefully worded account of his actions underlines this.

Beyond Sansome Street, he found that "several fires were burning fiercely, and that the city fire department was helpless, owing to water mains having been shattered by the earthquake." He realized then that a great conflagration was inevitable, and that the city police force would not be able to maintain the fire lines and protect public and private property over the great area affected. He at once determined to order out all available troops, not only for the purpose of guarding federal buildings, but to aid the fire and police departments of the city.

That decision to order in his soldiers—phrased in such a way, after the event, as to imply consultation—was in fact Brigadier General Funston's alone.

He arrived at it by the time he reached Sansome Street; now he set about putting it into force. Having tried unsuccessfully to telephone—the entire system had been disrupted—Funston found that he had to return to "first principles" in order to communicate with the commanding officers at the Presidio and Fort Mason, the two Army posts most convenient to the city: "Several men dashing about wildly in automobiles declined to assist me, for which I indulged in the pious hope that they be burnt out."

There is a curious anomaly in that wish; in the days to come observers detected other oddities in Funston's behavior.

Unable to flag down a car, he made his way, "running and walking alternatively, from Sansome Street to the army stable on Pine, near Hyde, a little more than a mile, where I arrived in so serious a condition that I could scarcely stand. Directing my carriage driver to mount my saddle horse, I hastily scribbled a note to Colonel Charles Morris, Artillery Corps, commanding officer at the Presidio, directing him to report with his entire command to the chief of police at the Hall of Justice on Portsmouth Square. I then sent a verbal message of the same import to Captain M. L. Walker, Corps of Engineers, in command at Fort Mason."

As an afterthought—at best no more than a token gesture to the civil authorities he had already decided were unable to cope with the crisis—Funston testified that "before leaving Sansome Street I asked a member of the city police force to inform the chief of police as soon as possible of the action I contemplated taking."

Again, this was a strange thing to do. Sansome Street was a mere six blocks from Police Chief Dinan's office in the Hall of Justice—a five-minute run for the Brigadier General. To have entrusted this momentous decision to call in the Army to the hands of a patrolman possibly reflects the attitude already prevailing in Funston's mind; he would act first and seek sanction later.

Events proved him right in not relying on City Hall's ability to act, but it was an attitude that in the days to come had a decisive effect on the people of San Francisco and on the attitude the soldiers displayed toward them.

Funston's scribbled instructions to Colonel Morris and Captain Walker were taken on horseback by Lieutenant Long.

From the Pine Street stable, he rode first to Fort Mason. There Captain Walker, the Commanding Officer, had gone back to bed, having assessed the earthquake as no more than a mild shaker. Roused by Long, the captain immediately mobilized his company of engineers.

By 7:00 they were marching on the city, muskets slung on shoulders, ammunition pouches filled.

By then Lieutenant Long had reached the Presidio quarters of Colonel Charles Morris and was knocking hard on his front door. It was finally opened by Morris himself. Long handed him Funston's orders: "By the time he had finished, the old gentleman was beside himself with rage." Morris controlled his temper long enough to say: "Go back and tell that newspaperman [Funston] that he had better look up his army regulations, and there he will find that nobody but the President of the United States in person can order regular troops into any city!"

With that he slammed the front door shut.

Lieutenant Long decided that the time had now come for him, too, to break Army regulations. He ordered the Presidio's bugler to sound the call to arms. In minutes the garrison had assembled. Before "anyone could interfere," Long gave the command, "Fours left!" and the soldiers marched toward San Francisco.

There were ten companies of Coast Artillery; the First, Ninth, and Twenty-fourth Batteries of Field Artillery; the entire Twenty-second Regiment of Infantry; troops I, K, and M, Fourteenth Cavalry; B Company, Hospital Corps—a small army, a mixture of seasoned soldiers and raw recruits.

Having made his moves to garrison the city, Brigadier General Funston decided to stroll to the summit of Nob Hill, only a few blocks distant. The General planned his coming strategy, every move of which turned on the black smoke spiraling from the densely populated region south of Market.

Satisfied that for the moment he had done all that was possible, he walked home to share a cup of coffee with his wife. He then ordered her to evacuate to the Presidio.

"But surely Washington Street is safe at this end?" she asked.

"Nowhere," replied her husband in a rare burst of eloquence, "is safe against the pestilence of fire."

Unaware that Funston had already acted, Eugene Schmitz was rapidly reviewing the resources left to him to save what remained of San Francisco. They were pitifully meager.

Like the rest of the city, he had been awakened as if "a huge dog was tossing a rag doll."

Any thought of the impending graft investigation or his relationship with Abe Ruef had been banished by the time he had dressed. By then he was aware of the fires.

Later, he reported that his first thought on seeing the smoke was: "I was Mayor of my native city. I could not let it burn and stand idly by."

He drove in his buggy toward City Hall. From downtown refugees he learned of its destruction. Bill Marston, President of the Chamber of Commerce, said later that the destruction of City Hall is "what comes of mixing bad politics and bad cement."

Schmitz headed his buggy toward the Hall of Justice, downtown on Kearney Street. The Hall, facing historic Portsmouth Square, had been badly cracked by the earthquake. When the Mayor arrived, huge flakes of masonry were still falling from the central tower.

Waiting on the steps were Jeremiah Dinan, Chief of Police, and John Dougherty, who for the past seventy minutes had found himself—only because of seniority in the Fire Department—holding an office he had never dreamed of assuming: Fire Chief of San Francisco.

Together the three men hurried down to the basement office where Dinan had set up a makeshift disaster headquarters. Desks, chairs, and a large map of the city had been hurriedly assembled.

From this bunker the three men faced the task of saving one of the most beautifully situated cities in the world. Each, in his own way, was ill equipped for the job.

Eugene Schmitz had never in his wildest moments seen himself as the protector of a city he had cheated and boodled for so many years.

Nor had Jeremiah Dinan prepared any contingency plans for the role his department would play following a major disaster. Virtually all the communication links within the force had been severed;

the telephone lines to the police stations were cut, the street call boxes smashed. His seven hundred men were scattered, working according to no set plan.

The Mayor listened in silence as his police chief painted a dismal picture. Then Schmitz gave his first orders of the day: the Police Department's sole patrol car was to be sent around all the precincts to establish their condition; every available officer was to close down every liquor-selling outlet: saloons, hotel bars, grocery stores. On his way to the Hall of Justice he had noticed something that frightened him: saloons and bars seemed to be filled—often only a dozen blocks away from where smoke was rising. Mayor Schmitz, a teetotaler, knew enough of the effects of drinking to realize that it would produce additional problems in a situation already fraught with danger.

"Damn the lot," he ordered. "Closed."

Dinan left the room to implement the order, surprised at the "calmness and authority the Mayor displayed."

The Mayor turned to Fire Chief Dougherty and looked into the lusterless eyes of the old man before him. Dougherty was sixty-nine years old. He was "worn and drawn," a man even his friends said had become deafened and bowed by twenty-eight years of chasing fire bells.

Haltingly, he outlined the scope of the disaster from the point of view of the Fire Department. By 7:00, over twenty major fires had been reported. At each one his firemen had found the hydrants useless. They had been forced to fall back, leaving the flames to spread.

"No water anywhere?"

Dougherty shook his head.

"Where can you start a fire line?"

After a pause the old Fire Chief began to speak again. There was no chance of saving the area south of Market—though some of the buildings were of brick, "which would slow up the fire." Meanwhile he would order his men to make a stand along Market.

The pair moved over to the map. Schmitz listened as Dougherty sketched out a proposed plan of action. Every available appliance would head for Market, the city's widest street, and prepare to repulse the flames with water drawn from the Bay through a series of interconnected hoses. They would be helped in their efforts by the fact that both sides of the street were lined with buildings their constructors had assured the Fire Department were "fire-resistant."

It was a plan that Dennis Sullivan had drawn up shortly after he had entered office. Its implementation required the same boldness that had gone into its conception. Mayor Schmitz could have been forgiven for doubting the capacity of the old fireman Dougherty to execute the plan.

As John Dougherty left the basement room, a tumult came from the direction of Chinatown.

9. Appeal for Dynamite

FIVE-YEAR-OLD CHINGWAH LEE clung to his father, one of Chinatown's most respected doctors, and watched in terror what was happening yards away. A huge tawny bull, bawling with pain and fear, its flanks bright with blood from wounds already inflicted on it, was lurching toward them. Sixty-five years later, he recalled that scene as one that convinced many that Chinatown was doomed.

Doctor Lee had gathered his wife, eight months' pregnant, and little Chingwah together in their living room. From outside came the first babble of fear, mingled with the crash of temple gongs and the wail of moon fiddles.

The street was packed. Coolies, merchants, children, crib girls, all were jammed together, many of them shouting in terror at the mad animal lumbering among them.

For many of the Chinese, the animal was the incarnation of their belief that the world was supported on the backs of four bulls. This was one of them—and in deserting his post he had caused the earth to tremble. In an attempt to drive him back to that post they had pelted him with stones and slashed him with knives, crying as they did so: "Go back! Bull, go back! Your brothers need you under the world!"

Now, as Chingwah watched, a coolie hurled a huge machete at the animal; the steel buried itself deep in the bull's side, sending new blood into the air.

Stumbling, its great head lowered in death, the animal staggered on past the flimsy tong rooms, banner-hung bazaars, joss houses, opium dens, brothels, cellars, and tenements, pursued by a screaming horde which finally burst into Portsmouth Square, not far from the Hall of Justice.

There, Police Officer Leonard Ingham shot the bull dead.

For over an hour Ed Gleeson, the young reporter on the *Daily News,* roamed the streets, recording the chaos on a pad of paper. Making his way back toward his newspaper's office, he desperately tried to make some sense of the disaster he had seen. Everywhere, he scrawled, the "people are frightened, terror-stricken; families are moving their belongings helter-skelter, moving aimlessly about, keeping in the open."

Wherever he turned, he saw the dead and the dying; at the Essex Hotel, Police Patrolman Max Fenner lay dead under the rubble; on Seventh Street, an unidentified woman lay buried. In a burning lodging house Gleeson "heard someone buried beneath a basement floor cry—'For God's sake, help me!' "

In the years to come Gleeson became a legend among West Coast newspapermen because of his unusually sensitive reporting, but at that moment he could find no way of describing the enormity of what he had seen. "It would have been like trying to reduce Hell to a single paragraph."

As he reached the *Daily News* office on Ninth Street, Gleeson wondered what his mission had accomplished; without water, electricity, or gas, the presses could not turn to publish even the meager facts he had recorded.

Inside, he found that William Wasson, the editor, had achieved the seemingly impossible; he and the printers had fixed a monkey wrench and flywheel to a press. "By foot and hand power," the *Daily News* was going to print the scoop of its lifetime. It was the only one of the city's six newspapers to publish that day.

Shortly after 7:00, as Ed Gleeson began to dictate his story to the city editor, he wondered about the fate of Nell, the girl he loved. Before leaving his home, he had collected all his unframed pictures of her and stuffed them into his jacket pocket. But there had been no sign of Nell herself—in spite of his searching inquiries during the past two hours.

Gleeson studied the proposed layout of the extra edition of the *Daily News.* A banner headline proclaimed: "HUNDREDS DEAD!" In slightly smaller type the three-deck heading announced: "FIRE FOL-

LOWS EARTHQUAKE, LAYING DOWNTOWN SECTION IN RUINS—CITY
SEEMS DOOMED FOR LACK OF WATER."

Nell, Ed Gleeson knew, lived downtown.

Arnold Genthe, photographer, dressed carefully that morning
in riding habit and high black boots. He felt personally immune to
disaster, even though it had touched virtually everything he prized.
His collection of Chinese porcelain lay in fragments under his feet;
his photographs were scattered everywhere. Yet for some unexplained
reason his winecellar, including his precious bottle of Johannisberger
Schloss 1868, was hardly touched. He brought the wine bottle up-
stairs and placed it in a cooler. Then he set about gathering up his
photographs.

Two hours later, he felt hungry. He decided to walk up Van
Ness Avenue before going downtown.

As he left his studio home on Sutter Street, he noticed a column
of Brigadier General Funston's soldiers wheeling left, toward the
center of the city. The sight puzzled Genthe; he could not imagine
what possible use they would be in subduing the smoke rising in
the distance.

Mrs. Marjorie Brown saw the troops approaching as she, her
husband, and her sister toiled up a hill toward a small hotel where
she planned to rest awhile with her grandmother. The soldiers, the
detachment from Fort Mason, kept to the center of the street, forcing the refugees onto the sidewalk. A block away from Mrs. Brown,
the troops swung right, heading toward Portsmouth Square.

To Geneve Shaffer, the troops were an added excitement. Re-
covering from her initial fright, she scrambled out of bed, dressed,
and rushed downtown, anxious for news of her hero. But when she
reached the Palace Hotel there was no sign of Enrico Caruso.

Undaunted, Geneve set out—"frankly sightseeing," but also to
see if she could spot the singer in the crowds. She crossed Union
Square and walked up toward Portsmouth Square in time to see the
soldiers deploying themselves in a long line outside the Hall of
Justice.

Standing facing them were Mayor Eugene Schmitz and Police
Chief Jeremiah Dinan, looking, it seemed to Geneve, "a little
frightened."

Just over a mile away, Father Charles Ramm was trying to ease another kind of fear—the dread that swiftly approaching death often brings. For an hour the young priest from St. Mary's Cathedral had been moving among the dying who lay in crude litters on the floor of the cavernous Mechanics Pavilion.

From the high rafters, colored streamers and grotesque cardboard cutout faces looked down on the scene below—the same streamers and masks that only twelve hours earlier had fluttered above the final races in the annual Mardi Gras roller-skating carnival.

At 6:00 that morning, the Pavilion's doors were forced open by two doctors from the wrecked Central Emergency Hospital across the street. Minutes later, the few survivors from the hospital were moved across to the Pavilion. The first tremor buried most of the medical and nursing staff, along with the patients, under a mass of bricks which buckled the massive iron cross beams of the building.

Nearly all the city's hospitals had suffered some damage. The newly built St. Luke's Hospital was almost totally wrecked. In less than a minute, the operating theater fell into the main kitchen below. Nurses, asleep in their second-floor rooms, were dropped, some still in their beds, with bone-jarring suddenness into the main dining room. Patients' beds collapsed under the impact of the earthquake.

By 7:00, when Father Ramm reached the Mechanics Pavilion, the dying from St. Luke's were arriving, joining the hundred other victims, all severely injured, who had already been brought to the building. Water was scarce, and medical aid was restricted to little more than bandaging.

For some, bandages were not enough. Without pain-killing drugs and anesthetics, all Father Ramm could offer them was spiritual preparation for another world. Kneeling beside the litters, he gave absolution wherever it was needed.

For some minutes John Conlon, one of the nine battalion chiefs in the Fire Department, debated whether to accept the offer that the railwayman had made to him shortly before 8:00.

Two and a half hours had passed since Conlon had led the crew of the No. 30 engine to meet the biggest fire the city had ever known. In that time they raced from one harrowing situation to another: each time they found that without water there was little they could do.

Retreating before the flames, trying every hydrant as they fell back, Conlon's crew reached Eighth Street. A huge fire raged, the flames crackling a hundred feet or more into the air as they moved swiftly from one wooden building to another.

Then, from out of the smoke, the railwayman materialized with his suggestion of help.

"Even if you have water, you will not stop it now," he shouted above the roar of flame. "You need dynamite."

Conlon looked bleakly at the man. "I suppose you have a few sticks in your pocket!"

"Better! I've got a whole wagonload!" said the railwayman. "It's yours."

Conlon, like all those in the Fire Department, had never used dynamite before. The battalion chief looked at the blaze again. While he had been speaking, the flames had ignited two more frame structures.

"Go get it!" he ordered.

In minutes the railwayman returned with a wagon full of cases.

Under his guidance the firemen carried cases into a corner house, placing them along the walls nearest the approaching fire. Fuses were run out and touched off, and the dynamiters ran for safety. They were still running when the house collapsed in a cloud of dust, leaving an open space that no flames could easily leap.

Swiftly the firemen moved to the next building, planning to extend the fire wall a few yards farther. Again, the structure exploded as planned, its three floors collapsing in a roar.

By now, the blaze had reached the building only two doors away, eating its way upward, floor by floor.

Once more dynamite was placed against the walls whose other side the flames were approaching. The firemen barely had time to clear the house, and had still to light the fuses, when the fire touched off the dynamite and the building exploded outward. Arcing over Conlon and his crew, blazing timbers igniting houses that until then had not been endangered.

There was nothing to do except fall back.

Three blocks away, Captain Charles Cullen and fire engine company No. 6 were fighting a desperate battle to save a couple trapped on the top floor of the Corona House Hotel. The building had sagged, killing over forty people in a series of crushing telescopic movements.

Cullen and his men had given up trying to cut out the bodies when they heard faint cries for help from the top of the building. Scaling the side of the tilting structure, firemen still had some feet to go when the flames reached the back of the hotel.

"My men didn't hesitate," Cullen said later, "they climbed on, chopping away the debris which imprisoned the couple, and removed them to safety. By then the fire was raging around our engine. It would have been fatal for us to stay there any longer, so with wet sacks around our heads, we all assisted in pulling our engine clear of the blaze."

A few hundred yards away, at the corner of Harrison Street, Battalion Chief Pat Shaughnessy was also waging a losing battle. For twenty minutes he and his crew had tried to reach a man buried beneath the structure of a burning building. They could not see him, only hear his piteous pleas for them to hurry. "But he was hopelessly trapped. The timbers lay feet thick over him and we would have needed lifting tackle to clear them."

Shaughnessy and his crew were reaching the limit of their endurance. As they worked, the flames blistered their skin. Suddenly there was a roar as the flames leaped forward, driving the firemen back. The screams of the trapped man were lost to them.

All along a line sweeping from Spear Street down to Tenth Street, a mile and a half away, the inferno raged unchecked. Before it, often only yards away, the Fire Department retreated: thirty-eight steamers, thirty-seven hose wagons, ten hook-and-ladder trucks, and eight chemical companies, all rendered useless by the lack of water. When they found a hydrant yielding even a trickle, they coaxed it onto the flames. Then they tried pumping from the sewers. When the sewers ran dry, they tried beating out the flames with their hoses, gunny sacks, and tunic jackets. In the end they were still forced back. In their wake they left at least two hundred bodies interred where they lay in the ruins. Nobody ever knew exactly how many died in those first hours.

As the firemen withdrew, they noticed that the wind had picked up, blowing in from the sea, sending cinders high into the air over them toward Market Street, where John Dougherty had planned to make a fire line.

The plan was doomed before the new Fire Chief could position a single fireman. The blaze Bill Marston had noticed in the produce district a good hour earlier had not been checked. It was now rampaging from one building to another. The heat was so intense that it created its own wind: scorching drafts of air, meeting above the streets, whipped the flames to a frenzy, carrying in their upward rush a pall of smoke that could be seen nearly one hundred miles out to sea.

Mayor Eugene Schmitz came face to face with Brigadier General Funston in the bunker beneath the Hall of Justice soon after 8:00.

Funston made it clear that the troops would remain under Army command. There would be "two to each block, with instructions to shoot instantly any person caught looting or committing any serious misdemeanor."

Brigadier General Henry E. Noyes, himself in the city, had no doubt at all about what Funston was doing. In the *Journal of the Military Institution* he stated: "At eight o'clock General Funston took charge of the city."

Before presenting the Mayor with a military *fait accompli,* Funston sent off a terse telegram to Secretary of War William Howard Taft, in which he outlined the situation in the city and included a request that the War Department "authorize any action I have to take."

Funston sent the wire from the Phelan Building, headquarters of the Army's Department of California. He also considered the situation grave enough to send for still more soldiers. An aide was dispatched aboard the Army tug *Slocum* to pick up "at once" the battalion of the Twenty-second Infantry, stationed at Fort McDowell on Angel Island in San Francisco Bay. On landing they were to march to the Phelan Building to await further orders—military orders.

Then, and only then, did Brigadier General Funston make his way to the Hall of Justice.

There would be, he informed the Mayor, "consultation at all

times" with the civil authorities as to how the troops were used; indeed, Funston saw to it that the first detachments were deployed under the "guidance" of Police Chief Dinan. The men were sent to patrol the north side of Market Street with bayonets fixed. Funston had already earmarked the area as a potential flash point for panic, since it was crowded with "excited, anxious people."

The military martinet and the former violinist might have recognized things in each other's behavior that they detested; they would also have seen the weakness of their positions if one of them had balked at a time when events were already moving too quickly. Funston could not possibly have hoped to maintain his hold on the city if the Mayor had refused to accept what had happened. Eugene Schmitz had seen enough already to know that *every* bit of help would be essential in the coming hours, however highhanded it might be.

Whatever his private thoughts were, the Mayor brushed them aside when he showed Funston a telegram he had drafted to the naval station at Mare Island: "EARTHQUAKE. TOWN ON FIRE. SEND MARINES AND TUGS."

Common ground had been found. Funston hurried back to the Phelan Building to summon more soldiers from Fort Baker in Marin County, Alcatraz Island, Vancouver barracks in Portland, Oregon, and the Presidio at Monterey, nearly a hundred miles away. Later they were to be joined by detachments of the National Guard, turning San Francisco into a military fortress.

The telegram Eugene Schmitz sent to the naval station was not the first he had dispatched. One had gone to Governor Pardee, outlining the scope of the disaster. Another had gone to Mayor Frank Mott of Oakland, across the Bay: "SEND FIRE ENGINES, HOSE, ALSO DYNAMITE, IMMEDIATELY."

10. A Shared Drink

OAKLAND AND ITS NEIGHBOR, Berkeley, the third and fourth largest cities in California, escaped the full impact of the rip. In both, it rocked their façades, but the toll in human lives was small. In Oakland five people died when a wall collapsed on a rooming house over the Empire Theatre. In Berkeley there were no deaths reported.

Elsewhere, stretching from Santa Rosa in the north and south to San Jose, the death toll was mounting.

By 8:00, fifty-one bodies had been dug out from beneath poorly constructed buildings in Santa Rosa. Santa Rosa had stood and fallen as a monument to shoddy workmanship. Lime mortar and poor-quality sand had been used to cement bricks. Hardly a structure had proper cross bracing.

Fires started at once. The town's fire department—two steam engines, a hose company, and a ladder truck—soon found that even with limited water supplies, the task of containing the blaze was far beyond them. Within a few hours Santa Rosa was a funeral pyre.

Southward, San Jose, in the bright morning light, was a pitiful sight. The earthquake left over eight thousand people homeless.

At Agnews State Insane Asylum, the reclaimed bodies were being laid in neat rows on the grass. Fifty-five had already been placed there by the time a young priest, Ernest Watson, arrived on the scene from Santa Clara University. He still remembers the disturbing cries of "bloody murder" from the more violent patients who had been strapped to trees. From one of them came the apocalyptic warning: "Jesus of Nazareth is passing."

Sheriff Ross, leading the rescue teams, recalled years later the shrieks of a demented man: "I'm going to heaven in a chariot of fire! Don't you hear the rumbling of the chariot wheels!"

In San Francisco, the rumble in the streets came mostly from fire engines racing over cobblestones, seeking the unobtainable: water.

By 9:00 there was virtually no water in the entire area south of Market Street. Twenty-three cisterns, each one of which held between sixteen thousand and one hundred thousand gallons, had been drained dry. Their combined output had little effect on the inferno.

Scores of other cisterns which Fire Chief Sullivan had wanted to refurbish lay empty. The supplementary salt-water system, like the dynamite squad, was no more than a tragically unrealized dream.

Sullivan himself, unconscious from his injuries, was moved shortly after 9:00 from the Southern Pacific Hospital by horse-drawn ambulance to the Letterman General Hospital at the Presidio, where doctors pronounced him beyond their medical aid. Sullivan lingered for three days in a coma.

With him died the detailed plan he had evolved for the sort of emergency San Francisco now faced.

In its wake the fire left Walter Courtney Bennett, Britain's Consul General, without an office. The flames gutted it in a few minutes.

Back in his room in a hotel overlooking Union Square, he sat down to draft an official report of his loss to the Right Honourable Sir Edward Grey, the Foreign Secretary, in London.

After establishing the course and length of the earthquake, the Consul General went on to reveal how close the Foreign Office had been to losing him.

The earthquake and fire left him with an administrative problem. In the midst of a disaster which minute by minute was changing the very shape of the city, the Consul General informed the Foreign Secretary: "I am without fee stamps, official seals, etc., etc."

It was a very human reaction, this desire to reduce a massive tragedy to manageable, everyday proportions. Days later, when he had finally completed the report, the Consul General added comments that indicate he was not altogether successful in keeping the disaster in perspective. He wrote that "martial law was declared at once, looters and rioters were shot by the dozen."

He, like many others, was a victim of the trauma he had undergone.

In the lobby of the Palace Hotel that morning, Olive Fremstad bought a copy of the *Daily News*—one of the nine thousand copies sold that day, many for a dollar each.

In a single sheet, Ed Gleeson and his colleagues summarized the disaster in human terms. "At 8:40 there were one hundred dead and dying at the Pavilion, and more arriving each minute. All of the city hospitals threw open their doors, and within a short time their wards and halls rang with the agonizing cries of scores of crushed and burned victims of the awful catastrophe. At the Protestant Orphan Asylum on Haight Street, fearful damage was done, and three little children were badly injured. Insane patients were taken from the Emergency Hospital to Mechanics Pavilion. Many of them were hurt. Some broke loose and ran among the dying, adding horror to the scene . . ."

The only notice that Madame Fremstad might easily have identified with was: "The Majestic Theatre is almost a complete wreck. The rear end, on the Ninth Street side, fell out, while the roof caved into the auditorium of the building."

There was no review of *Carmen*.

At about the time she bought the newspaper, the fire was sweeping through the dressing rooms backstage at the Grand Opera House. Eventually it gutted the entire building; in the process, eight carloads of sets and costumes belonging to the touring company were lost.

By then the flames had enveloped the offices of the *Examiner, Call,* and *Chronicle,* sparing Madame Fremstad the pain of reading the castigation the critics of those newspapers had reserved for her.

The earthquake itself did little damage to the newspaper buildings, but the fires south of Market Street swept swiftly toward the *Examiner* and the *Call*.

The *Call* building was the first to go. The eighteen-story tower caught fire from the top—a quirk in keeping with the unpredictable editorial line the newspaper often presented. The temperature rose to an estimated 2000° F., and the firemen watched helplessly as it melted window frames. The windows blew out, sucking in still more blasts of air to turn the whole structure into a blazing furnace.

The *Examiner* burned less dramatically, but in the end the flames won and Linotype machines, fonts of type, typewriters, telephones, were all mangled beyond recognition.

On the south side of the city, the Southern Pacific Railroad headquarters on Townsend Street—long the target of the *Examiner*'s vitriol—survived. In the days to come the railroad terminus became a rallying point for refugees.

On the north side of Market Street stood the *Chronicle* and *Bulletin* buildings. The editorial staff of the *Chronicle* had been on duty since 6 A.M., urged to work by the newspaper's founder and publisher, M. H. de Young. His managing editor composed himself enough to write an editorial minimizing the extent of the disaster. It was a piece of optimism that the newspaper would never again equal.

An edition was prepared, "and the printers were cajoled into standing by the presses, despite the intense heat from the fires across the street. When the presses were ready to roll, the engineer sent up word that the water supply had been cut off and it would be impossible to start the presses."

Shortly thereafter, the *Chronicle* building caught fire—also from the top. In a short time tons of zinc, used by the printers to make press castings, poured down onto the Linotype machines. The accumulating mass crashed through the building, carrying everything with it—including the editorial intended to reduce nearly total disaster to a few comforting paragraphs.

It next was the turn of the headhunting *Evening Bulletin.* Editor Fremont Older's plans to reveal the full story of Rudolph Spreckels' scheme to finance an investigation into the corruption at City Hall had to be temporarily postponed.

When the newspaper appeared again, printed on a borrowed press, it managed to maintain its knack for interpreting a catastrophe on the level it believed its readers best grasped. Its attitude toward the earthquake and fire was perfectly expressed under a bold black headline: "FATHER, MOTHER, SON . . . FOUND DEAD IN RUINS."

All morning the fearful din continued in the city jail, unchecked. To the prisoners the building seemed on the verge of collapse, as it creaked and groaned like a worn-out sailing ship in a storm. Then a chilling rumor swept through the cell block. San Francisco was being evacuated—but they would be left to die as an object lesson to future sinners.

It was then, prisoner Chuck Connors recalls, that he began to laugh, "from sheer hysteria."

He was still laughing when the soldiers arrived, the bayonets on their muskets fixed.

In the dining room of the St. Francis Hotel, Enrico Caruso dug into a breakfast of fried eggs, bacon, toast, marmalade, and coffee.

His whole bearing was that of a man completely divorced from the panic in the streets only yards away. It was the only protection he had. Like a child donning a toy uniform and assuming the fantasy role that went with it, Caruso, in his striped trousers and jacket, had dressed himself perfectly for his exercise in autism.

To Talbot Williams, crossing the lobby of the Palace on his way to raise the Stars and Stripes over the hotel, the singer "looked dignified standing there, staring straight ahead, not talking to anybody."

Caruso also surprised Alfred Hertz by a sudden shift in behavior. The conductor had returned to the hotel, warmed with whiskey, and started to describe the scenes outside to Caruso. Without warning, the singer moved away toward a hotel employee, a Chinese. The man, Hertz later recalled, "was quickly and calmly cleaning the easy chairs and carpets of the lobby as if all this were just a daily occurrence."

Caruso ordered the Chinese to stop. The Chinese, either unable to understand English, especially Caruso's heavily accented speech, or believing guests had no jurisdiction over him, ignored the order and continued to polish. Whereupon Caruso hit him.

A fist fight was averted by Hertz and Antonio Scotti, who swiftly intervened and made peace. "Caruso looked as if nothing had happened. He said, quite calmly, that he wanted a drink. I think we all needed a drink," Hertz recalled.

Flanking Caruso, who still clutched his signed portrait of President Roosevelt, Scotti and Hertz led him out of the hotel.

Pushing their way through the crowds, they took the singer to a drugstore on a corner of Union Square, run by Charles M. Wollenberg. "Just as I was about to give them a drink," Wollenberg remembers, "a soldier came in and said all liquor was banned. Caruso didn't get his pick-me-up." The three men made their way across to the St. Francis Hotel and ordered breakfast.

The waiter who took the order, Larry Lewis—still working in the hotel at the age of 103—told us that Caruso "was the only guy with a really big appetite that morning. I took his order into the kitchen and Charlie Olson, the cook, prepared it. Mr. Caruso had, I recall, three fried eggs, sunny side up, half a dozen rashers of bacon, and a mountain of toast. It would have kept two ordinary guys going for a day. But Mr. Caruso polished it off with no trouble. He didn't say much, just kept on eating."

After finishing breakfast, Caruso tipped the cook and waiter two dollars and fifty cents each—an outrageously large tip, quite out of keeping with the singer's careful attitude toward money.

By the time the trio left the hotel, Union Square had become a staging point for the columns of refugees trudging up from the Market Street area, clinging to what little they had been able to save: bundles of clothing, steamer trunks (often with roller skates nailed to the bottom to make them easier to trundle), wheelbarrows piled with crockery, sewing machines, tubs and buckets filled with cutlery, cooking pans filled with whatever food there had been to snatch. Anything that could be wheeled or pushed had become a wagon. Prams were stuffed with bedding; children dragged their mattresses behind them. More than one man carried a piece of furniture—a small wardrobe or a bureau—on his back. Others trundled pianos: for many families an upright piano was a symbol of affluence.

If Caruso noted any of this, he gave no sign. He led the others rapidly through the crowds. In the center of the square he turned and faced Scotti and Hertz.

His voice, he informed them, had "gone" again. Hertz, who had been through the routine once already, said: "Then we must find it again!"

The conductor ordered Caruso to open his mouth and peered down his throat. Standing back, Hertz told Caruso that if he sang, his voice would return. Obediently Caruso once more sang of Don José's tortured love and jealousy for the hoyden Carmen.

People all around hardly glanced at the tenor, who only hours before had thrilled many of them with his singing. Their interest now lay down the route they had traveled. Along it, straddling street after street, came the fire in steady pursuit.

Suddenly Caruso broke off the melodious flow, as if he were

aware for the first time in hours of the darkening clouds around him. Oscar Lewis, the splendid reporter of the San Francisco scene, recorded later that "Caruso insisted he must get out of town at once. He asked Scotti to return with him to the Palace while he packed his trunks."

The two men had a row when Scotti refused to join Caruso: "We exchanged some words," Scotti remembered, "but he announced his determination of returning to the Palace. I sought to dissuade him without success."

It was approaching 10:00 when Caruso walked into the hotel lobby.

Alfred Hertz followed at a distance. He was one of the first to detect the changed atmosphere inside the hotel, and Caruso's response to it. "The place had an air of evacuation. Whereas before people had often tried to pay their bills before leaving, they were now rushing out, wanting to get clear of the place at all costs, taking what they could with them. This had a disturbing effect on Caruso."

For a moment the singer took in the bedlam. Then, with a bellow, he plunged into the crowd. Four Chinese were making off with his trunk. From his pocket, Caruso drew the revolver he had bought in New York and shouted: "You give me my trunk or I'll shoot." For a second the four stunned Chinese and the singer confronted each other. All around people stood frozen.

"I will shoot!" Caruso's voice took on a new, dangerous pitch. There is no doubt in writer Bruce Charles Williams' mind that Caruso would have shot. Williams believes that at this moment in the hotel lobby something snapped inside Caruso; a man who rarely allowed himself to be humbled by circumstances had for nearly five hours been involved in events over which he had no control. The earthquake had "disrobed this regal being and reduced him, for one inglorious moment, to a simple, terrified, angry mortal."

Once again Caruso commanded the Chinese to drop the trunk.

"Put that pistol down!"

From across the lobby came the third actor in the drama, a soldier. In seconds Hertz and Martino, Caruso's valet, lined themselves up beside the singer.

High drama gave way to farce. Martino explained that the four Chinese were acting under his instructions; for some hours the valet had been methodically packing Caruso's vast wardrobe, and the

Chinese had been hired to carry it to a wagon parked at the rear
of the hotel. The soldier took the gun from Caruso and broke open
the breech: in his anxiety, the singer had failed to load the weapon.
If the trooper recognized Caruso, or found the episode amusing, he
did not show it. Without a word he turned and walked out of the
hotel.

Turning to Martino, Caruso mumbled: "I want my sketching
pad."

Pad and presidential portrait under his arm, the singer walked
through the lobby and out into the street.

For an hour Brigadier General Funston inspected his men—a
line of mounted and foot soldiers in khaki, strung out in a loose line
a block ahead of the fire. He noted with satisfaction that battle-
seasoned men—cavalry, coast artillery, armed and equipped as in-
fantrymen, and field artillerymen mounted on their battery horses—
had taken over the task of shepherding the crowds back. Younger
and more inexperienced soldiers were helping the police to close
down the saloons and liquor shops. There was, Funston noted, no
friction.

"Abundant use was now found for all the troops at our disposal; the conflagration, with a mile of front, was rapidly eating its
way into the heart of the city, and the streets were black with tens
of thousands of people kept at a distance of two blocks from the
fire by strong detachments of troops.

"Before 10:00 the troops from Forts McDowell and Miley arrived. They were used in various ways—guarding the people, patrolling the streets to prevent looting, maintaining fire lines, and taking
a hand at the hose wherever there was sufficient water pressure to
enable the firemen to accomplish anything."

By midday Captain Charles Cullen and the men of No. 6 engine
company found their role as firefighters temporarily ended. At Fifth
and Folsom Streets flames had charred their hoses. It was one more
small frustration on a morning in which the Fire Department had
been completely overwhelmed. Few argued with William Bronson
that "too few men, little water, and a total lack of centralized direction hamstrung their efforts."

Well before noon, Fire Chief Dougherty virtually abandoned

hope of a planned fight against the flames—along Market Street or anywhere else. All morning, landmark after landmark crumbled; the Emporium, Holbrook, Merril, and Stetson were all burned out. Hundreds of acres south of the Slot were reduced to ash. In places, the heat had buckled rail tracks until they reared like ocean waves. By noon the fire had spread north of Market Street to devour blocks up to California Street. Expensive real estate, the offices of insurance companies and banks—all perished.

But it was an inferno to the west that had finally stunned Fire Chief Dougherty into hopelessness. It had been kindled at about 9:30 A.M. by a woman preparing breakfast.

The unknown woman lived out in the Hayes Valley, an area bounded by Van Ness Avenue and Octavia Street on one side, and McAllister and Market Streets on the other. It was a community of simple, two-story houses, the homes of workmen and their families.

The woman's house had suffered no worse than the surrounding ones from the tremors. Windows were broken, plaster was strewn on the floor. But the house still stood—and her family was probably hungry.

She started to light a fire in the kitchen stove. Legend has it that the earthquake-damaged flue allowed sparks to set the walls and roof alight.

In minutes the "ham-and-eggs fire" destroyed her home and scores around it, burning them as if they were matchwood. Then the inferno looked for something more substantial to devour. It advanced on Van Ness Avenue, leaped the thoroughfare in a jump of 185 feet, spread across Larkin Street, and began to eat into what was left of City Hall. Churches, a college, hotels, offices, rooming houses—all fell to the flames.

Now there was nobody in the city who didn't believe the worst.

Photographer Arnold Genthe had a strange, relaxing morning.

At the other end of Van Ness, he abandoned his plans for breakfast downtown.

"Some friends called out 'come in and have a drink.' Raising my glass, I toasted the hostess with a line from Horace, 'and even if the whole world should collapse, he will stand fearless among the fallen ruins.' "

It was a brave sentiment. Having delivered his toast, Genthe set off to walk to the Bohemian Club, then as now the refuge of male society. He did not complete the journey. A friend stopped him with the news that property in the path of the flames was being dynamited.

"This was the first time I thought of such a possibility. Turning back I hurried up Sutter Street to find a militiaman guarding the entrance to my studio! 'You can't get in here,' he said, handling his rifle in an unpleasant manner. 'But it's my house,' I said. 'I don't care whether it is or not. Orders are to clear all houses in the block. If you don't do as I say, I shoot, see?' "

Martial law, whether it had been officially declared or not, had come to Sutter Street. That morning, on his way to the Bohemian Club, Genthe heard that "some of the militia, drunk with liquor and power, had been shooting people."

He resolved the problem of gaining entry by inviting the soldier to join him for a drink. The offer was eagerly accepted. Together the two men entered the studio. Genthe went to the cooler holding his vintage bottle of Johannisberger Schloss 1868. "A special occasion had arrived. I knew that to my unwelcome guest, it would mean nothing, so I brought him a bottle of whisky, and while he poured himself drink after drink, I sipped the wine, if not with the leisurely enjoyment that it called for, at least getting some of the exquisite flavor without having to gulp it down."

At last the soldier had drunk his fill. Rising to his feet, he ordered his host out—"or I'll have to shoot you, see?"

In silence the two men stepped back into the street. All Genthe was able to salvage was film. At 12:30 he set off to use it.

12:30 P.M. to 6:30 P.M.

April 18, 1906, 2:30 p.m. By the time the fire died down the entire area in this photograph would be destroyed (*Roy D. Graves Collection*)

11. Last Evidence of Life

AMADEO PETER GIANNINI FINALLY reached the outskirts of the city. The journey of seventeen miles from his home in San Mateo took more than five hours, the last few against a tidal mass of humanity fleeing from the pall of smoke that hung in the air.

The refugees told stories that threatened even the banker's iron control. Fissures had opened in the streets, swallowing up whole families. Looters were being executed after summary drumhead courts-martial. Other miscreants were being hanged even without trial. Ghouls had been lynched when caught cutting fingers and ears off corpses for rings and earrings. Rioting Chinese had swept through the business area in a wave of vandalism that even General Funston's soldiers had been unable to check.

Some of the reports of local happenings had a grain of truth in them, but an air of fancy surrounded the stories concerning the fate of the rest of America.

New York had collapsed, and the Hudson River had surged over the remains. The Great Lakes had done the same thing at Chicago. Seattle and Portland had been wiped out by a tidal wave. Los Angeles had been demolished by the earthquake.

It was impossible for Giannini immediately to reject these stories as preposterous. The rip itself had raced past only a few miles from the Giannini home. Little damage occurred inside the big frame house, but the surrounding countryside underwent radical change. Evidence of the great earth slip was everywhere. Sidewalks rose and fell; the road he was traveling resembled a roller coaster in places, and was cracked wide open at a number of points.

117

But what shocked the banker most were the people—"the little people," for whom he had created his bank. All along the streets—walled on either side by one great fire in the south and another in the east—he could see families sitting helplessly on their front doorsteps, hoping that the flames would be stopped or diverted.

At noon when he reached the Bank of Italy, he found a situation that caused him to lose his composure long enough to say: *"Cra—zy! Are you cra——zy!"*

The outburst was not entirely unjustified.

Assistant cashier Armando Pedrini and clerk Ettore Avenali were standing at their desks. Between them were three heavy canvas bags, which held eighty thousand dollars in gold and silver—every cent that the Bank of Italy had in hard cash.

"Have you been out in the streets?" Giannini rumbled.

They nodded.

The two men had arrived at the bank early in the morning. They were both amazed to find the building intact.

Pedrini decided to open up for business as usual. The decision made, the pair "hitched up a bouncy little white mare to a snappy buggy" and rattled off through the rubble-filled streets to the Crocker Woolworth National Bank. There they collected the three bags from the vaults.

After counting the money, the two men rode back to the Bank of Italy, "opened the doors, and were ready for business, provided anyone was interested."

That was a little after 9 A.M. For the first hour, records bank chronicler Paul Rink, "they stood in the doorway, thumbs in vest pockets, looking out into the bright morning."

By 11:00 Pedrini and Avenali were beginning to have second thoughts about the wisdom of their action. "The morning had taken on a kind of ominous quality."

Businessman Charles Harley thought the pair looked rather incongruous standing there, hopefully waiting for customers. In a three-hour tour of the area, Harley saw one scene repeated time and again: fire crews seeking and failing to find water. The implication was clear; the unattended fire would inevitably spread, and "it had become merely a question of rescuing what could be carried away."

The other banks had been following this "policy" for some hours.

At the Wells Fargo Bank, F. L. Lipman, the chief cashier, was supervising the storing of all the bank's records in a vault below Pine Street.

Lipman arrived at the bank, carrying a dress suit in a case. In spite of the fires, clearly visible by this time, he had left home still hoping to go to the opera that night. By 9:00 all thoughts of a seat in the stalls vanished in mushrooming clouds of black smoke. He went promptly to the telegraph office and cabled the bank's New York correspondents, "instructing them to call loans we had out and to send us three million dollars."

At the Crocker Bank, a steady stream of customers brought ledgers, records, and money for storage in the vaults. Unknown to them, William Crocker, the bank's president, had hired a boat to take all the bank records out into the center of the Bay—"and just sit there." By 10:00 dozens of heavy boxes and bulky bags had been carried off to a point near Alcatraz Island; the boat remained on station for many hours.

Since early morning two tellers at the Anglo-California Bank had been carting negotiable bonds in a wheelbarrow down Market Street to the Ferry Building for shipment across the Bay to Oakland. In three hours they shifted one million dollars' worth of bonds. The unregistered bonds would have been ready currency for any thief, but not one was lost.

At the London, Paris, and American Bank, sacks of United States registered mail were placed in the vault. Manager Sigmund Greensbaum entered them in a ledger, along with deposits of jewel boxes and family deeds.

Eleven o'clock came and went, and still no customer appeared at the Bank of Italy. Its two employees became increasingly alarmed: they, too, were aware of a change in the mood of the people. Earlier they had been lighthearted; now they were nervous and apprehensive.

Refugees toiling toward Russian and Telegraph Hills brought rumors to the bank, a wood-frame building on the corner of Washington and Columbus. They told ugly stories of fighting and looting by organized gangs, of firemen powerless to stop the flames, of troops shooting at will.

There could be no thought of "business as usual" now. Not a little frightened at their predicament, Pedrini loaded the only weapon in the bank, a ten-dollar six-shooter, placed it beside the sacks of money, and prepared to defend the bank's assets with his life.

The two men were standing there when Giannini came through the doors.

Giannini hotly declared that "only an insane man would open a bank on a day like this. You should have left the money at Crocker. At least it would have been safe."

By 1:00, having locked the doors of the bank, he had regained his composure.

Leaving Avenali to guard the sacks, he took Pedrini with him on an urgent mission: to establish how much time they had left to mount an operation no other bank in the city had attempted.

Giannini planned to shift everything movable in the Bank of Italy to safety outside the city.

By early afternoon, some homeowners on the higher slopes of the city were filling tubs and buckets with water in preparation for any threat from the flames. In the hours to come these little reservoirs made the difference between survival and smoldering ruin.

In the Italian quarter on Telegraph Hill, and along North Beach, wine cellars were opened and barrels uncorked, ready to douse the fire.

By 2:00 John Barrett, the *Examiner* newspaperman who had actually seen the earthquake striking, concluded that it was now impossible to reach the Postal Telegraph office near the corner of Market and Montgomery Streets.

The New York *Journal,* for which he acted as a local correspondent, received no more news from him that day. Since early morning he had fed the newspaper a running commentary on the disaster. At midday he began a message with the words: "I write believing this report to be my swan song."

From Union Square, a wall of smoke and flame barred the way to the telegraph office. A soldier told him that the building had been abandoned.

The soldier's warning was premature. The chief operator was still on duty, with the flames licking the walls of adjoining buildings.

All morning he supplied New York and the world beyond with a series of stark bulletins.

At 6 A.M. he tapped out:

THERE WAS AN EARTHQUAKE AT FIVE FIFTEEN THIS MORNING, WRECKING SEVERAL BUILDINGS AND WRECKING OUR OFFICES. THEY ARE CARTING DEAD FROM THE FALLEN BUILDINGS. FIRE ALL OVER TOWN. THERE IS NO WATER, AND WE HAVE LOST OUR POWER. I'M GOING TO GET OUT OF THE OFFICE AS WE HAVE HAD A LITTLE SHAKE EVERY FEW MINUTES AND IT'S ME FOR THE SIMPLE LIFE.

Then the telegrapher changed his mind. Over the wire went this laconic statement:

WE ARE ON THE JOB AND WE ARE GOING TO TRY AND STICK.

By mid-morning crowds were gathering outside telegraph offices in a dozen American cities, as New York relayed the reports coming 2600 miles from San Francisco.

At 10:30 A.M.:

THE CALL BUILDING IS IN FULL BLAZE NOW AND IT IS ONLY A QUESTION OF MINUTES FOR US HERE.

At 11:05:

FIRE WITHIN FEW DOORS NOW.

The flames were in no hurry. In graphic bursts the operator continued to transmit news of the mounting horror to a shocked world.

At 2:20 P.M. he sent this message:

THE CITY PRACTICALLY RUINED BY FIRE. IT'S WITHIN HALF BLOCK OF US IN THE SAME BLOCK. THE CALL BUILDING IS BURNED OUT ENTIRELY, THE EXAMINER BUILDING JUST FELL

IN A HEAP. FIRE ALL AROUND US IN EVERY DIRECTION AND WAY OUT IN THE RESIDENCE DISTRICT. DESTRUCTION BY EARTHQUAKE SOMETHING FRIGHTFUL. THE CITY HALL DOME STRIPPED AND ONLY THE FRAMEWORK STANDING. THE ST. IGNATIUS CHURCH AND COLLEGE ARE BURNED TO THE GROUND. THE EMPORIUM IS GONE, ENTIRE BUILDING, ALSO THE OLD FLOOD BUILDING. LOTS OF NEW BUILDINGS JUST RECENTLY FINISHED ARE COMPLETELY DESTROYED. THEY ARE BLOWING UP STANDING BUILDINGS THAT ARE IN THE PATH OF FLAMES WITH DYNAMITE. NO WATER. IT'S AWFUL. THERE IS NO COMMUNICATION ANYWHERE AND ENTIRE PHONE SYSTEM BUSTED. I WANT TO GET OUT OF HERE OR BE BLOWN UP.

San Francisco was cut off abruptly from the outside world.

For six hours the jets on the roof of the Palace Hotel played their streams protectively. From the flagpole the Stars and Stripes continued to fly. For hundreds of people, the water and the emblem symbolized the city's refusal to concede defeat.

Abe Ruef watched the fight to save not only the Palace, but Market Street, with "unashamed pride"; the struggle along the broad thoroughfare had been lost for the most part. But the hotel still remained, the bonanza inn of a bonanza town.

A few blocks away from where he stood, his own property lay in ruin. The mighty A. Ruef Building had cracked under the force of the tremor; a dynamite squad completed the destruction.

For Ruef the loss of the building could not be so great a shock as the threat to his whole future. Earlier that day he had learned of the move, initiated by Rudolph Spreckels, to clean up City Hall and to indict him and Mayor Eugene Schmitz for corruption.

Over the years there have been attempts by some writers to present Ruef as a last-minute convert to honesty, a man standing firmly beside the Mayor, working to make amends to the city he had cheated so copiously.

It is an attractive thought, one that lends a piquant touch of glamour to a man who essentially lacked it. Whatever else Ruef did that morning, he did not make his presence known at the Hall of Justice until after midday. Then he stayed only long enough to discover that Eugene Schmitz had invited a cross section of fifty of the city's most prominent businessmen to form a committee in whose hands the civil administration of San Francisco would rest. Among those he had asked to serve were Rudolph Spreckels and James D. Phelan, the former Mayor, both dedicated opponents of Schmitz and Ruef. Neither Ruef nor a single member of the Board of Supervisors had been included.

Schmitz and Ruef met, briefly and alone, in the basement bunker the Mayor had occupied since arriving at the Hall of Justice. No details of their conversation were made public.

But at the end of it, Ruef could hardly fail to notice the change, which Brigadier General Funston had first detected, in the Mayor.

In his hours of trauma, Trilby found he needed no support from Svengali. It might have been little more than a finely developed sense of self-preservation on the part of the Mayor, signs of which could be seen in his decision not to inform Ruef immediately of the impending graft investigation. Instead, Schmitz turned for help to Downey Harvey, whose social standing was equaled only by his wealth.

Harvey had hurried to the Hall of Justice early that morning; later he was on hand to help the Mayor select the fifty key men; he also arranged to summon them to their first meeting. If Eugene Schmitz felt the need for somebody to prop him up, Harvey was present to supply the morale, with no motive except that "the Mayor needed all the confidence possible to cope with the crisis."

Psychologists later speculated that Schmitz was a man who "needed" a crisis to help correct the imbalance in his make-up.

Until the earthquake broke into his sleep, Eugene Schmitz—according to a later Mayor of the city, Joseph Alioto—was "fundamentally a weak man—yet one who, immediately after the disaster happened, showed a new side of his character." Schmitz himself said later that for him "life had really begun again" that morning.

Whether this refreshing thought troubled Abe Ruef nobody will ever know.

By early that afternoon he watched "almost entranced," as the flag over the Palace Hotel avoided the flames. At times a shower of sparks from a nearby burning building rained upon the emblem, giving it the appearance of a fiery fringe. Repeatedly the cloth shook off the sparks in a bit of by-play that brought a lump to Ruef's throat.

As he watched, a squad of General Funston's soldiers approached, running with cases of dynamite on their shoulders. They entered the Monadnock Building, a newly built office block opposite the hotel.

In minutes the soldiers placed their explosive charges and detonated them. When the roar died away, the iron-frame building still stood. Once more the dynamite squad placed fresh boxes of dynamite; again the building withstood the blast. The squad withdrew. The road was open for the flames advancing on the Palace Hotel.

At that moment Abe Ruef and the handful of other bystanders on Market Street noticed that the jets of water on the roof were dying. Seven tanks, holding 130,000 gallons, were nearly empty. Moments later the fountains stopped.

It was half past two.

John P. Young, the editor of the *Chronicle,* and a friend joined Ruef. The three men said nothing; no words were needed.

As they watched, two unidentified men ran from the hotel— the last evidence of life in the Palace.

12. Explosives in
Inexperienced Hands

FOR THIRTY YEARS the hotel had stood as a symbol of San Francisco. It was larger, in every way, than any legend. Within its two and a half acres had slept, loved, and hated the famous and the notorious.

In the ballroom Lillie Langtry had stunned guests with her dancing. Sarah Bernhardt had taken an eight-room suite for her entourage, which included a parrot and a baby tiger. Henry Irving and Ellen Terry had fought with the management over the style of their marble washbasins. They had a choice among nine hundred specially designed styles all bearing the Palace monogram, as did twenty thousand plates, ten thousand cups and saucers, eight thousand vegetable dishes, seven thousand cuspidors, and six thousand silver-plated knives and forks.

Kipling had complained of the poor service; Oscar Wilde had pronounced it excellent. Mrs. Patrick Campbell, the British actress, had quarreled and made up with Ella Wheeler Wilcox, the American poet, in one of the luxury suites. At one time, the hotel had been home to kings, the daughter of Queen Victoria, and knaves. They had all ridden in its five redwood-paneled elevators and tramped its miles of corridors. Some had died there peacefully; one had been murdered.

Now the hotel stood abandoned by all save "one last sinister guest." Oscar Lewis wrote, "Late in the afternoon, this guest began stalking through the corridors, the lobby, the banquet halls, mounting stairways, entering the hundreds of rooms. Trailing his scarlet robe, he advanced inexorably, permeating every corner of the structure, silently at first, then more boisterously, until presently the grand court vibrated with an immense humming roar."

It was an epitaph matched only by the purple life the hotel had led.

At the corner of Market Street, Ruef and Young could feel the intense heat generating from within the building. For a short time the two-foot-thick walls of the hotel masked the full fury of the flames.

To Young, "it was impossible to state positively whether the fire which destroyed the great hostelry, once the glory of San Francisco, attacked it from the east, but it seemed to our little group that it surrendered to the assault from that direction. But from whatever point it came, the hotel presented the appearance of being afire in every part. The spectacle was one calculated to inspire awe, despite the fact that all around it were structures which had already succumbed to the destroyer."

The heat steadily drove the onlookers back. At a street corner, Young turned to leave.

"Where are you going?" asked Ruef.

"Hall of Justice," replied Young, surprised. "Aren't you coming? We're all meeting to see what can be done."

Ruef turned back to watch the Palace being destroyed.

For over an hour Adam Gilliland, the insurance agent, had been digging a hole at the foot of his garden. In it he planned to bury all the records of the Hartford Insurance Company that he had been able to save before fire leveled its offices. It was not much—a few roughly penciled maps showing the exact location of the properties which were covered against fire.

One map showed the two-thousand-dollar fire insurance premium he had written up for Patrolman Leonard Ingham. The policeman's recurring nightmare had predicted the fire with uncanny accuracy— the course it would travel, beginning south of the Slot, sweeping up Market Street to engulf the Palace Hotel.

Gilliland paused in his digging to stare downtown. Looking closely he saw a strange sight. The hotel was a mass of flames. From the rooftop the Stars and Stripes still flew. Smoke obscured the flag for a moment; then a current of hot air whirled the smoke away.

From the hillsides all around came cheers and a chorus of "Long live the red, white and blue!"

Completely fascinated, the insurance man watched the drama run its course. The flames burned up through the hotel roof; at last one tongue reached up the pole and fastened on the flag itself. It burned immediately.

The last symbol of the Palace Hotel's defiance was gone.

On Ninth Street another battle with the flames had been lost. A squad of soldiers arrived to dynamite the *Daily News* office. The staff had only minutes to leave.

Reporter Ed Gleeson said that the venture had "been a good try. We'd got out two editions. Soon after the second run was started the white paper gave out, and it was necessary to use colored paper— red, yellow, pink, anything that would show print.

"We all knew it had only been a matter of time. The fire was traveling with incredible fury. The flames were rapidly eating their way toward us. Outside you could see all the signs of panic. People just dumped things they found too heavy to carry, dumped them and ran. So there was little surprise when the dynamite squad appeared."

Not many minutes later the building was in ruins. The dynamite squad had done its job.

San Francisco's last newspaper fell. Now there would be no way to check the rumors.

All morning the rumor had spread that an armed gang was massing to storm the United States Mint at the corner of Fifth and Mission Streets and rob it of over two hundred million dollars in coin and bullion stored in its vaults.

Frank Leach, the mint's superintendent, heard the story as he stepped off the Oakland ferry. By the time he reached the mint, the rumor had gained credence enough to warrant precautionary measures. Brigadier General Funston dispatched a company of troops from the Sixth Infantry, under the command of Lieutenant Jackson, to guard the building.

The troops took up defensive positions on the roof. From there they could fire directly along Mission and Fifth Streets and across Turk and Eddy Streets.

Shortly afterward, Captain Jack Brady of the Fire Department arrived to supervise the building's defense against the inferno.

Built in 1874, the mint was a monolith of granite and sandstone blocks, a tiny federal island in the heart of the city. Even the earthquake had succeeded in inflicting only minor damage on the huge building.

With the threat of armed attack receding in the face of the inferno—"the devil himself couldn't have come very close after midday," Leach said—he marshaled the sixty men in the mint to prepare to meet the approaching flames. The heavy iron shutters across the ground-floor windows were bolted. Now the men attacked the tarred roof, ripping it away with iron bars and pick shovels. Then buckets of blue vitriol were hoisted up from the refinery and the liquid was mopped over the exposed roof beams.

The mint had its own water supply, but the tremor had broken the pump from the artesian well buried beneath the vaults. Brady was able to do a makeshift repair job, and soon after midday the pump could be hand-operated.

By then the mint was completely surrounded by the flames, which extended for blocks on either side. On the exposed roof the defenders, blackened by smoke, deafened by the crash of falling buildings, were faced with a fresh menace.

At about 3:00, a fire stream of cinders flew toward them, borne on the wind.

It swooped over their heads and plunged into the mint's inner courtyard, setting fire to the stripped tar there. The men were still standing, dazed, when Lieutenant Armstrong grabbed a bucket and dropped down between the exposed rafters.

Mayor Eugene Schmitz was holding his eleventh conference of the day. Each one produced a spate of directives, but none had as far-reaching an effect as the order that came out of the meeting going on now in the basement bunker.

Most of the meetings had been devoted to short situation reports from the Fire and Police Departments.

Fire Chief John Dougherty reported the fifty-first individual outbreak at 1:00; the Mutual Life Building on California Street had burst into flames. By then the fire line north of Market Street stretched from Pine Street to the Appraiser Building on Washington.

There, the first relief company to reach the city—a fire engine from Oakland which was ferried across the Bay—was battling to save the structure; it was one of the firemen's few victories that day.

By then the fight to save the waterfront had begun; that struggle lasted four long days.

Inside the Post Office, ten employees were beating out the flames with mail sacks.

Elsewhere, the flames met with little resistance. Everywhere the fire stoked up its temperature on marble and brick and concrete blocks, withering and crumbling them to heaps of lime and brick and wire-draped junk.

Police Chief Jeremiah Dinan brought disturbing news of the first cases of exploitation. His officers reported that draymen were charging seventy-five dollars to carry household effects a distance for which they had asked two dollars the day before. Some saloonkeepers were being truculent when ordered to close down.

The Mayor issued explicit orders. Profiteers were to be arrested on complaint; saloonkeepers who were uncooperative were to have their stocks destroyed on the spot.

To reinforce these orders, issued without reference to a single law book or the advice of any law officer, the Mayor swore in a thousand armed volunteer patrolmen. His acts were reminiscent of the days when vigilante law was the only one San Francisco understood. Now, the "policy" defeated its purpose. On hearing the news, Brigadier General Henry E. Noyes, a senior Army staff officer in the city, noted the "curious spectacle of a city patrolled and guarded by federal troops, state troops, municipal police, and amateur safety committees. As a result there was continued friction and many clashes of authority." Results from the Mayor's decision to enroll the volunteers took hours to materialize.

Earlier that morning Schmitz had ordered a ban on all indoor cooking, to avoid the danger of starting new fires. But by then the "Ham-and-Eggs Fire" had already destroyed a large portion of the city.

Eugene Schmitz listened attentively to Judge Cabiness, who was detailing the legal precedent that provided for the judicious use of dynamiting to protect property.

By 2:00, Cabiness—a solemn-faced man of forty-five whose interpretation of fine legal points later enhanced his reputation as Presiding Judge of the Superior Court of the State of California—found what he had been seeking.

Clearing his throat, the Judge started to read from the case book: *"Pascal Surocco et al.* versus *John W. Geary.* Volume Three. California Supreme Court Reports. Appeal from the Superior Court of San Francisco. This was an action brought in the Superior Court of San Francisco by the plaintiff against recovery of damage for the blowing up by gun-powder and destroying his house and store with the goods therein on 24th December 1849. Damages laid at sixty five thousand dollars. The defendant answered that the said building was at the time of entry upon the same and the destruction thereof, certain to be consumed by public conflagration then raging in the City of San Francisco, and communicate the said conflagration to the other adjacent buildings in the said city."

(The 1849 case referred to the city's first great fire, which started in Kearny Street and caused $1,500,000 damage before burning itself out; then dynamite had been scattered in a futile bid to stop it spreading.)

"The right to destroy property to prevent the spread of a conflagration has been traced to the highest law of necessity and the rights of man independent of society or civil government," Cabiness read.

The Mayor and Cabiness looked at each other. Judge Cabiness had just provided the Mayor with the legal authority to destroy any building in the public interest.

But a legal way to destroy property had been found a full eighty minutes after Brigadier General Funston, on his own initiative, sent in the first military demolition squad. The promise of "consultation" with the civil authorities had already been broken.

At 12:45 P.M., Lieutenant Martin Briggs and six men began systematically blowing up buildings on California Street. Like Fire Battalion Chief John Conlon and his men—who failed with their dynamiting earlier south of the Slot—Briggs and his men had no experience in the proper placing of charges. All the windows in the first building they detonated were blown out; this in turn started another fire a full block away from the main fire line.

Undaunted, the squad moved on. In an hour they blew up over a dozen buildings—and started four other fires.

Many echoed John Conlon's comments: "They were useless, spreading, more than stopping, the fire."

The troops were more effective in dealing with looting. By early afternoon—again acting on orders issued solely by Brigadier General Funston—about a dozen looters in various parts of the city were summarily executed without trial.

They were the first of many—and their deaths provoked argument for half a century.

For many years now there has been a systematic attempt to minimize these executions. Even William Bronson gives them only brief mention in his exciting picture book, dismissing the executions with, "There were, to be sure, several on-the-spot executions of looters the first day"—surely a curious denial of the constitutional right to be judged innocent until convicted. Others, conceding that what was done was illegal, have tried to rationalize the killings as no more than what might be expected of hard-pressed soldiers doing a thankless job. But the citizens of San Francisco were under equal stress, and their panic might have caused them to do many things which would have appeared criminal under normal circumstances. Perhaps they deserve understanding more than the soldiers. There has also been a determined attempt to reduce the actual number of killings to a mere handful—and to maintain that in any case, the deaths were those of villains nobody would miss.

Under pressure Funston admitted that two killings—both at the hands of the volunteers Mayor Schmitz had engaged—were "reported" to him. He did not investigate the circumstances surrounding those two deaths.

Even if he had, a large number of deaths by shooting and hanging would still have remained unexplained. Three men allegedly rifling through a basement were executed on Stockton Street after midday. Their deaths were reported to Mayor Schmitz early that afternoon. If they shocked him there is no evidence of that; later he used their deaths as a warning to the public. There were the five bodies that photographer Moshe Cohen saw. At the age of eighty-seven he still remembered vividly "that they'd been shot on the brick; they'd been shot and left to lie there." Ed Gleeson also had little doubt that troops gunned down anyone "even suspected" of pilfering.

A. J. Neve, manager of one of the city's larger drugstores, testified that looters caught at this work were "shot without question." Oliver Posey, a wealthy mining operator, reported: "Instant death to scores was the fate for vandalism; the soldiers executed summary justice."

Gleeson and Cohen were in the city when the earthquake struck, and yet their testimony on looting has never been sought by those who have attempted to play down the executions. We were able to question the reporter and the photographer, along with a number of other witnesses, closely; the testimony of others is also available in the archives of the Presidio garrison, the California Historical Society, and the Society of California Pioneers.

All the evidence indicates that the executions were carried out without proper authority—or warning.

The authority was never legally given; the warning was not published until midafternoon—five full hours after the first soldier shot a man in a ruined building in Market Street. It was the opening shot in a deadly game, at the end of which, the city's newspapers reported later, the soldiers had bagged up to one hundred citizens of San Francisco.

It took Garret McEnerney, a lawyer and friend of Eugene Schmitz, and the Mayor only a short while to compose the wording of the warning that was both dictatorial and unconstitutional:

PROCLAMATION
BY THE MAYOR

The Federal Troops, the members of the Regular Police Force, and all Special Police Officers have been authorized by me to KILL any and all persons found engaged in Looting or in the Commission of Any Other Crime.

I have directed all the Gas and Electric Lighting Companies not to turn on Gas or Electricity until I order them to do so. You may therefore expect the city to remain in darkness for an indefinite time.

I request all citizens to remain at home from darkness until daylight every night until order is restored.

I WARN all Citizens of the danger of fire from Damaged or Destroyed Chimneys, Broken or Leaking Gas Pipes or Fixtures, or any like cause.

E. E. SCHMITZ, MAYOR
Dated April 18, 1906

It was, the small group of men around the Mayor's desk agreed, a bold step. Each one was well qualified to have advised on the illegality of the proclamation. Not only McEnerney, but Franklin Lane, a former city attorney, or Judge John Hunt, could have issued a timely warning that the Mayor had no authority to order any forces he commanded to shoot down the population.

But they said nothing when the Mayor ordered his Chief of Police to have the proclamation printed. In an hour, five thousand copies were run off in the printing shop on the outskirts of the city.

Dinan had been gone only a few minutes when the basement room began to fill with the men the Mayor had invited to help him run the city.

The first to arrive—promptly at 3 P.M.—was a young, heavily built man with a thick mustache: Rudolph Spreckels, the thirty-four-year-old sugar refinery millionaire, who had provided one hundred thousand dollars to investigate Schmitz. Behind him came the short, sandy-haired James D. Phelan, a former Mayor of the city who later represented California as Senator. He, like Spreckels, helped to prosecute Schmitz and Ruef in the coming months.

Today, Phelan and Spreckels were joined in another common purpose: the salvation of the city they had helped create.

The earthquake and fire had made Spreckels and Phelan poorer by nearly three million dollars. Phelan lost one million dollars with the destruction of his uninsured office building at the junction of O'Farrell and Market Streets. Near Salinas, the six-story Spreckels sugar factory, built on filled ground near the Salinas River, was reduced to a shell. Spreckels himself had another, more pressing personal concern: his wife was expecting a baby at any moment.

Herbert Law, the next to arrive, came from Market Street, where he had left the Monadnock Building—which the soldiers had failed to dynamite—a smoking ruin.

Others followed: Charles Sutro, Joseph Tobin, Rufus P. Jennings, M. H. de Young, owner of the *Chronicle;* each one of them was capable of raising one million dollars with no trouble under ordinary circumstances.

"But these are," Downey Harvey reminded them, "abnormal times; the disaster can already be counted in tens of millions, probably hundreds of millions of dollars."

James Phelan probably reflected the mood of those gathering in the bunker when he addressed them with characteristic optimism: "San Francisco is no ancient city. It is the recent creation of the pioneers and possesses the accumulated stores of only a couple of generations. Its temples, monuments, and public buildings are not of conspicuous merit or of great value. There is, in fact, nothing destroyed that cannot speedily be rebuilt."

Outside, James Hopper watched the men hurrying into the Hall of Justice. They seemed to be weighed down by "their fearful burden," talking "in tones that unconsciously sank to whispers." The strident tones of David Mahoney were muffled as he arrived with Claus Spreckles. Bishop William Nichols and Archbishop Montgomery had shared a buggy; the two men strode swiftly into the Hall of Justice. On their heels came Henry Crocker, then John McNaught and Irving F. Moulton. In a group came a knot of businessmen: Frank Anderson, Hugo Asher, Maurice Block, and Albert Castle.

Some, like John Martin and Benjamin Wheeler, stopped and talked to the waiting reporters; others, like Willis Polk and Ralph Harrison, swept past them. The newspapermen noticed not only who had been invited to join the decision making, but who had been overlooked. Abe Ruef's absence was noted with surprise; the nonappearance of Brigadier General Funston caused less comment—the newspapermen had yet to discover the iron hand he was clamping on the city.

As the last man—the saturnine Benjamin Wheeler—entered, Hopper was aware of two things. An invitation had not been sent to A. P. Giannini, the "people's banker." The fifty men chosen to administer civil government in San Francisco in fact represented only employer interests; virtually the only voice the masses had among those who were deciding their future was that of the Roman Catholic priest Father O'Ryan.

Of more immediate interest to Hopper was the wind. It had risen and changed direction. With its help, a solid curtain of flame was now bearing down on the Hall of Justice itself.

By 4:00 the evacuation of the Bank of Italy was underway. It did not take long. Giannini and his cashier, Pedrini, had returned with a produce wagon. A second cart, driven by Frank Rossi, a bookkeeper who worked for Giannini's brother, followed the first.

The bank's fixtures—chairs, desks, cabinets of records—were

loaded into the wagons. The three bags of gold and silver were placed under crates of oranges in the first dray. There was no room for the bank's new $375 adding machine. Giannini climbed up and took the reins. The other three climbed aboard the second wagon.

Keeping close together, the two drays rumbled up Columbus Avenue. Though none of them knew it then, the journey was the beginning of a venture which eventually turned the small Bank of Italy into the largest banking house in the world—the Bank of America.

The first leg of that momentous journey was short; for security reasons, Giannini decided to travel only the four miles to the home of his brother-in-law in daylight. Now, at the start of that two-hour journey, Giannini permitted himself a last quick look back down Columbus Avenue. Smoke was already drifting up the street.

To Brigadier General Funston, Enrico Caruso seemed to display commendable calm. The singer was seated high up on Telegraph Hill, drawing pad on his knee, sketching the devastation sweeping below, along a front ten streets wide, less than a mile away.

Caruso included himself in the sketch—a self-portrait in which he looked like some plump Napoleon looking toward his Moscow.

The officer paused briefly to watch, then continued on his way to find new targets to dynamite. He said later, "I doubt if anyone will ever know the amount of dynamite and gun cotton used in blowing up buildings, but it must have been tremendous, as there were times when the explosions were so continuous as to resemble a bombardment."

The casualties from this demolition began to accumulate: a police captain was seriously injured when he went to investigate a misfire, and later an Army lieutenant was killed when a charge blew up in his face.

Now Funston moved to extend his pattern of strategic destruction to completely encircle the heart of the city. If that failed to contain the fire, he planned to dynamite a wider circle, fanning out into the suburbs. He was determined to halt the flames, even if, some cynics said later, "it meant blowing up the last houses to do so."

In the gathering gloom inside the city jail, prisoner Chuck Connors heard the prisoners' renewed screaming, cursing, and crying.

"They banged their fists, boots, and food bowls against the bars, yelling for help."

Late in the afternoon it came. From the Hall of Justice, where he had been in conference with the other leading citizens, Judge John Hunt arrived and ordered the prisoners to be taken outside. The cell doors were swiftly unlocked. The inmates, watched by the detachment of soldiers who had guarded them all afternoon, were herded out into Portsmouth Square.

To Connors the scene in the square had some of the hallmarks of hell about it. Piled all over the ground were the bodies—over fifty sheeted forms—which had been carried out of the Hall's morgue. Shovels were thrust into the hands of the prisoners.

"Dig!" commanded a soldier.

"What?" asked a prisoner.

"Graves!"

With ash raining on them, and ringed by bayonets, the prisoners dug shallow trenches in which they buried the dead.

Then at 5:00, handcuffed in pairs, they were marched toward the waterfront.

It was a journey, Connors recalled, that "not even the most hard-boiled among us was likely to forget. In one street, we came upon a man who had been trapped in the wreckage for hours. I think his legs were crushed, because he couldn't move much. He just kept shouting, 'Shoot me—for God's sake shoot me,' and crying like a kid. A policeman came up and shot at him twice, but didn't hit him properly because he just kept on yelling. Then a young fellow snatched the cop's revolver and held it to the trapped man's head and blew out his brains."

Scenes of equal horror were being enacted in other streets the prisoners marched through. Fifty-five hours passed before they were safely behind bars again. They were ferried across the Bay to San Quentin Prison, and were refused admission because "they were federal prisoners in the charge of troops." The steamer returned to San Francisco, received new orders, and made the shorter crossing to Alcatraz Island. There, before being locked up, they got their first real meal in over two days.

But now, shortly after 6:00, the line of prisoners was being marched past a drugstore at the corner of Clay and Kearney Streets as a demolition squad busied itself.

The soldiers had chosen to blow up the drugstore with the only explosive they had—black powder.

Twenty minutes after the prisoners passed, the powder was detonated. It exploded with such force that bedding from a flat above the drugstore was hurled, flaming, across the street—and landed in Chinatown.

At 6:30 P.M., the Chinese quarter, which had remained free of fire all day, became another victim of the folly of allowing explosives to be put in inexperienced hands.

6:30 P.M. to Midnight

Market Street with the Ferry Building in the distance
(*Worden Collection, Wells Fargo Bank History Room*)

13. Hemmed in by Flames

THE EVENING SHADOWS lengthened and the glow at the base of the great fire wall deepened to a tawny red. As the wall rose to a clear two hundred feet, it lengthened to pink flecked with black. Above, like a headband, lay a pall of smoke, extending upward for about two miles. From somewhere in front of the advancing curtain of flame came the regular concussional shocks of dynamite. The conflagration was also sending out its own advance guard, softening up the path ahead with showers of hot cinders and belches of hot air.

For Margaret Edith Robertson, a seventeen-year-old schoolgirl standing on the upper slopes of Nob Hill, it was not so much the spectacle below which had stunned her, but the sudden and dramatic change in the behavior of Enrico Caruso.

The outward calm the singer had shown as he sketched earlier in the afternoon was gone. Once more he was a confused and frightened man, close to tears.

The change came as darkness approached. Until then, Caruso and the schoolgirl had chatted pleasantly. The devastation downtown seemed light-years from their talk of opera and travel. They had met quite by chance, but to the schoolgirl it came when the memory of her restless behavior the previous night at the Grand Opera House was still fresh in her mind.

She had sat with her parents in some of the best seats in the house. But the curtain had hardly risen on *Carmen* before Margaret experienced an overwhelming desire to leave—"a horrible feeling that I had to get out."

It was a premonition which spoiled her night at the opera; the performances on stage were little more than a miasma of sound and color. Overriding everything was her conviction that the ceiling was about to collapse. Hours later, it did.

Following the earthquake, she spent most of her day, like thousands of others living on the hills around the city, watching the inferno spreading below. "It *looked* bad as it raced from block to block," Margaret recalled, "but we were sure that the Fire Department would handle it in the end."

Late in the afternoon she spotted Caruso wandering aimlessly up Nob Hill. "If he hadn't looked so lost, I probably wouldn't have talked to him," she remembered. Caruso was "delighted to talk, especially since I could speak Italian."

For two hours the granddaughter of Britain's Governor to Madras and the son of an Italian peasant talked happily of places he had only vaguely heard of and she had seen only in picture books. Caruso spoke of Naples, Rome, and the palaces of Venice. She told him of her own background, the genteel manor house life of nineteenth-century England. She had been born in the Manor House at Wandsworth, "where all Queen Anne's children were born"; her maternal grandfather had designed the lions for London's Trafalgar Square monument to Nelson. It had been a world of tea parties and gracious manners. Then her family had immigrated to America, where life continued its pleasing pattern until the earthquake.

Responding almost as if her last comment were an emotional cue, Caruso peered anxiously down the hill, toward the center of town.

At that moment a fresh, orange-red column of flame exploded as Chinatown began to burn. The wall of fire had been extended and was advancing briskly toward Nob Hill.

Caruso's calm façade crumbled.

"The poor man was almost out of his mind with fear. He was really frightened, really terrified, he really was."

Still in that state of terror, Caruso plunged on up Nob Hill and down the other side onto Jones Street. Had he looked back over his shoulder, he would have seen the spectacle of Chinatown ablaze.

All afternoon, photographer Arnold Genthe had been capturing on film some of the classic moments of the disaster. He concentrated on the human aspect, leaving others to catalogue the fallen buildings and ruined sidewalks. All Genthe's pictures were deliberately out of focus, frequently lit from the rear—calculated to produce an effect that would distinguish his work from all the other pictures taken that day.

Early in the evening he returned to his favorite area—the streets of Chinatown.

For the first time in fifty years, its streets were silent. The population had fled on the heels of the steer they tried to kill a full twelve hours earlier.

The signs of panic-stricken flight were all around Genthe. Crates of vegetables—bamboo shoots, bean sprouts, and *gaichoy,* a type of spinach—were stacked, unopened, outside grocery shops beside boxes holding dried fish of all kinds—sea slugs, shark's fin, seaweed. A general store had been in the process of changing its window display when the tremors sent its owner fleeing, leaving lichee nuts, Chinese backscratchers, and artificial flowers in a jumble.

Chinatown's three newspapers—the *Occidental News,* the *Chinese World,* and *Chong Sai Yat Po*—were all going to press when the tremors came. The staff escaped, but the type cases of Chinese ideographic symbols were scattered all over the floor. The telephone exchange, usually occupied by eight kimono-clad girls who connected the two thousand Chinese subscribers, was deserted, lines still plugged in. The operators had joined the rush out of Chinatown.

Now, apart from Genthe, only two other things moved in the deserted streets: flames and the rats fleeing before them.

The rats had been in Chinatown since it was founded: black, brown, red, and gray—all infested with parasites of one kind or another: trichina worm, flukes, roundworm, and threadworm. Often they brought diseases from distant Chinese provinces. Traveling halfway around the world in Chinese boats, the rats brought bubonic plague to San Francisco.

It was first noticed in Chinatown in March 1900—a spinoff from a bubonic pandemic which killed 180,000 in Canton, China, 12,000 in Hong Kong, and swept as far north as Russia, then back down to China, east to Africa, and west again to America.

A bacteriologist at Ann Arbor, Michigan, caught bubonic plague through a laboratory accident while he was working with germ cultures taken from rats in Chinatown at the end of March 1900. The case was hushed up, for "in San Francisco, plague met politics."

Nine years passed before even an inkling of what lay behind that statement was made public. Finally, in March 1909, a new civic administration permitted publication of *The Citizens' Health Committee Report on Eradicating Plague from San Francisco*. Only a handful of people ever knew of the report's existence.

"Instead of being confronted by a united authority with intelligent plans for defense, it [the plague] found divided forces among which the question of its presence became the subject of factional dispute. There was often popular hostility to the work of the sanitarians, and war among the City, State, and Federal health authorities."

The report details the extraordinary lengths to which Mayor Eugene Schmitz went while in office to cover up the presence of bubonic plague in the city.

"A Federal health officer was arrested for trying to do his duty as he saw it. Eugene Schmitz refused to approve the printing of health reports and vital statistics, and attempted to remove from office four members of the Board of Health who persisted in the statement that plague existed in the city.

"The State bacteriologist, Ryfkogel, found plague germs and lost his position and part of his back salary.

"The public drew its inferences from the voluminous misinformation furnished by the disputants. Plague was said to be a medieval disease. It belonged to the days of Charlemagne or James the Second, before the common people had soap.

"It was an Oriental disease, peculiar to rice-eaters. It was a Mongolian or Hindu disease and never attacked whites. In San Francisco it was not a disease at all—it was a graft."

Eugene Schmitz and Abe Ruef received generous backhand payments from Chinese crib owners for years; other kickbacks went to police officials and members of the port authority to allow slave girls to be brought freely into Chinatown. Not many years had passed since the *Chronicle* reported a cargo of Chinese girls as if it were a stock market commodity: "The particularly fine portions of the cargo, the fresh and pretty females who come from the interior, are used to fill special orders from wealthy merchants and prosperous tradesmen. They are all critically examined by those desiring to purchase, and are sold to the 'trade' or to individuals at rates ranging from five hundred dollars down to two hundred dollars per head, according to their youth, beauty, and attractiveness. The refuse, consisting of 'boat girls' and those who come from the seaboard towns, where contact with the white sailor reduces even the standard of Chinese morals, is sold to the proprietors of the select brothels."

Lincoln's Emancipation Proclamation was ignored by the grafters of City Hall when there was money to be made from such trade. And bubonic plague, once publicly acknowledged, would have a disastrous effect on the brisk turnover in the cribs and parlors.

"For a while the people were in the gravest danger, and it seemed impossible to convey any adequate warnings to them. Intimations from medical conventions of Eastern state boards of health that unless San Franciscans got together and stamped out the plague, it would be necessary to enforce a general quarantine against the city, actually brought forth a demand from certain quarters that the Marine Hospital fellows go back to Washington where they belonged."

To rid the city of the plague required "unremitting toil, trapping and poisoning rats and destroying their harboring places; tearing the sodden planking out of light wells that were prehistoric Chinese garbage dumps; letting the sun into noisome old cellars that had not seen the light of day for forty years; inducing, persuading, and compelling landlords and their agents to pave back areas and basements and fill the spaces in the under-pinning of tumble-down shacks with concrete, and tear down and rebuild where the problem was hopeless of solution any other way."

While this campaign was being waged— with City Hall actively hampering it wherever possible—a hundred and thirteen people, mostly Chinese, died between March 1900 and February 1904 from bubonic plague.

Now, the carriers of the plague—tens of thousands of rats—were the last to leave Chinatown, said the report, renewing the menace "to a people stripped of their natural defenses and left naked to the enemy by unparalleled circumstances."

Some of the rodents would die in their nests in the walls, roofs, and under the floors of Chinatown. But Arnold Genthe knew that thousands would escape into the city, carrying with them a danger every bit as great as the flames. As he watched, a pack of rats darted across the road to a huge cupola. The dome had dropped from a roof and landed on its base, still intact. The rats swarmed over it.

Puzzled by their behavior, Genthe approached the cupola. In falling it had crushed at least two Chinese; on the far side a leg and an arm protruded. These stumps were being gnawed by some of the rats; others were desperately trying to find a way under the dome.

Sickened, Genthe turned and ran.

All day another photographer, Moshe Cohen, did some philanthropic moonlighting. An employee of the *Call,* he set out to photograph the disaster for the newspaper early in the day. The pictures he took also bore the individual stamp of a craftsman—they were stark, gaunt portraits of confusion and helplessness. He tried to make his way to the *Call* office, but was still several blocks away when it went up in flames.

"It somehow seemed rather pointless to go on taking pictures when there was no paper to publish them," Cohen later recalled.

At that point he found himself in a small park.

"The place was a junk yard; people had just dumped all they could from their houses and run, hoping that the flames wouldn't destroy the park. There was a small fortune in paintings, furniture and carpets. What interested me was the food lying around. There was sugar, coffee, and bread, enough to feed a lot of people. I figured it would be a shame to let it lie there, so I started to get it all together."

In a short time he had also tapped a water supply: at the bottom of a nearby garden he found a small windmill giving a steady supply of water. Cohen carried bucketfuls into the park. He kindled a fire, and began brewing coffee in a tin bathtub. While it brewed, he sliced and buttered bread.

Rummaging again, he found a wide assortment of cups and saucers. He laid these out in neat rows; Cohen's coffee shop—"as much as you like for nothing"—was ready for business. All day, the photographer dispensed coffee and bread to scores of grateful refugees. But as night fell, the supply of water dried up. There was another reason to move: rats "as big as tomcats" had begun to move boldly up to the fire.

Picking up his camera, Moshe Cohen resumed his duties as a news photographer. But he took no pictures that night. As he left the park, a soldier warned him that his flash powder for lighting could be mistaken for dynamite and cause panic—"and the sergeant made it quite clear that could lead to a bullet coming my way."

When Cohen reached O'Farrell Street, he got proof that the soldiers were not to be trifled with. Three of them were deployed outside a store, grouped in a rough half circle, their rifles pointed toward the door.

"Suddenly this fellow came out. He was loaded up to the eyeballs with stuff. His arms were full and so were his pockets. He took one look at the soldiers and then ran past them, figuring that was the only chance he had. He was still running when one of the soldiers dropped him with a shot clean through the back. The fellow just pitched forward, and all the stuff he was loaded with flew into the air. The soldiers just looked at one another and resumed patrolling, never giving the dead man a second glance.

"They had their orders. The Mayor's Proclamation had been posted by then. But it all made me sick. The stuff the man had taken would have been burned anyhow. The fire was only a block away, but that had made no difference. I think they would have still shot him if the flames had been right inside the shop.

"And there's always the question that kept dogging me. How did they know that he wasn't entitled to the stuff? He could have worked in the place, or maybe even been one of the owners. Maybe he ran because he was scared, and as sure as hell he was entitled to be, with three guns pointing at him.

"But none of those soldiers even bothered to find out. They just stood there, guns pointing, and then one of them let fly."

As the evening wore on, the Oakland *Tribune,* which sent its own reporter from across the Bay to investigate reports similar to Cohen's, considered the situation serious enough to merit a special extra edition, headlined: "PEOPLE SHOT DOWN BY SOLDIERS IN STREETS OF SAN FRANCISCO." "It is estimated that at least twenty people," the story began, "have been shot for stealing from unprotected stores and families. The city is under martial law and the soldiers do not hesitate, but shoot down anyone seen in the act of thieving."

The suspected thieves were left for cremation in the inferno.

By 8:00 the fire covered a three-mile crescent-shaped front. People fifty miles away, in the counties of Sonoma and Santa Clara, north and south of the city, recalled "a sky so bright that you could read a newspaper by it."

Jack London, reporting for *Collier's* magazine, was on his way to Union Square. "I was walking through miles and miles of magnificent buildings and towering skyscrapers. There was no water. The dynamite was giving out. And at right angles two different conflagrations were sweeping down. I knew it was all doomed."

He stood at the corner of Kearney and Market Streets, in the heart of the city. Kearney was deserted; half a dozen blocks away the flames occupied both sides of the street. Silhouetted sharply against the wall of flame which danced along the pavements, two mounted cavalrymen watched calmly.

"That was all. Not another person was in sight. In the intense heat of the city, two troopers sat on their horses and watched. Surrender was complete."

By the time London reached Union Square, the area was well established as a makeshift refugee camp—a staging post for more permanent encampments being set up at the Presidio and in Golden Gate Park.

"In Union Square thousands of them had gone to bed on the grass. Government tents had been set up. Supper was being cooked, and the refugees were lining up for free meals.

"I saw a man offering one thousand dollars for a team of horses. He was in charge of a truck piled high with trunks from some hotel. It had been hauled there to what was considered safety, and the horses had been taken out."

But in the darkness, hemmed in by flames only a block away, with the paint varnish melting on the St. Francis windows, the teamster could see that the "safety" was relative at best.

"There was another man beside the truck. He was old and on crutches. Said he, 'Today is my birthday. Last night I was worth thirty thousand dollars. I bought five bottles of wine, some delicate fish and other things for my birthday dinner, and all I own now are these two crutches."

14. Eager Hands

THERE WERE SOME who, fully aware of the risks they took, stuck at their posts. All day, the handful of men inside the Post Office beat down the flames with mail sacks. It became part of the splendid record of the United States mails during the disaster; in the end not a single letter or package was lost.

At the United States Mint, a seven-hour battle was ending. The blackened building, its heavy iron shutters buckled by the heat, still stood. The artesian well continued to pump, and a bucket chain kept the walls and exposed rafters damp.

In the courtyard Lieutenant Armstrong, a young Army officer, lay on a pile of coats, his eyes covered, his hands and face burned by the vitriol he had poured on burning tar stripped from the roof.

From the roof the mint's superintendent, Frank Leach, looked out upon a scene of nearly total devastation. He turned away and climbed down to the courtyard where the sixty men who had saved the mint sat exhausted.

Dazed, he told them: "Appears to be nothing left out there. It's all gone. Most of the city seems to have burned out."

He was not far wrong. Nearly four hundred people were dead; over five thousand were injured; one hundred thousand were homeless. The cost in property ran into hundreds of thousands, mounting to a final figure of nearly five hundred million dollars.

To James B. Stetson, a testy seventy-year-old veteran of the Gold Rush who ran the California Street Railway Company, the damage to property was compounded by the way the dynamite squads went about their work.

"They lacked good sense and judgment, or perhaps it may have been that some incompetent officers gave senseless orders."

All afternoon Stetson, who had working knowledge of explosives from his days among the miners on the Comstock Lode, watched Funston's demolition squads in action with mounting dismay.

Without checking the direction of the wind, or the path the inferno was traveling, the dynamiters inexpertly blew up a building, left it smoldering, and moved on to the next one. Frequently, the result was that when the main blaze reached the dynamited structure it found ready-made kindling.

When the soldiers ran out of explosives, they had another, cruder, method—legalized arson.

"I saw a soldier enter a premise, holding a vessel like a fruit dish containing some inflammable stuff," Stetson recorded. "He climbed on to the second floor, went to the front window, opened it, pulled down the shade and curtain, and set fire to the contents of his dish. In a short time the shade and curtain were in a blaze. When a fire started slowly, to give it a draught, the soldiers threw bricks and stones up to the windows to break the glass."

These tactics had no effect at all in containing the fire. But the soldiers, acting under orders initially given by Brigadier General Funston, created their own mayhem as they retreated up Dupont and Stockton Streets, ignoring any advice offered by the few civilians still in the area.

By 9:30 in the evening, the city had begun to resemble an experimental military area.

Fourteen hours after General Funston's troops marched from Fort Mason and the Presidio into the city to a fairly universal welcome by the fleeing population, many men and women experienced or witnessed something of the military's muscle-flexing. The veneer of politeness which the soldiers showed at first quickly evaporated in the heat of the fire lines. Harsh, impatient orders were reinforced by bayonet jabs, and there were some acts of wanton viciousness.

The soldiers could not be entirely blamed for their behavior. They had been on duty since dawn, with little food and water. Many were young and not a little frightened of the havoc all around them. None had experienced a disaster on this scale.

Those in front of the fire lines saw little of their officers during most of the day. Most were confused by the variety of armed patrols on duty: police patrols, volunteers, the National Guard. Frequently orders were issued and then countermanded.

But it is difficult to excuse the behavior of the patrol that broke into Delmonico's Restaurant on O'Farrell Street. The restaurant—where in the early hours of that morning some members of the touring opera company had celebrated the opening of *Carmen*—was several blocks ahead of the advancing fire. The soldiers, it was said, were "thirsty and tired." Unlike other military patrols, who looted liquor shops during the day and continued to do so under cover of darkness, this particular patrol wanted only coffee.

They lit a fire. In minutes the restaurant roof caught fire. The patrol fled—fading into the protective obscurity an army in action affords its men.

Swiftly the blaze spread. By the time firemen reached the scene, it was beyond control, sweeping up O'Farrell Street.

Union Square, the multimillion-dollar St. Francis Hotel, and a number of other buildings were doomed even before an attempt could be made to stop the fire.

Hundreds of refugees camped in Union Square were forced to flee, often with no more than what they wore, leaving behind the precious belongings they had carted about all day.

Twice in the space of seven hours the Committee of Fifty was forced to scatter and re-form as the fire burned down its meeting places. By 5:00 the Hall of Justice was untenable; two hours later, the Plaza, on the other side of Portsmouth Square, had to be abandoned.

Herbert Law and his brother Hartland, who had made his money from patent medicines, suggested they try a third venue—the Fairmont Hotel, which the Laws owned.

At 8:00 the Committee of Fifty assembled in the hotel ballroom, sitting along the edge of the stage and on packing cases. From there they had a clear view of the burning city; the reflected light gave the ballroom a warm, cozy effect.

James Phelan told Rudolph Spreckels that Mayor Eugene Schmitz ran things "as he would a hurried rehearsal; he swung his baton and played his new band with as much aplomb as if he had been conducting it for years."

No minutes were kept of any of the committee's sessions; M. H. de Young, owner of the *Chronicle,* and the newspaper's editor, John P. Young, both members of the committee, were obviously not there as professional observers.

The group had been in conclave for some time when they were joined by Brigadier General Funston. For many in the assembly it was their first close look at the military commander of San Francisco. It was a reassuring sight. Red-eyed from the smoke, the lines on his face etched in grime, Frederick Funston looked as if he had walked off some Civil War battlefield. With him he carried that prerequisite of all military leaders—the latest situation map.

Introductions were brief. The committee gathered around Funston as he spread his map on a crate.

"Dynamite," he said impassively. "Dynamite is the only answer. From here, down to here, round to here."

His jabbing forefinger traced a line across the map of the city. The line began far out in the suburbs, at Herman Street. Then it swung across the city, bisecting over sixty blocks, and slashed down through Bay Street to the sea.

For such a plan, he assured his stunned listeners, he could get ample supplies of dynamite from military garrisons all over California and from the railways.

"In fact," he added unemotionally, glancing at his watch, "the first supplies should be here within the hour."

Turning back to his map, Funston slid his finger over the area he had condemned to destruction. "There is no water. The only hope I have of slowing up the advancing fire is by using dynamite. A fire wall can be blasted that will hold the flames until water can be provided."

Funston did not specify how long it would be until the water could be provided. In the meantime, as far as his listeners were concerned, he was advocating large-scale destruction of property still well clear of the fire.

Turning to Mayor Schmitz, Brigadier General Funston said that he had already instructed his officers to evacuate civilians from the whole area below the line. He had also sent patrols out to guard property above the line. In doing so he reinforced his orders that

miscreants were to be shot; it was, he added with a measure of satisfaction, a policy he had seen endorsed on the Mayor's proclamation.

If Eugene Schmitz and the committee hoped for any hint of
reassurance from the officer, they were disappointed. No comfort
could be drawn from his remarks: "You have no resources to hold
the fire below that line. None at all. Dynamite is the only answer."

There was silence in the ballroom. The civic leaders and the
General stared at each other. The pause lengthened uncomfortably.

"Very well," Mayor Schmitz nodded, breaking the silence, "we
are to be kept informed of each building to be destroyed." His remark was no more than a pathetic invitation to maintain the promised
"consultations" between Funston and the Mayor.

Funston, having obtained the necessary consent, left the room.

During the two hours that followed his departure, a number of
subcommittees were set up. The designations of the committees
described their functions: Relief of the Hungry; Housing the Home
less; Relief of Sick and Wounded; Drugs and Medical Supplies;
Relief of Chinese; Transportation of Refugees; Citizens' Police; Aux-
iliary Fire Department; Restoration of Water Supply; Restoration of
Light and Telephones; Restoration of Fire in Dwellings; Restoration
of Abattoirs; Resumption of Transportation; Resumption of Civil
Government; Resumption of the Judiciary; Resumption of Retail
Trade; Organization of Wholesalers; Finance, History, and Statistics;
Sanitation.

The nineteen subcommittees, John P. Young believed, "exhibited
in a remarkable degree the American capacity for organization, and
the ease with which a people appreciate self-government in the hour
of need, and place their dependence on men who have exhibited their
capacity to do things."

It was a noble sentiment.

Shortly after 11:00, the ballroom began to empty. The subcommittee members planned to meet again in the morning for further
discussions.

Apart from setting up those committees—a further full eighteen
hours passed before they began to operate to any real degree—what
else was achieved by the Mayor and the civil authorities by the end
of the first day of the disaster?

Over the intervening years a legend, one of many clouding the actual events, has grown up that this *de facto* local government achieved immediate miracles. *The San Francisco Disaster* by Monica Sutherland and *Earthquake* by Allen Andrews are just two of the books that have helped to foster the engaging picture of Eugene Schmitz heading a band of civic-minded stalwarts into action. William Bronson in *The Earth Shook, the Sky Burned* endorses this story, too, with his portrait of "swift action" by the Mayor, followed by the committee turning "to the problems of greatest need."

Other writers have conjured up a civic extravaganza in which the Mayor and his fifty men raced through the streets like an early Hollywood version of Robin Hood and his merry men, dispensing food and money, encouraging the firemen, finding fresh supplies of water when all seemed lost.

The truth, alas, falls somewhat short of this attractive legend. On that first day, apart from the three meetings, very little of a practical nature was actually achieved. Although Eugene Schmitz may have "needed" the crisis, which enabled him to indulge in the illusion that "life had really begun again," and although he may have shown an unusual degree of moral fiber during the day, in the end, little had been done for the people of San Francisco.

At 11:00 that night, confusion in the streets was as great as ever. Natural instinct—to get as quickly and as far away from the flames as possible—rather than an organized plan of retreat—prevailed. No attempt was made to marshal the remaining means of transportation into any real order; communications, where they existed, were haphazard, and verbal messages were frequently distorted.

Overriding everything was the effect of Brigadier General Funston's decision to send in armed men. From early on, Mayor Schmitz and his Committee of Fifty could hardly fail to be aware that in the end they would be subservient to the military.

What effect the show of military strength had on Eugene Schmitz and his citizens' committee is debatable. But the fact was that on that first day, many of the important decisions had been made and implemented by the time they became aware of them.

Funston himself did nothing to dispel their feeling of helplessness. While he might have recognized earlier in the day that the military occupation of the city could be facilitated with the cooperation of the local authorities, it is clear that by late evening he would not allow civic laggardness to impede what he believed to be the right—indeed, the only—course of action.

He welcomed the Mayor's proclamation—though a good nine hours elapsed between the earthquake and first fire and its publication. But for him it represented little more than a gesture. The real authority was his armed troops. For some hours they had clamped down on San Francisco with a firmness—and, some later said, harshness—that few American cities had felt until then.

At the end of their third meeting, Mayor Schmitz and his Committee of Fifty were still riding little more than a paper tiger.

By 11:30 P.M. Brigadier General Funston could look with satisfaction from his new command post at Fort Mason, at the north end of Van Ness Avenue, and judge the effectiveness of his measures. Over a thousand regular soldiers were stretched in a line from the Fort down the length of Van Ness. No civilian without a military pass could pass the cordon. From below it came the renewed booming of exploding dynamite.

Describing this night, the city's self-appointed military governor later noted: "San Francisco had its class of people, no doubt, who would have taken advantage of any opportunity to plunder the banks and rich jewelry and other stores of the city. But the presence of the square-jawed, silent men with magazine rifles, fixed bayonets, and with belts of cartridges, restrained them."

Undoubtedly they were an effective police force. The tragedy was that too often they could not distinguish between a potential thief and an honest householder anxious to reclaim or save his personal effects.

On the road to his home in San Mateo, A. P. Giannini turned in the driver's seat of his wagon. Fifty feet behind, the second wagon followed. In the glow that filled the night sky, he could see that Pedrini and Avenali were close to exhaustion.

"Not far now," he shouted encouragingly. "A few more miles, that's all."

"How many more hours?" asked Pedrini.

It had taken them four hours to cover the last five miles. Minutes before, Giannini had led the way off the refugee-filled main road to San Mateo, and they were now traveling on a side track.

He had chosen this new route because it was less congested, and jolting over the rutted ground would help to keep them awake. He cracked the whip over his two dray horses, and the Bank of Italy was once more on its way.

At about the moment Giannini drove onto the side track, a train was pulling into Oakland Station, across the Bay from San Francisco. It carried food and medical supplies as well as nurses and doctors who had traveled all night from Los Angeles.

The first measurable relief from the outside world had reached the devastated area. It came just nineteen hours after the first tremor —a remarkable tribute to swift and smooth organization.

As the clock tower of Oakland City Hall chimed midnight, eager hands opened the doors of the freight train.

THURSDAY
APRIL 19, 1906

Midnight to 6 A.M.

The remains of City Hall (left) (*Roy D. Graves Collection*)

15. Foreign Affairs

THE DRAB BASEMENT storeroom of the Presidio military hospital held a beauty all its own for Mrs. Eda Funston and General George Torney. Neatly folded on tiers of shelves were blankets. By the light of a storm lantern the wife of Brigadier General Funston could see that there were hundreds of them.

Turning to her companion, the commander of the Letterman Military Hospital at the Presidio, the tall, regal woman, dressed in a severe black blouse and long skirt, announced: "At a blanket each, there should be enough for two thousand. Mothers with babies and children first."

General Torney nodded. He had spent a great deal of his time agreeing with Mrs. Funston since her arrival early in the afternoon of the previous day. Some of her husband's qualities had rubbed off on Eda Funston in eight years of marriage. She knew what she wanted and how to get it by direct, forceful action.

She made the journey to the Presidio on foot. By the end of it she had come to one inescapable conclusion: the injured and homeless needed help—Army help.

Like her husband, Mrs. Funston firmly believed that only the Army could really cope with the situation. Not just wifely pride, but a deep-rooted conviction that the United States Army, with its vast reserves of money, manpower, and supplies, convinced her that it was the only force capable of assuming control. Needless to say, she approved of the swift action her husband had taken.

At the Presidio a relief operation gathered momentum all morning.

159

The garrison's cookhouses were mobilized to make bread and brew large cauldrons of coffee.

Shortly after the first fires began, urgent messages were sent to the commissaries at Portland and Seattle; six hours after the earthquake, seven hundred thousand rations were on their way from these bases. In Los Angeles, supply officers ordered the first of two hundred thousand packs of emergency food.

The Presidio itself lost nearly $250,000 worth of tinned foods when two large warehouses it rented downtown were burned out by the fire north of Market. Three thousand tents and thousands of blankets which were stored at the garrison were distributed to early refugees.

Mrs. Funston made her way to the Letterman Hospital, just inside the Presidio perimeter. The hospital had been totally rebuilt and re-equipped following a fire that had gutted it a few years earlier. The hospital was looking after a steady stream of seriously wounded from the downtown area, including the unconscious Fire Chief, Dennis Sullivan. An additional operating theater was set up; beds were crammed together to make more space.

For General Torney, Mrs. Funston was a welcome sight; her control and calmness were bywords among the garrison's officers. But she also confirmed his worst fears; her report indicated that the catastrophe was greater than anybody realized.

For twelve hours, Mrs. Funston worked tirelessly for the refugees. She seemed to be, Major C. A. Devol, the garrison quartermaster, recalled, everywhere at once. "She was quite determined that anything she thought would be useful was done—and things like Army regulations didn't apply here and now."

Shortly after midnight, she located the supply of blankets in the storeroom in a far corner of the garrison. Within a short time they were distributed to new arrivals.

All day and night the refugees spread through the military compound, setting up camp between rows of Army huts and tents. By early morning, an estimated thirty thousand were camped out.

To Fred Hewitt, a feature writer on the *Examiner,* they resembled "herds of huddled creatures, not knowing what would happen next. Every person I saw was temporarily insane. Laughing idiots commented on the fun they were having. Terror masked their faces, and yet their voices indicated a certain enjoyment that maniacs have when they kill and gloat over their prey. Women, hysterical to an extreme point, cried and raved for those they loved when they were standing at their elbow. Mothers searched madly for their children who had strayed, while little ones wailed for their protectors. It was bedlam. Strong men bellowed like babies in their furor. All humanity within eyesight was suffering from palsy."

In the glow of cooking fires, Hewitt—by his own admission not the most sensitive reporter observing the scene—saw something that stirred him.

Mrs. Eda Funston was leading a group of women and children seated around the campfire in Psalm Twenty-three. Sweet and clear above the fear all around came the timeless chant of comfort, of one who, in another time and place, had come through the valley of death; "the valley of death was all around," the reporter remembered.

Over two and a half thousand miles away, in New York, Hewitt's employer, William Randolph Hearst, sent off his first sponsored mercy squads to San Francisco.

Fifteen hours had elapsed since the newspaper tycoon finally realized the full magnitude of the disaster which had befallen his native city; the loss of the *Examiner* building alone depleted his own fortune by one million dollars. The hasty editorial he had published in his New York *American* was forgotten; the earthquake had proved itself the equal of other natural calamities in its killing power.

Colleagues recalled that "the Chief was deeply shocked at the loss of the city of his birth." From New York an urgent message went to senior executives in the other two main Hearst publishing centers, Chicago and Los Angeles: publications under their control were to organize charity bazaars and theatrical benefits. Every reader was to be urged to donate a dollar, dime, or nickel, and thereby to earn a place in Hearst's "World Roll of Honor."

The money was to be used to speed relief trains to San Francisco. The freight cars and locomotives would be provided by the Southern Pacific Railroad for the run into Oakland Station. Railway stock that Hearst newspapers once castigated as being "in the last stages of decay" suddenly became acceptable.

By 3:30 A.M., New York time, Hearst approved arrangements for twelve trains to make the long haul across country to the Pacific Coast. The Chief's latest instruction was sent to the entire Hearst chain: the disaster was to be played up for all it was worth. It was not the first time William Randolph Hearst had changed his editorial mind.

Two hundred miles down the track from New York en route to San Francisco, Edward Harriman, President of the Southern Pacific Railroad Company, sat in the observation car of the freight train. In rapid order he dictated a series of typically crisp dispatches to a secretary. "To general managers at Omaha, Salt Lake, Portland, and Houston. Offer immediate and all assistance including free transportation to refugees from disaster area." "To office, general manager, Los Angeles. Confirm your authorization spend ten thousand dollars purchase relief supplies." "Manager, Oakland. Our entire facilities at the disposal of refugees."

Each time the train stopped the messages were dropped off for transmission; then, resuming its journey, the train, with its cargo of baked beans, canned meats, biscuits, and rice, moved on toward San Francisco.

Farther up the line, the Negro conductor aboard the New York-to-Chicago night express picked up a top-priority message for a passenger, Dr. Edward Thomas Devine. Although he had never heard of Dr. Devine, asleep in his Pullman coach, the conductor did know the name of the sender, Theodore Roosevelt, President of the United States.

Deferentially, the conductor knocked on Dr. Devine's first-class compartment. The sleepy-eyed General Secretary of the Charity Organization of New York snapped on the light and blinked as he read the telegram: "I REQUEST THAT YOU REPRESENT THE RED CROSS IN RELIEF OPERATION IN SAN FRANCISCO. THEODORE ROOSEVELT."

Completely awake now, Dr. Devine read the presidential request again, then asked the conductor: "How do I send a telegram from here?"

"From here? It's not possible—"

"It's to the President of the United States."

"We'll get it off at the next station, sir!"

Devine scribbled on a piece of paper that he was honored to accept the President's invitation.

In those few words, Edward Thomas Devine and the fledgling American Red Cross both took a momentous step forward.

All Devine's adult life had been preparation for that presidential summons.

He had been Professor of Social Economy at Columbia University. His book on the principles of relief was acclaimed by social workers throughout America; a chapter on relief of disaster caught the imagination of Roosevelt. The President noted that Devine was "probably the best qualified director of relief in the country; he has undoubtedly made a more extensive study of disaster than any other practising social worker and is familiar with the techniques employed and the mistakes made during previous disaster relief operations."

Two years after making that comment, President Roosevelt summoned the soft-spoken Midwesterner to assume responsibility for Red Cross action in San Francisco.

Devine took control of an organization which had been practically reconstructed a year earlier. Professional workers were brought in to man the local societies and state branches; amateurs, however well-meaning, were gently eased from office. In their place came seasoned fund raisers who knew where to tap money and how to spend it wisely.

As part of the reorganization, Secretary of War William Howard Taft was appointed President of the Red Cross Corporation. On January 5, 1905, Congress had granted the Red Cross a new charter and Taft provided a Washington office—Room 341 in the War Department—for the organization.

But none of this could entirely remove the feeling in some government quarters that the National Red Cross was superfluous—that relief could be handled best by local organizations. Untried, with virtually no funds, its terms of reference not clearly understood, the Red Cross spent the whole of 1905, and up until April 1906, striving for recognition.

Now, in one terse telegram to Dr. Devine, President Roosevelt solved the one problem the re-formed Red Cross still faced—lack of dynamic leadership in the field.

As the train thundered toward Chicago, Dr. Devine sat on his bunk and prayed for guidance. In the days to come he needed more

than prayer to cope with civic fury in San Francisco over his appointment to administer relief funds of more than nine million dollars.

President Roosevelt's draft of the proclamation announcing Devine's appointment lay on the desk in the President's darkened White
House office. It would be promulgated on receipt of Devine's telegram accepting office.

The proclamation read: "To the people of the United States.
In the face of so terrible and appalling a national calamity as that
which has befallen San Francisco, the out-pouring of the nation's
aid should as far as possible be entrusted to the American National
Red Cross, the national organization best fitted to undertake such
relief work."

After appointing Devine, the President requested that donations
be sent to the Red Cross headquarters in Washington, "in order that
the contributions which I am sure will flow in with lavish generosity
may be wisely administered."

The proclamation, the first of its kind, established a policy, subsequently followed by all Presidents, which gave the Red Cross the
moral support of the White House; ultimately it also helped establish
the Red Cross as the recognized leader of mass-scale emergency
relief in America.

All day Roosevelt closely followed reports coming out of San
Francisco. California's Governor Pardee telegraphed a dramatic as-
sessment of the situation; Secretary Taft brought news that Brigadier
General Funston, on his own authority, had sent in the troops;
Washington newspapers carried frightening stories of terror and
destruction.

To Governor Pardee the President telegraphed: "It was difficult
to credit the news of the calamity that had befallen San Francisco.
I feel the greatest concern for you and the people, not only of San
Francisco, but of California in the terrible disaster. You will let me
know if there is anything the government can do."

On hearing of Funston's action, the President confided to Taft:
"This alone would have vindicated General Funston's rapid promotion from volunteer rank, had such a vindication been necessary."

All day accredited diplomats called at the State Department, ex-
pressing national condolences. One of the callers was Chentung

Liang-cheng, the Chinese Ambassador, who in addition to sympathy offered money.

President Roosevelt ruled that foreign aid of any sort, from any source, would be firmly refused: America could look after its own.

But it was some time before the world at large learned of this decision. By then money was already on the way to Washington: the donations caused presidential embarrassment and brought him under bitter attack—from the Hearst newspapers—for snubbing friendly nations.

But in the twenty-two hours since San Francisco had been stricken, America had indeed lived up to the self-sufficiency of which, in Roosevelt's judgment, the nation was capable.

In Denver, Colorado, a boxcar filled with fresh meat was loaded in the morning—one of fifty similar cars being filled at points as far away as New Jersey and Texas.

At the Indian School in Chemewa, Oregon, senior pupils spent the night kneading and baking 830 loaves of bread. The first batch was put on a Wells Fargo coach at 3 A.M. to begin the two-day journey to San Francisco. In Ogden, Utah, the town's bakers announced that all they could bake would be shipped directly to the disaster area.

In New York the Merchants' Association followed up an initial gift of fourteen freight cars of tinned food with an express boxcar holding $60,000 worth of drugs.

In Chicago—where many still remembered the holocaust in which two hundred had died—relief efforts were begun on a massive scale. Religious and business committees set up their own plans for help; by early morning three freight trains were on their way from Chicago to San Francisco. Along with a wide range of supplies, the first train also carried ten senior detectives from the Chicago police force to help maintain law and order in San Francisco. "Happens San Francisco always was a frisky place," Chicago's Police Chief announced; "be friskier still now." Upon their arrival in San Francisco, the law officers were promptly turned around, with a polite word of thanks from Police Chief Dinan.

All through the night financial pledges arrived by telegraph in Oakland, the point nearest the city that was still intact. Philadelphia promised $500,000; Pittsburgh, $100,000; St. Louis, $200,000; the state of Massachusetts, with the help of Boston, undertook to raise $3,000,000.

In Pontiac, Illinois, the city council donated $100; in Toledo, Ohio, the Mayor decreed California Day: the fund-raising effort netted $5000.

Archbishop Farley of New York asked Catholics to pray and donate: in the early hours of the morning, St. Patrick's Cathedral was filled with worshipers.

The Salvation Army set its machinery in motion; girls in blue bonnets stood through the night on thousands of street corners in hundreds of towns and cities, accepting donations.

The Grand Army of the Republic, the Freemasons, Odd Fellows, and Elks, all held emergency lodge meetings to plan fund-raising forays.

A money order for $100,000 was wired by John D. Rockefeller; William Waldorf Astor and Andrew Carnegie promised similar amounts. The Guggenheim brothers of New York gave $50,000; "a friend of humanity" sent $25,000.

Nearer to San Francisco—from Los Angeles, Seattle, Stockton, and Sacramento—the first medical relief trains were on their way. In two days so many doctors and nurses arrived in the disaster area that an official appeal was made that no more come.

In Los Angeles, the retired heavyweight boxing champion Jim Jeffries stacked a wagon full of oranges; in the coming hours he raised $600 selling them.

Early that morning, businessman A. R. Stringer sailed from Sacramento on a steamer crammed with foodstuffs and medical supplies, doctors, and nurses. As the boat chugged through the night, Stringer addressed his assembled rescue team: "San Francisco can count on Sacramento for the last bit of bread and meat in the house, can draw on us for every dollar we have, and then can have our blood if it needs it."

Halfway across the world, in Tokyo, the city's late editions were carrying long dispatches about the "total destruction" of America's great Pacific seaport.

To Dr. F. Omori, Professor of Seismology at Tokyo Imperial University, the "vast death toll" which the newspapers reported was at least partially predictable. His specially designed seismographs had recorded traces well before the big rip; there was enough warning to have taken some preventive action. (Two years before, San Francisco's weather man, Alexander McAdie, had in fact written to the Professor inquiring the cost of a seismograph. Omori replied that for two thousand dollars San Francisco could acquire a seismograph which, sited properly, would give advance warning of an impending earthquake. The matter was not pursued.)

Elsewhere in Japan, which itself lay on an earthquake belt, the country's Red Cross organization and the Imperial Government began a relief collection which in the end contributed $244,960.10. China raised $40,000; Mexico, $14,480.31; Cuba, $734; Australia, $385; Ceylon, $32.33.

All over Europe, eight hours ahead of San Francisco, the morning newspaper stories were helping to speed the collection of relief funds.

In Paris, United States Ambassador McCormick had accepted several large donations by midmorning; in the end France subscribed nearly $27,000. From Czarist Russia came $199.02. Austria, Belgium, and Germany raised $50 each, and Scotland managed to raise another forty cents on that figure.

In London, British Foreign Secretary Sir Edward Grey received several communications from his aides during the morning, indicating a national sense of shock which was reflected in the morning newspaper headlines.

The *Daily Express* relegated a report from Pietermaritzburg, South Africa, a story on a revolt in Zululand, and an invitation for the Royal Family to make a state visit to Canada to single columns.

Following the *Express* policy of always finding a local angle for any world-shattering story, a reporter was sent to the Isle of Wight to interview Professor John Milne, described in the front-page story as "one of the greatest living authorities on seismic disturbances."

Beneath the headlines—"EARTH OFF ITS AXIS? PROFESSOR MILNE ON THE CAUSE OF THE EARTHQUAKE"—followed one of the more original views on the cause of the disaster.

Arriving home after a round of golf, the Professor found that his seismograph had registered an earthquake. "It took me a few moments to calculate where it had taken place, and I found that only two spots were possible. It was either North West India or San Francisco."

If he had been a little unsure as to where it occurred—after all, several thousands of miles separated the Golden Gate from the Khyber Pass—Professor Milne had no doubt as to the cause. "Sometimes the earth gets a little bit off its course, and the reaction in swinging back to its true position involves a tremendous strain on the center. This is so great that it results in the breaking of the earth's crust."

Professor Milne was not the only Englishman with a novel theory. Sir Hiram Maxim, "the noted British inventor and scientist," told readers of a London evening newspaper, "Ever since the solid crust of earth was formed there have been certain lines of least strength, and as the earth shrinks the solid crust yields at these weakest points. It will now be found that California is not so large as it was before the earthquake, but the difference will not be so great."

Even if the whole world was shrinking, England was determined that a reduced California should receive relief benefit. Early in the day Foreign Office officials informed Sir Edward Grey that donations for the relief of San Francisco were pouring in from all over the country; in the end $6570.88 was raised.

The money would not be forwarded, decreed Sir Edward, until there was definite news from the Consul General in San Francisco as to the state of the city.

16. A Row of Guns

WALTER COURTNEY BENNETT, the British Consul General in San Francisco, never dreamed the day would come when Britain's senior diplomat in the city would roll himself up in a blanket beneath a bush in Golden Gate Park, head pillowed on his bulky briefcase. The case held all that remained of the Consul General's documents—the rest had been destroyed in the fire.

Beside the diplomat lay his wife and daughter, sleeping at last.

The Bennetts were one of thousands of families who fled to the relative safety of the park. Refugees were still arriving in droves. Like many others, the Consul General's family escaped with only the clothes they wore; the fire had pounced on their hotel, enveloping it in flames in minutes.

At the park's main entrance, an emergency hospital was set up in the open air. Patients from the burned-out Mechanics Pavilion, and from other hospitals, were laid out in rows on the grass.

To Ed Gleeson, still hunting copy, the emergency hospital seemed pitifully short of everything—"cots, nurses, doctors, the lot."

In the course of his day-long search for news, the reporter discovered that his girl friend, Nell, had escaped through the back door of her home as the frame building creaked and groaned in the grip of the tremors. The couple met briefly on Market Street; Nell insisted that Ed eat a quick cold snack before resuming work.

At Golden Gate Park, Gleeson saw "strong men, too exhausted to speak after pulling a steamer trunk several miles," sitting stunned on the grass. By nightfall, a semblance of order was beginning to emerge. Soldiers supervised a bread line; cooking fires sprang up all over the grounds.

The shortage of water was critical. At the emergency hospital there was barely enough to sterilize the instruments.

When Gleeson arrived at the hospital, he was pressed into medical service. "I was going to assist Dr. Charles Miller, chief surgeon of the city, while he performed a major operation."

The operating table was set up in a small tent. A bottle of chloroform was the only anesthetic; two storm lanterns provided light; instruments were sterilized in a bucket. "Dr. Miller put the patient under by holding a wad of cotton wool soaked in the chloroform under his nose. I don't remember much about the operation, except that the surgeon looked worn and gaunt. He had been operating all day, wherever he could set up his instruments."

In emergency hospitals all over the city, the night was a long one for the staff.

At St. Mary's, the wearying hours began late in the afternoon, when the Hayes Valley fire started to sweep toward the hospital.

An evacuation plan drawn up several hours earlier was put into effect. Surgical dressings, trolleys, instruments, drugs, were dumped into laundry boxes, loaded onto trucks, and rushed to the Pacific Mail dock where the river paddle steamer *Medoc* had been berthed all afternoon with steam raised.

Doctors and nursing sisters from St. Mary's quickly transformed the riverboat into a floating hospital.

Back at the hospital itself, Mother Euphrasia, the matron, supervised the final stages of the evacuation. "As our patients were removed from their beds, the mattresses were thrown through the windows, and the patients were carried to waiting trucks. Just before I locked the door, I took one more look inside the lobby. I was struck by the beauty of a painting hanging on the west wall, a Madonna and Child by Franz von der Frigger. I walked back into the lobby and removed it.

"Large cinders were beginning to fall around us, and the fire was already invading the upper side of our block. Someone handed a small baby in swaddling clothes to a nurse, completing our human cargo; nobody knew to whom it belonged. An eight-year-old boy was our last passenger; he came along, rapping the fence pickets with a stick, saying he had gone out to see the fire and upon his return had found his home burned down and his parents absent. He was invited for a boat ride and readily accepted."

With the decks strewn with mattresses—and often two patients to a mattress—the doctors and the nursing Sisters of Mercy tended to their charges while the paddle steamer headed for the safety of the Bay.

All night the groans of the seriously ill echoed across the decks of the floating hospital; of the 170 patients aboard, ninety were acute bed cases.

The dead were carried aft and laid inside a lifeboat; the click of rosary beads and murmured Hail Marys were a somber accompaniment to the more mundane calls for bandages and bedpans.

Back in the city, the situation was deteriorating. The only good news was that the Ferry Building still stood, and that the ferries were carrying hundreds to safety. Firemen had also saved the Southern Pacific sheds on Townsend Street.

The mansions on Nob Hill were a different story. These homes represented a financial empire that stretched to Washington and back again, embracing thousands of miles of rail track, ranches, vineyards, and even whole towns. For years they had stood like castles over the city—the homes, the Hearst newspapers declared, of robber barons who grew fat through bribery and corruption.

First to burn was the Mark Hopkins mansion. During the night students and teachers from the University of California struggled to carry to safety art treasures stored in the gabled palace, which had been given to the university for use as an art school and gallery. Hundreds of canvasses and statues were rescued, but late in the evening troops were forced to clear the area as the flames approached.

The fire was in no hurry. For several hours it merely danced around the mansion, lighting up every stack, turret, and dormer.

Railroad executive Mark Hopkins, whom some called "the stubbornest man alive," had built a home completely vulnerable to burning. In minutes it became the funeral pyre of the Hopkins bad taste. The Palace of the Doges drawing room; the carved English oak dining room; the master bedroom of ebony, ivory, and inset jewels; the library where Mrs. Mary Hopkins had indulged her passion for bad novels—all burned within an hour.

By then Leland Stanford's home next door was blazing brightly. The mansion had stood for over thirty years, a fitting monument for a man who saw God through the eyes of a Methodist, and who happily accepted the evaluation of a contemporary commentator that "in an earlier age Leland would have been a Christ or a Confucius."

The house was fronted by high marble steps which led into a huge circular hallway rising seventy feet. The hall's only visible support was a marble pillar. The floor was covered with signs of the zodiac inlaid in black marble. Other unusual features, including a hothouse conservatory, and an East Indies room where staid waltzes were played "in a misty Victorian elegance," distinguished the palatial residence.

The Stanfords were no dynasty breeders. They had been married for nearly twenty years before their only child, a son, was born. His death from typhoid in Florence, Italy, at the age of fifteen, unhinged his parents. They cast around for a fitting monument to their boy; the suggestion of a railway train—Stanford had at one time been President of both the Southern Pacific and Central Pacific Railroads—was discarded, as was a statue. Finally, urged on by a spiritualist whom Stanford believed to be in direct contact with God, he founded a college. In October 1891, Stanford University opened.

The earthquake that struck the city almost fifteen years later wrecked a large portion of the Stanford campus and gardens. With equal thoroughness the fire now destroyed the mansion of its founder.

The Collis P. Huntington mansion was a slow burner. The massive structure kept the flames at bay for several hours, protecting a collection of innocuous paintings which Huntington had collected in the belief that in acquiring them he would also acquire the manners and tastes of a gentleman.

He died in 1900, unaware that for years he had been victimized by unscrupulous art dealers. His mansion, with its French château-style roof, remained conspicuously empty. The memories of his wholesale bribing of Congress, courts, judges, and newspapermen faded. A railroad tycoon of no small stature, he saw himself as the reincarnation of a Renaissance Pope, swift to punish, equipped with boundless guile and strength, a catalyst through which money would be made and plots fomented. In the end he became the victim of his own illusions of infallibility—"I know that God will let me reach one hundred and ten years." He still had a number of years to go when he died, leaving behind his sleazy objets d'art and an embalming-house décor.

When Charles Crocker, consolidator of the Southern Pacific and Central Pacific Railroads, erected his home on Nob Hill across the street from Huntington's, he was preoccupied with the style of architecture in medieval Europe. He told the builder exactly what he wanted: "early Renaissance."

What came of the architect's plans was something Pinocchio might have designed in a childish dream. Fifty wood carvers hired by Crocker to ornament the mansion produced scrollwork never before— or since—seen in San Francisco. Stylistically, the result combined a Bavarian schloss and a Venetian château with something that could only be called early Swiss cuckoo-clock.

Dwarfing it all was a seventy-six-foot tower; for years the city gossips swore that there were outlets concealed in its walls for the purpose of pouring hot lead down onto any mob that dared to storm this wooden citadel.

Inside, the house looked like a small-town museum. Eager for recognition as an art collector, Crocker bought pictures by the job lot; he never tired of telling his acquaintances that he *"owned* the Crocker Meissonier on the coast."

At 5:00 the morning after the earthquake, a tongue of flame leaped from the main fire wall and wrapped itself around the tower. It flared brightly, showering sparks all over the main roof. In moments one and a half million dollars in real estate was doomed.

Among them the four magnates had given the city a transcontinental rail link. Their belligerence, their "lust for the aphrodisiac smell of money," had driven them to build these monstrous structures on Nob Hill.

Shortly after the Crocker mansion caught fire, flames began to advance on the seamy quarter at the foot of Telegraph Hill, which for years had catered to a more basic kind of fetishism than that practiced on Nob Hill.

Firemen made no attempt to save the Barbary Coast. Feeding on the wood-plank tables, benches, and sawdust on the floors, the flames ate their way through the winecellars, where for years deadbeats, drifters, panhandlers, and whores had drunk crude alcohol at five cents a pint.

The flames devoured a score of brothels in minutes: the Living Flea, the Sign of the Red Rooster (a red cock with a light in its beak), and Ye Olde Whore Shop crumbled.

Dance halls, where the latest dance steps had been the Chicken Glide, the Pony Boy Ponce, and the Bunny Hug, went with equal speed.

Bawdy houses and crimping establishments—where victims were drugged and shanghaied—pawnshops, fandango palaces—all burned in the fiery sirocco that also consumed the Dew Drop Inn, Canterbury Hall, and the Opéra Comique, all three of which had specialized in erotica of a high order.

Like Chinatown, the Barbary Coast hid a secret private network of tunnels through which men, women, and booty were smuggled. The Coast existed on blackmail, extortion, and protection rackets. Now the fire swept through Dead Man's Alley, Murder Point, and Bull Run Alley, scouring the dark, dank tunnels of an accumulation of filth.

At 5:30 A.M., the Fairmont Hotel's windows cracked from the intense heat surrounding the building.

Minutes later Fire Chief Dougherty saw a red flash from a ground-floor room. It spread rapidly. By 5:45 A.M., the hotel had succumbed.

Close to tears—exhaustion and the futility of everything he had tried were having an effect on him—the old fireman walked wearily up toward Van Ness Avenue. The broad street was the last possible line of defense. If the fire broke through here, all of San Francisco would burn.

When he reached Van Ness, an astonishing sight greeted him. Field-artillery pieces were lined up on the far side of the avenue, their muzzles trained point blank at the elegant houses on the opposite side.

6 A.M. to Noon

General Funston brought troops from over one hundred miles away (*Ed Gleeson*)

17. Harsher Tones

THE CANNONS ENHANCED an already bizarre scene materializing on Van Ness Avenue this second morning of the disaster.

From the grim industrial area downtown and the slopes of Telegraph Hill and Russian Hill, from the narrow alleys around Chinatown and the far reaches of Fourth Street, a steady stream of refugees had poured onto the broad street. On the far side they stopped and faced the fire.

Behind the field guns, the firemen, and the lines of patrolling soldiers marshaled along the avenue, the dispossessed constructed their own barricades against the enemy. Piles of personal effects were heaped along the sidewalk from Filbert down to Haight. At dawn there were dozens of these heaps; an hour later there were thousands.

At the corner of Union Street a man sat beside a wheelbarrow piled with books, all he considered important enough to save.

Already the city's magnificent libraries, holding over one million volumes from all over the world, had been destroyed. The Mercantile, Bohemian Club, Pioneer, French, German, B'nai B'rith, and Law Libraries were burned to the ground. The libraries' losses were estimated at around five million dollars.

Near the junction of Green and Van Ness, a large Italian family formed a little fortress of trunks, a sewing machine, mattresses, and three bird cages stuffed with silverware. In the middle of this strange collection sat the family, guarding the household goods they had been able to salvage.

Between Washington and Clay Streets, the area along Van Ness was piled high with Morris chairs, kitchen tables, sewing machines, boys' coasters, and baby carriages. In the midst of it all stood an upright piano, which a couple of men polished and polished.

The heaps seemed to dare the flames to reach them. Fred Hewitt, the feature writer on the *Examiner,* felt that many people seemed "oddly apathetic, considering they were still alive."

What he saw was a phenomenon that doctors later diagnosed as delayed mass shock. A long day and night had passed since the population had been rudely tumbled from their ordinary routines. Sleep had been virtually impossible in the city for a full twenty-four hours. Half choked by the hot, cinder-filled air, San Franciscans had for the most part lost track of time.

The disaster seemed to have brought its own madness. Civil leadership floundered, and armed troops, often without specific instructions, roamed the streets, enforcing order with rifles and bayonets. The soldiers' weapons were powerful deterrents to argument, however reasonable. The cumulative result was traumatic. The "oddly apathetic" behavior Hewitt saw was the reaction of people for whom enough had become too much.

On the steps of St. Mary's Cathedral, Father Charles Ramm blinked his bloodshot eyes in the daylight and squinted in the direction of Van Ness Avenue. For over twenty-four hours the forty-three-year-old priest—once one of the University of California's great halfbacks—waged a one-man war against the disaster. He ministered to the refugees in the Presidio, at the Golden Gate Park, and along Van Ness Avenue; more than once he gave absolution.

All night as he went about his ministry, he heard reports of places of worship that had been destroyed. Standing outside St. Mary's Cathedral, the priest vowed that if it were necessary he would risk his life to save the Cathedral.

As he turned and entered the Gothic structure, Father Ramm saw something he would never have believed possible. The congregation, with every seat and space in the aisles occupied, had crept forward to sit on the steps of the high altar. From above, the massive redwood figure of Christ looked down on them.

Long after Father Ramm rose to high office in the church, he still recalled the "silence, total and absolute except for the clacking of rosaries and a murmured prayer."

In the charge room of North End Police Station near Telegraph Hill, Archbishop Montgomery led a distinguished congregation in the Lord's Prayer. The members of the Committee of Fifty who were present mumbled their responses quickly. A loud "amen" from Mayor Eugene Schmitz was the signal for the group to seat themselves.

At 6 A.M., Chief of Police Jeremiah Dinan had driven the Mayor to the police station in the Police Department's patrol car, and the police station became the newest emergency headquarters of the *de facto* civil government.

By 7:00 over thirty members of the committee were already assembled. The gloom cast over them by the destruction of the Fairmont Hotel increased further with the arrival of R. B. Hale, owner of one of the city's largest department stores.

The past few hours had been particularly unnerving for him. He had been forced to stand by and watch as his emporium and stock were dynamited. General Funston's soldiers did not even allow him time to rescue a bolt of cloth. Now the dynamite squads appeared to be working at random. "There is no set pattern, just blast, blast, blast," Hale told his colleagues.

All were uncomfortably aware that through the humid and depressing hours of darkness the dull booming of dynamite had increased in intensity.

There was nothing, Eugene Schmitz said, that could be done now. He had approved the measure—now it had to run its course.

"But surely," protested Hale, "people should be given time to take what they can."

That thought recurred in one form or another time and again. Before coming to this meeting, committee members had toured the disaster area. Their reports presented an alarming picture.

Water supplies were low everywhere. Casualties were mounting. The conflagration was spreading. There was a shortage of food for the survivors; a lack of coffins for the dead. Bodies were being left everywhere to be consumed by the flames.

Rats had been seen at a dozen points; the specter of bubonic plague rose again.

As far as committee member Dr. Marcus Herstein was concerned, the threat of plague was potentially the most dangerous the city faced. The fire, he maintained, was a short-term threat; the presence of a huge rat population was a menace that would utterly destroy any hope.

"Gentlemen, there will be quarantine. People will be afraid to help us rebuild in case they come into contact with the plague."

"There is no plague," said Eugene Schmitz.

"There will be—unless the rats are controlled," Dr. Herstein predicted. "When the ruins cool we will find ourselves living in a rats' paradise."

Angry murmurs came from several present. "We have heard that before. It's people, not rats, that we are here to discuss," someone growled.

"We should think of everything," retorted Dr. Herstein.

"The Chinese will suffer most," said another, attempting to dismiss the matter.

They would all suffer, insisted Dr. Herstein. The earthquake had undoubtedly also smashed the sewers along with the water mains. When the flames finally died the whole city would be covered with the stumps of open sewer pipes. The rats would have easy access to all parts of the city, with "the main sewers as boulevards."

Franklin K. Lane, one of the lawyers on the committee, said that while it was doubtless a matter for careful observation, there was a more pressing problem at the moment: the military had requested more dynamite.

In the days to come Dr. Herstein's prediction was not referred to again.

Several months passed before the knowledge "suddenly" became public that bubonic plague was rife in the city, attacking clean, well-fed, white people in good houses and killing them swiftly. In one month fourteen died. There was no single focus for the outbreak, no area that could be isolated. Bubonic plague was no longer "a typically oriental disease"—though the illusion was hard to dispel, even with the evidence furnished by white men's funerals. Of the 160 cases of plague, only eight victims were Chinese or Japanese, and only three contracted the disease in Chinatown.

But all that was in the future. On this morning the committee faced the immediate question of more dynamite. The members quickly agreed to grant the request.

The committee had made its first collective decision. Others swiftly followed.

Tirey L. Ford, attorney for the United Railroads, raised "the question of identification"; he felt that committee members should have proper passes to move unhampered through the fire lines.

The lawyers lost no time drafting a suitable authorization. In a booming voice Ford read: "The Bearer is a member of the Relief and Restoration Committee of Law and Order, and is invested with the same powers that I possess. You are therefore notified to give him every assistance possible in the prompt performance of his duty and cheerfully comply with any request that he may make. Signed: Eugene Schmitz, Mayor."

Everyone agreed that it was concise and authoritative.

Next the committee turned to the matter of proper transportation for its members. Judge John Hunt of the San Francisco Superior Court told a doleful story of having to hitchhike his way to the police station; he felt it was undignified for his office to be reduced to this mode of travel. What was needed, he felt, was speedy transportation for the exclusive use of the committee.

Mayor Schmitz produced a simple solution. In the name of the committee he would issue his first public edict of the day: all automobiles in the city were to be placed immediately at the committee's disposal until further notice. Those cars not voluntarily surrendered would be commandeered.

Other promulgations followed. Strict food and water rationing was to be enforced. Supplies, where and if they were found, could be taken in the name of the committee and distributed at the discretion of the committee members. Profiteering would be ruthlessly stamped out. The grounds of the Presidio and Golden Gate Park were designated as the main refugee camps. The police and the vigilante force of one thousand volunteers were to be reminded that looting was still punishable by summary execution. Young children caught stealing were to be beaten, and then adorned with placards bearing the legend "I AM A THIEF."

"I want it given out as widely as possible that looters have been shot dead and that they will continue to be," concluded the Mayor.

After the meeting broke up, committee member Downey Harvey wondered how these edicts could be brought to the fleeing masses.

In front of the police station a crowd of journalists and townspeople had gathered. From now they became a regular fixture outside the station, waiting for news of the committee's latest deliberations. Harvey's concern was taken care of.

In the crowd stood Charles Rea, a member of the city's elected Board of Supervisors, who had been overlooked in the Mayor's invitation to serve on the committee, and James Hopper, the *Call* reporter.

As the committee members trooped out, Rea offered his own rather jaundiced assessment, repeated many times in the coming days: "All talk and little action. Many of them are simply hungry for publicity and are worthless in our present emergency."

What intrigued Hopper more than Rea's opinion was the absence of Rudolph Spreckels and James Phelan. He wondered whether the truce the two men had declared in agreeing to serve on the Mayor's committee was coming to an end.

It was not. At that moment the two millionaires were engaged in an unfamiliar task—loading chalices, prayer books, and other holy objects into a wagon outside the Convent of St. Peter in the Mission District. Around them the sisters and Christian brothers handled the convent's heavier items: tall candleholders, statues, a box containing the Eucharist. They worked in silence, and the speed with which they loaded was the only indication that the near-stampede going on all around them was having an effect. The fire was less than a dozen blocks away. At the rate it was traveling it would engulf the convent in a short time.

Spreckels and Phelan had chanced upon the evacuation of the convent during their tour of the fire lines in Spreckels' car. Driving ahead of the two great columns of fire—one sweeping through the Mission District, the other cutting up toward Van Ness—the two men discussed the handling of events to come. By the time they reached the Convent of St. Peter, they both wondered, in particular, how they could ease the military stranglehold clamped around the city, and, if nothing else, stop what they regarded as pointless dynamiting.

As they watched the nuns and monks haul their wagon away, the familiar heavy and sickening boom came closer.

The two men looked at each other.

"Good God!" said James Phelan. "They'll blow the whole city apart if they go on like this."

In Fort Mason a plan to do almost just that was being discussed.

In his temporary office at Fort Mason, Brigadier General Frederick Funston listened impassively as Captain Coleman, who had supervised dynamiting operations during the night, outlined a new dynamite proposal. The plan bore an uncanny resemblance to scorched-earth tactics. Coleman wanted to blow a trench fifty yards deep almost the whole length of the south side of Van Ness Avenue down to Golden Gate Avenue, through to what was left of upper Market Street, and finally along the whole length of Dolores.

It was, insisted Coleman, the only sure way to halt the fire.

The area earmarked for destruction was almost twice the size of that proposed by Funston to the Committee of Fifty.

Coleman's men could obtain enough explosives to complete the task. More dynamite was on the way. All night naval tugboats had ferried supplies from the California Powder Company at Pinole; a demolition squad at the Mare Island Naval Shipyard had been ordered to bring all the gun cotton they could find. To speed up the operation, Coleman continued, the gun crews along Van Ness Avenue itself could begin the systematic destruction of all the houses along the south side of the street.

To Funston, Coleman's presentation was convincing, professional, and militarily sound. It was a piece of staff work the Brigadier General could not fault. The fire break the Captain proposed would create an effective barrier against the approaching flames. Moreover, reports of the night's dynamite operations had disappointed Funston. While "whole frame and old brick buildings were reduced to piles of rubbish by these explosions, the modern steel and concrete structures are as impervious to the heaviest charges as they had been to the earthquake." Coleman planned to make use of the explosives in areas where they would be effective.

There was only one thing in Coleman's plan that Funston quarreled with: the timing. Coleman insisted that the operation should begin at once.

Funston was unconvinced. He believed that dynamiting so far ahead of the flames might create a "corridor" along which the inferno's high winds could sweep, actually accelerating the fire. Then there would be a real risk that the fire might leap even the wide ditch of rubble that Coleman proposed to "dig." Launching the plan too early would work against them; orders to start would come later.

In the meantime the evacuation of the area to be demolished was to begin without delay.

All night situation reports came into Fort Mason. By 9:00 in the morning, the overall picture Funston saw was a grim one. Summing up the incoming reports he wrote: "Block after block, street by street, hour after hour, the firemen, police, and soldiers fought the conflagration in the hope of possible success. Scores of buildings were blown down . . . others were set on fire in order to check the flames by back firing . . . every hotel and bank, every large store and nearly every storeroom and warehouse in the city had been destroyed. Three hundred thousand people were homeless, and thousands more were left without means of livelihood. The rations, tents, and blankets on hand at the army posts adjacent to the city were dealt out to the sufferers."

In some ways the United States Army did some sterling work. Inexperienced in the matter of relief on the massive scale now required, the Presidio garrison coped splendidly. Staff officers, quartermasters, and enlisted men had provided whatever comfort they could. Squads of soldiers spent the night preparing breakfast for the multitude camped around them. Others ran a shuttle service from as far away as Twentieth Street, bringing additional supplies of bread from a large bakery there which was still intact. It was the first food many of the refugees received in twenty-four hours.

Cooking pits were dug, latrines prepared. One could not praise too highly the work of the Presidio's garrison—or at least those who had remained behind.

Along the fire lines, events took on a more dangerous turn.

18. Magical Powers

FOR SOME HOURS it seemed to Henry Anderson Lafler that he had strayed into some medieval scene of siege. Lafler, a journalist, retreated behind the cordon of soldiers, where an atmosphere of a "city captured in war" seemed to prevail. "We were strangers on our own streets, refugees from our own houses. Were we children—we, the citizens of San Francisco—that we should have been suddenly gripped by the throat by a stupid soldiery and held fast till our city burned?"

Dr. Alfred Spalding, one of the medical team forced to flee from the doomed Mechanics Pavilion, was clear about the exact moment the military had taken over complete control: it had happened at 4:00 the previous afternoon.

Years later he recalled, "There were all sorts of good and bad acts committed. While our man transported us at regular rates, another man carted a family and demanded twenty-five dollars. The man offered his last five dollars. The drayman refused to give up the stuff. Soldiers told him to take the five dollars and unload. He again refused. Then they gave him three minutes to 'get busy,' and one held a watch. At the end of the time, the man still refused, and they ran him through with bayonets.

"All along the streets I saw dead bodies placarded 'shot for stealing.' Ten men were shot while trying to get into Shreve's. One man was shot for refusing to carry a hose."

Charles Eugene Banks, a journalist, also catalogued some of the deaths he had observed: "A policeman saw a man crawling through the window of a bank and shot him dead. In several instances thieves were run through with bayonets and their bodies left lying where they

185

had fallen. At one place, five men were shot, two killed, and three badly wounded. The troops had thrown open a corner grocery with the usual order that the crowd might carry off all it contained except the liquor. A large party of men made a rush for the place and emerged with quantities of whisky. When called upon to drop them, they failed to obey and a volley was fired upon them.

"No mercy was shown to those who defied calls to halt. The rifle was levelled with the first order, and on the failure of a second command to stop was discharged.

"One man on Market Street who was found digging in the ruins of a jewelry shop was discovered by a naval service man and fired upon three times. The fellow sought safety in flight, but the reserve man brought him down by running his bayonet through him."

Daylight did not stop the killing. A shopkeeper who demanded seventy-five cents for a loaf of bread was frog-marched outside his shop and executed—in keeping with the Mayor's directive that profiteering be curbed.

James Code recalled the man he saw shot down on Clayton and Oak Streets. Code was thirteen at the time; ahead was a distinguished career in the U. S. Army. Yet at the age of seventy-seven the execution was still vivid in his memory.

None of these drumhead deaths were ever officially investigated; they certainly put Funston's later claim of only a tiny handful of deaths in a strange light.

One reason the killings were not investigated, according to Ed Gleeson of the *Daily News,* was simply that "when daylight came, none of the sentries would admit to having participated."

Common law, as Gleeson and many others were discovering, had largely been suspended in San Francisco.

On Russian Hill, Mr. Edward Dakin, Civil War veteran and collector of historic flags, switched his attention from the holocaust raging in the city itself to the Bay. Peering through his telescope he was able to identify quickly the flag on the dreadnought which led a flotilla of warships through the Golden Gate as the ensign of Admiral Goodrich, commander of the U. S. Navy's Pacific Squadron.

The Admiral was aboard the *Chicago,* which had been cruising twenty miles off San Diego when the flagship's wireless operator picked up a message that San Francisco lay in ruins. The battle squadron immediately sailed for the Golden Gate.

Edward Dakin could see that the decks of the ships were lined with hundreds of men. He shouted the good news to refugees streaming past the house to safety: "It's going to be all right! The Marines are here!"

At 11:00 the Marines and sailors of the Pacific Squadron began to disembark. It was a smooth, swift-moving operation. The *Chicago* tied up on Pier 24; the *Marblehead* lay alongside Pier 26; the *Boston* docked at Pier 8; the *Paul Jones,* at Pier 17; and the *Princeton,* at Pier 7.

Immediately the naval task force went into action. Squads of sailors formed firefighting teams. Two naval fireboats, the *Active* and the *Leslie,* had berthed on Pier 8 ahead of the squadron. The pier became the focal point of the firefighting operations. Five thousand feet of hose pipe was run up to Telegraph Hill seven blocks away, and jets of water were immediately turned on the inferno.

Other firefighting teams raced along the three-mile length of the waterfront, seeking out points from which they could fight the flames most effectively. By then other ships had arrived. The destroyer *Perry* arrived with the *Preble,* a well-staffed floating hospital. The water tender *Soto Komo* ferried fresh water for the city's fire engines.

It was a magnificently coordinated operation, planned to the last detail.

Admiral Goodrich, on hearing that communications with the outside world were tenuous, sent a signal party ashore. They flagged situation reports to the flagship, which were then relayed to the Navy base on Mare Island. From there they were transmitted directly to Washington. One of the first requests was for drinking water. Within a few hours, lighters, each carrying fifty thousand gallons, were on their way from Mare Island.

Some Marines were deployed to guard the waterfront and the remaining property immediately beyond. They did so with good humor and firmness that brought widespread praise. Not one incident of naval misbehavior was reported.

In the initial bustle of movement and crisp commands which

followed the order to disembark, nobody paid any attention to the naval tug tying up at the wharf at Fort Mason.

The tug had ·sailed from Mare Island at the request of Captain Coleman, who had just completed his presentation to General Funston. On board were a three-man demolition squad that consisted of Captain MacBride of the Marines and two Navy gunners, and one and a half tons of gun cotton.

For several hours, Adam Gilliland, the insurance agent, had been laboring over columns of figures. The figures, translated into destroyed bricks and mortar, meant that the Hartford Insurance Company had liabilities of at least seven million dollars.

All over the city, officials of over a hundred other insurance companies were doing similar calculations.

William Dutton, President, and Jacob Levison, a director of the Fireman's Fund Insurance Company, realized that it was the death knell for the company as they knew it; the claims they would eventually face were likely to be far greater than the company's total assets of seven million dollars. They were right: Fireman's Funds was not able to meet final liabilities of $11,500,000. The company was closed down only to be re-formed as a new company, free of debts. Claims were settled in a novel fashion; claimants were offered 56.5 percent cash and 50 percent stock in the new company against their losses in the earthquake and fire.

Fireman's Fund and the Hartford Insurance Company behaved with compassion and honor in making their settlements.

This was not always the case.

Only six major companies—four American and two English—honored their liabilities in full, without delay, with no demands for cash discount. Forty-three American companies and sixteen foreign ones spent months, and sometimes years, fighting delaying paper battles to avoid meeting their commitments.

German-based firms had a uniformly bad record. Among them, they had nearly $100,000,000 worth of policies. When asked to meet their legal obligations, four of them promptly stopped trading in North America, to avoid paying out anything. One company, the Hamburg-Bremen Fire Insurance Company, settled most of its $4,500,000 debt by making arbitrary discounts of up to 25 percent on what it should have paid. The Credit Men's Report—the watchdog of the American insurance world—castigated the company for "insulting and discourteous treatment, and also for displaying in its New York office a misleading notice, to the effect that it was pleased to inform its friends and patrons that funds had been sent over from Hamburg for the purpose of promptly paying its San Francisco losses."

Of more immediate concern to National Guardsman Elmer Enewold than dishonest insurance companies was the long line of "hard cases" from the Broadway Street jail in the Italian quarter, whom he was trying to keep moving at a brisk pace. Enewold and fifty-nine other Guardsmen were escorting the column to Fort Mason. From there the prisoners were to be shipped to Alcatraz.

The prisoners lagged along Van Ness Avenue, almost as if they hoped to make a concerted move for freedom in the confusion all around.

"The first of you that steps an inch out of line gets a bullet right between the eyes," Elmer Enewold warned.

He was not making an idle threat. The night before he had been involved in an incident that lent weight to his warning. "I saw a man about a quarter of a block away from me bending over something on the ground. I yelled at him to get out but he paid no attention to me. So I up and fired at him.

"I missed, of course, but the shot must have scared him for he started to run. I was just getting ready to shoot again when a shot was fired from across the street and the fellow toppled over.

"This was fired by a regular who had seen him run after my shot was fired. When the two of us reached the fallen man we found he had been shot through the neck and was stone dead.

"An officer came along and ordered us to throw the body into the still-burning ruins. So in it went. We went back to see what the would-be thief had been after and found a body of a man half buried under a heap of bricks. We dug it out and laid it beside the twenty or more that had been killed in the collapse of a lodging house."

Now Elmer Enewold repeated: "The first one of you moves gets it for sure. Don't try anything."

Nobody tried anything. The column trotted up Van Ness Avenue on the double.

If the aim of the emergency edition of the *Call-Chronicle-Examiner,* which was now being distributed free of charge, was to dispel rumor, it failed.

All morning wild stories flew through the city. In the end fact and fiction became so blurred that few people could distinguish between the two.

Once more the wildly improbable legend that the mint was about to be attacked by an armed gang was passed along the fire lines with growing conviction. The Oakland *Tribune* actually printed the "scoop" under the splash headline: "ATTEMPT TO ROB MINT: 14 SHOT."

The same newspaper reported that "a committee has examined the bank and safe deposit vaults in San Francisco and found them all intact. This makes it certain that the money and paper on deposit are safe." According to the *Tribune,* the books and records in the San Franscisco Hall of Records "also escaped serious injury."

A brief check would have established the fact that there was never any attempt to rob the mint, that no committee had inspected any vaults, and that most of the city's records had been charred.

The *Tribune* was not the only newspaper playing games with the truth: papers all over America were happily printing fiction.

In San Francisco, newspapermen spent hours that second day trying to trace a story being repeated by any number of people. A certain John Spencer had originated the chilling story of a lynching near the Palace Hotel. After relating the "incident" in Mission Hills, the storyteller disappeared before the truth could be established; later he turned up on Van Ness Avenue with a ghoulish yarn of a man he had seen biting off the fingers of a dead woman to get at her rings—"and the vampire was shot down by a squad of soldiers." Again he vanished before newspapermen could catch up with him.

The result of these rumors was to produce a credibility gap in later years. The wild stories have been remembered, while the real tragedies—the senseless killings, the painful mistakes with dynamite, the arbitrary bullying of the shocked people by soldiers—have been largely forgotten.

In 1956, a San Francisco newspaper printed an anniversary edition in which the following "factual" item appeared:

"Fourteen men were shot, picked off like birds, trying to loot the United States Mint. Fourteen soldiers, caught by other soldiers in the act of looting a saloon, were hanged."

When—and where?

Streaked with grime, eyes red-rimmed from exhaustion, banker A. P. Giannini reached Van Ness Avenue late in the morning.

He had been on the move for many hours. Upon reaching his home in San Mateo, he sought a safe hiding place for the bank's eighty thousand dollars. Eventually he buried them in the ash pit of his living-room fireplace. Then he returned to San Francisco to find the business section gutted. The Bank of Italy was a charred heap of embers and the Crocker National Bank was gone. Its fireproof vaults were a mass of sizzling steel that would need weeks to cool before they could be safely opened. The same situation prevailed in banks all over the city; though their money was secure it was also virtually useless, locked in safes that could not be opened because of the danger of spontaneous combustion the moment their contents came into contact with the air.

The knowledge shattered many bankers. All they could do was wait—and hope. Paul Rink records that "these staid and conservative gentlemen seemed to be at a loss for ideas."

To help them through the crisis, Governor Pardee had that morning declared the days to come official bank holidays—in effect placing a moratorium on debts.

To Giannini this seemed "negative rather than constructive" thinking. People would want as soon as possible to *"feel* real hard coins in their hands."

He had eighty thousand dollars' worth of those coins in three bags buried in the fireplace back in San Mateo.

Giannini hurried to his brother's home on Van Ness to make plans to use the money to help his customers, at the same time seizing what he could see was a tremendous opportunity for the tiny Bank of Italy.

At about a quarter to twelve Captain MacBride and his dynamite squad selected a house above Sacramento and Larkin Streets as a test bed. In moments the gun cotton had reduced it to rubble.

The dying echoes of the explosion were then replaced by screams coming from Bush Street. A throng of running people panted up the street's steep slope, pursued by a maddened bull. The animal had escaped from a nearby stockyard, where it was penned with other cattle rescued from downtown. As the flames approached, the bull escaped, charging up Bush Street in a series of short, vicious bursts. The beast was about to charge again when a Marine dropped him, stone-dead, with a single shot. Now that the danger was over, the crowd turned back and laughed uneasily.

They were still laughing when a wagon driven by a squad of soldiers arrived on the scene. The troops ordered the men in the crowd to load the carcass onto the truck.

"Where are you taking it?" somebody asked.

"The Presidio," replied a soldier.

Another rumor started. Within an hour many San Franciscans believed that animal carcasses were being collected from "all over the city" to feed refugees. The next day reports of famine in San Francisco appeared in the Washington and New York newspapers. Within forty-eight hours, London, Paris, Berlin, and Tokyo all read news stories of people dying of starvation.

Nearly twenty hours after being disconnected, the chief operator of the Postal-Telegraph Cable Company tapped a line from his shack on Goat Island in the Bay that had linked him to Oakland. From there his reports were bounced to New York and relayed around the world.

At 9:45 A.M. he began transmitting:

FIRE STILL SPREADING. EVERYTHING IS GONE FAR BACK AS 27TH STREET AND SOUTH AS FAR BACK AS THE FOOTHILLS. COMING DOWN BROADWAY TO WATERFRONT ON NORTH SIDE, LAST PART OF BUSINESS SECTION. NO TICKETS ON FERRIES ARE BEING SOLD TO FRISCO. NO ONE IS ALLOWED TO RETURN FROM OAKLAND. SCORES OF DEAD ARE LYING ALONG THE STREET, BUT WILL BE TAKEN CARE OF FROM NOW ON. DYNAMITING HAS STOPPED UNLESS TO TRY TO CHECK FIRE. SMOKE CLEARING OVER THE BURNED SECTION. PALACE AND GRAND HOTELS, CALL, EXAMINER, AND CHRONICLE BUILDINGS STILL STAND BUT ENTIRELY

GUTTED. HALL OF JUSTICE AND CITY HALL ENTIRELY DE-
STROYED. PRISONERS ARE UNDER GUARD OF SOLDIERS AND SAIL-
ORS. WOMEN AND CHILDREN WERE IN PITIFUL CONDITION
YESTERDAY, BUT ARE BEING CARED FOR NOW. CRUISERS CHICAGO
AND MARBLEHEAD LANDED SAILORS AND MARINES FOR DUTY IN
GUARDING AGAINST PILLAGING.

At 10:25 he sent:

FAIRMONT HOTEL ENTIRELY BURNED. FLAMES SPREADING NORTH
TO WASHINGTON SQUARE AND NORTH BEYOND NOB HILL. SWEEP-
ING AROUND BASE OF HILLS TO SOUTHWEST OF CITY DESTROYING
WHAT WAS THOUGHT TO HAVE BEEN SAVED TWENTY-FOUR
HOURS AGO. AUTHORITIES SHOOTING PILLAGERS LEFT AND RIGHT.
FOOD IS VERY SCARCE. PRICES MORE THAN DOUBLED. WATER
CAN HARDLY BE OBTAINED EVEN FOR DRINKING PURPOSES. THE
ENTIRE CITY WITH NO EXCEPTION IS DOOMED. GOLDEN GATE
PARK ONE VAST HOSPITAL. LOSS OF LIFE AT LEAST ONE THOU-
SAND AND STILL GROWING. LOSS OF PROPERTY ESTIMATED SEV-
ERAL BILLIONS. RUNNING OUT OF DYNAMITE AND THE POLICE
ARE COMPELLING PEOPLE TO WORK AT THE POINT OF REVOLV-
ERS. THE STREETS OF OAKLAND ARE CROWDED WITH WOMEN
AND CHILDREN WITH NO PLACE TO SLEEP AND WITH NOTHING
TO EAT. THE HOSPITALS ARE ALL DESTROYED AND THE WOUNDED
ARE BEING CARED FOR BY MILITARY DOCTORS AND SURGEONS TAK-
ING THEM TO THE HOSPITALS AT THE PRESIDIO AND GOAT ISLAND.

At 10:50 the line suddenly went dead, adding to the dramatic
effect of the messages. They contained a number of errors—the
dynamiting had not stopped, the death roll would never reach a
thousand, bread lines had been set up in Oakland—but on the whole,
they gave a remarkably accurate picture of the situation.

Shortly after midday, the telegrapher at Oakland, across the
Bay from San Francisco, began sending:

FIRE IS STILL RAGING IN SAN FRANCISCO AND ENTIRE CITY IS
DOOMED. THEY HAVE NO WATER EXCEPT ALONG THE BAY SHORE
AND THEY ARE DYNAMITING BUILDINGS IN AN EFFORT TO CHECK
THE FLAMES. THE POWDER SUPPLY IS NEARLY EXHAUSTED EVEN
TO POWDER IN GOVERNMENT ARSENALS WHICH HAVE BEEN
EMPTIED. THE FIRE CANNOT BE CHECKED UNTIL IT BURNS OUT.
EVERY BUILDING IN BUSINESS SECTION AND NEARLY HALF OF
RESIDENCE SECTION DESTROYED NOW AND NOT A LARGE BUILD-
ING LEFT STANDING.

The world waited, and reporters in a dozen capitals searched for
new angles. The *Daily Express* correspondent in New York found
one. He was preparing a story speculating on the fate of Enrico
Caruso.

The singer was well into his second day of abject misery. Inside
the entrance to Golden Gate Park, Caruso waited helplessly for the
transport.

After spending a lonely and frightened night seeking his fellow
artistes from the touring opera company, he had made his way to
Golden Gate. There, "quite by chance," he ran into Martino, his valet.

"Where is my luggage?" the tenor wailed. "My trunks of clothes,
where are they?"

Martino explained that they were lost.

"Why?"

To Martino the question seemed an odd one under the circumstances. The streets were littered with people's belongings that had
been abandoned when the flames came too close.

Martino could not fail to notice the remarkable change in the
singer. Disheveled and unshaven, he hardly matched the picture of
the dapper, elegant opera star. More than his outward appearance,
though, Caruso's voice shocked Martino. The strong, powerful voice
which had so often held him spellbound—the voice that only two
days before had been so confident—had faded to a weak whisper.

"You must get me out of here," Caruso pleaded. "I don't care
how, but you must do it."

"The picture," Martino gently answered, indicating the signed portrait of President Roosevelt that Caruso still clutched. "Give it to me. It might help me get some official help."

"No! The picture stays with me! It's my passport."

Martino nodded and went off to look for transportation to carry them to safety.

While his valet searched, Caruso sat on the grass, nearly in tears, gazing at the portrait of the President of the United States, which by now he had invested with magical powers.

Noon to 6 P.M.

Flanked by flames, refugees rush down Market Street to the
Ferry Building (*Roy D. Graves Collection*)

19. Exodus on Market

SHORTLY AFTER MIDDAY, reporter James Hopper of the *Call* joined the crowds of homeless and hungry refugees who had been streaming down Market Street for an hour. On either side of the street the fires raged.

Between the two great walls of fire, Market—in spite of the crowds—seemed to be a dead street——"not one recently dead, but one overcome by some cataclysm of long ago and then dug out of the lava."

Everywhere there was a brooding silence: "contortion of stone, smoke of destruction, and a great silence." The silence had communicated itself to the refugees, who had come down out of the Mission Hills, drawn by the news that Market Street was still open, offering an escape route to the Bay.

At first only a few, then a hundred, then thousands surged down onto the street, dragging their belongings toward the Ferry Building at the bottom.

"People spoke little, or if they did it was in low tones," Hopper recalled. "The silence was acute. Everybody seemed to be overwhelmed by the terrible magnificence of the spectacle being enacted all around."

The air was stifling, the heat intense. People plodded on mechanically. The scope of the disaster seemed to have exhausted the senses. "Faces showed the strain, but there was no complaint. Disaster had taught us a powerful lesson—it taught all of us the 'value' of mere possessions.

"Fortunes, homes, factories, offices had all been swept away. It

199

is pitiable to see solitary old women tottering along under a load that would not tax the strength of a child. Women in opera cloaks dragged trunks. Bands of Chinese, dazed and helpless, drifted along with the mass of refugees. It was incredible what foolish things people clung to."

To boatman Tom Crowley, the Southern Pacific Railroad's city terminal was a reassuring sight. Unscathed by the flames crowding all around, the massive Ferry Building provided evidence that the waterfront had not been totally destroyed.

At the age of ninety-four, Crowley recalled the exultation he felt upon seeing the Ferry Building, still standing. Like the Palace Hotel, the terminal was a landmark, a symbol of hope, for many refugees.

Thirty hours before, Crowley had mobilized his fleet of eighteen launches to carry refugees from Pier 13 at the bottom of Vallejo Street. By the middle of the second day he had shuttled several thousands to safety. At fifty cents a head—if they could afford it—it was a real bonanza for the boatman.

Now, returning empty after ferrying yet another group of refugees, Crowley piloted his boat along the three miles of wharves and slipways.

The waterfront was a mass of people awaiting evacuation. In the twenty years he had been on the waterfront, Crowley had never seen such a tremendous—and diverse—group of men, women, and children gathered in one place. Any sound they made was lost in the steady roar of the burning city.

Crowley's fleet was not the only one doing record business that day. Operating from a dozen points, other boatmen turned the disaster to personal profit. Unlike Crowley, they demanded—and got—up to ten dollars for a cross-Bay trip that two days earlier had cost twenty-five cents. Skiffs, rowboats, coal and cargo lighters—anything that would float was pressed into service. Not until Dunkirk was a comparable fleet mobilized.

In contrast to the boatmen on either side of its piers, the Southern Pacific ran its rescue operation free of charge to all comers.

Since the beginning of the exodus, the railroad had moved seventy passengers out of the city every minute in a shuttle service that eventually transported three hundred thousand people from the disaster area. The cost to the company was five hundred thousand dollars for this service alone. Later, the Southern Pacific offered free transportation for any refugee to any part of North America. It also shipped thirty-seven thousand tons of relief supplies into the city at its own expense. At today's valuation of the dollar, the Southern Pacific commitment amounted to more than four million dollars—over and above its loss of equipment, supplies, and buildings.

During later investigations into the events surrounding the disaster, the Southern Pacific was one of the few agencies to escape criticism. Its flair for doing the right thing—and for being seen doing it—earned it widespread praise. It was favorably compared with a Russian counterpart, the Trans-Siberian Railway, which had once transported two hundred thousand Russian troops in eight months. It was an unfair comparison. The Southern Pacific accomplished that, and much more, in eight days.

At the foot of Washington Street and all along the waterfront, the fight to save the Bay Shore had been in progress for thirty-two hours. The Fire Department mustered twenty engine companies—each pumping a thousand gallons a minute out of the Bay. There were also half a dozen ladder companies, three chemical companies—although their foam was long since gone, they were still able to pump water—a water tower, and a mobile battery. The naval fire-fighting teams supplemented the municipal Fire Department.

It was a pitifully small force to repel the flames beating down on all sides, but to reporter James Hopper, "the men were an inspiration. When they dropped, exhausted, in the gutters, somebody would always be there to pull them to their feet and help them to carry on. Their helmets were baked to their heads and their turn-out rig was peeling off their backs. More than one of the fire horses had collapsed in its harness."

At 1:00 in the afternoon, the firefighters noticed a new development. The jets pouring onto the inferno were having an effect. The wind that had blown the flames down onto the waterfront had veered a point or two. Now it was curling the wall of fire back over areas it had already covered.

For the firemen along the waterfront, it was the first sign of hope.

Out in the Bay, people looked back toward San Francisco from the ships carrying them across to Oakland.

The wind had momentarily lifted the great cloud of black smoke to reveal the center of the city. There was nothing to be seen except shell after shell of buildings open to the sky, rising from acres of rubble. Block after block lay in ruins. Familiar landmarks had been obliterated.

On a fishing boat cutting through the wake of a larger ferry, a young Italian fisherman, Giuseppe Alioto, turned to the girl beside him and smiled. Things would not always be this bad, he murmured. The girl, Domenica, nodded, grateful for the reassurance.

They had never met before. Now, drawn together by calamity, they started to talk. It was one of the many romances which began that day. This one would blossom into a marriage that would produce a son, Joseph Lawrence—who became the city's thirty-third Mayor sixty-two years later.

At the Ferry Building, the arrival and departure of refugees had become a fast-moving and streamlined operation. Passengers were permitted to take with them on the ferries only as many personal possessions as they could carry with them.

One old man willingly gave up the wheelbarrow of things he had trundled down Market to the Ferry Building, but he firmly refused to part with a small box holding a white rat. It was, he explained to railroad officials, no ordinary rodent. "It's a performing rat," he insisted. "He's like a son to me. . . ."

Both made the crossing to Oakland.

It took some time to persuade a young man to part with a stiff bundle in his arms. Inside the bundle were two dead babies. The father kept telling the railwaymen that they were asleep, and were being kept warm by his own body. They were all he had left in the world.

In the end he made the crossing alone.

Celia Parker remembered the man who offered two hundred dollars if he could change places with her in the line of refugees waiting to board the boat—an exchange that would have gained him precisely one move up in line. Kathleen Norris recalled the continuous laughter of the Chinese women as they waited, bowed down with great swollen bundles of possessions—which they gave up with fresh laughter. Oliver Pritchett told of a man who asked repeatedly where he could get a shave.

Cecil Chard recalled "the harrowing stories that were whispered in low tones so that the general multitude would not be made more anxious—stories of women wandering in the ruins, clasping dead children in their arms, of men gone mad, of firemen crushed, of the sick and wounded buried under falling walls; stories of soldiers who had exceeded their orders, of unfortunate citizens who, upon a refusal to leave their treasures, had been shot. They told, too, of the swift retribution that overtook those who, under the cover of the prevailing excitement, attempted to rob and loot."

The Ferry Building became a clearinghouse for rumors of all kinds. The terminal even generated its own myth. More than one newspaper had already reported its destruction.

"Load!"

Southern Pacific's Chief Special Agent P. J. Kindelon's command roared over the railroad's freight yard at the bottom of Mission Street.

"Aim!"

The row of men kneeling on top of the line of freight cars swung their muskets up to their shoulders.

"Fire!"

A volley whistled above the heads of the mob swarming over and inside the boxcars twenty yards away. Startled, the looters turned round.

"Next time it'll be lower!" roared Kindelon. "Move away from those cars! And leave everything!"

"It isn't your stuff, mister!" bellowed a red-faced man.

"Move! Now!" Kindelon bellowed back.

The looters stood their ground. Kindelon looked at his force. He had a few dozen railway policemen to hold back about one thousand men and women surrounding the boxcars of oysters, wines, and canned foods.

Trouble had erupted swiftly when a small gang had forced open a freight-car door. In minutes they were joined by hundreds of the twelve thousand who had been given refuge in the yard.

Outnumbered, Kindelon had ordered his men to climb to the top of another parked freight train.

The red-faced man turned back toward the boxcar.

"You move one more step—and you're a dead man," shouted Kindelon, drawing his pistol.

The man turned to face Kindelon.

"Load!"

Still the mob did not move.

"Aim!"

The muskets swung down on the line of people.

There was total silence in the yard. A man stood frozen with a crate of oysters in his hands. A woman clutching a tin of canned meat started to tremble. "At the command of three—fire!" shouted Kindelon.

The railway official looked down at the mass of people below him. After the first volley he knew there would be no time to reload before they would counterattack; he also had no doubt about the outcome.

"One!"

The beefy-faced man stared hard at Kindelon.

"Two!"

The man cursed; then turned and walked away.

"Keep moving. All of you!"

In moments the looters were gone.

Kindelon's coolness averted a possible tragedy. The battle of wits began the moment he opened the freight yard as a makeshift refugee camp. Kindelon recalled: "They started fires over all the yard to cook and keep warm. I had a number of men go around to stamp out the fires. The use of smoking tobacco was also prohibited. About half a dozen were caught smoking and we clubbed them out of the yard."

Eventually he was forced to accept military assistance. Companies of soldiers began patrolling the yard; the slightest infringement of any order was countered by a bayonet thrust.

All too soon Kindelon came to regret having accepted the offer. The soldiers began to show they were no respecters of the property they had been sent to protect. At night a squad looted a boxcar full of whiskey—Boxcar S.P. 1911 standing on lead track No. 5—and got drunk.

It was the first of several occasions on which military patrols robbed the Southern Pacific. On one occasion twelve cars of beer and wine were pilfered; a patrol was caught red-handed tapping a puncheon of wine in Boxcar S.P. 85431; members of the 11th Infantry were arrested as they tapped a barrel in Boxcar 9618 under cover of darkness.

All these looters were turned over to Brigadier General Funston's command, to be dealt with under military law—which had deemed that stealing in the city during the crisis was a capital offense. No public record indicates that any soldier was court-martialed or punished for these infringements of the law. If nothing else, such a record would have undermined Frederick Funston's claim that his men had behaved in an exemplary way at all times.

The crimes committed by his troops hardly justified his very brief statement on the military occupation of the city: "If there is a lesson to be derived from the work of the regular troops in San Francisco, it is that nothing can take the place of training and discipline, and that self-control and patience are as important as courage."

20. A Passport Portrait

IN GOLDEN GATE PARK, plumber Oswald Jones had no doubt about what he would call the baby girl who had just been born on the grass. He told the young doctor who had assisted in the birth that he would christen his child April Francisco Jones.

She was the seventeenth baby born in the open that day. Another twenty-three arrived on the grounds of the Presidio before the day was over. One, the first child of Mr. and Mrs. Peter Campe, was christened Presidio Campe. The Williams family named their daughter Golden Gate.

At 4:00 in the afternoon the Committee of Fifty once again bestirred itself. Five hours before, the scorching heat had forced Mayor Eugene Schmitz and his men to give up their short-lived occupation of North End Police Station.

Clutching their special passports, they climbed into their commandeered cars, and drove off to seek yet another meeting place. At 2:00 they moved into Franklin Hall on Fillmore Street, a clear mile from the nearest fire line.

"Here," James Phelan rumbled, "here we stay."

Within an hour the municipal government was ready to set about the massive task of housekeeping.

If Eugene Schmitz is to be accorded an hour of glory, it would be the hour between 3:00 and 4:00 that afternoon, during which he organized Franklin Hall into the semblance of an administrative headquarters.

The various subcommittees—food, housing, medical supplies, and so on—were provided with desks and chairs. A chain of command was set up. Orders were given to speed up the commandeering of food supplies; they were to be paid for later at the going market price. Relief supplies arriving at Oakland were to be routed to the Presidio and Golden Gate Park; when supplies became more plentiful, other dispersal points were to be set up.

Police were ordered to conscript whatever manpower they could find for digging latrine trenches, and to organize the bread lines behind the fire lines. The ban on all indoor cooking was to remain in force. A dusk-to-dawn curfew was to be strictly enforced.

Franklin Hall—with its props of bare floorboards, plain desks and chairs, and empty window frames—was the ideal setting for the play Eugene Schmitz was now directing. Caught up in the stupendous drama of events, he saw himself as "the man of the hour," a popular hero whose brisk "Do it; I place you in charge" seemed to have a magical effect.

Rudolph Spreckels was placed in charge of food supplies. James Phelan was assigned to manage the finances, and to "keeping an eye on the dynamiting."

John P. Young, editor of the *Chronicle,* remembered that the mood now derived from the desire of everyone there to meet the demands of those who needed assistance, information, or relief.

"A large number of volunteers reported to assist in the work of relief, and asked only to do something useful. It was an extraordinary exhibition of unselfishness. Men who two days previously had commanded the services of hundreds of their fellows, obliged with alacrity when directed to do anything."

A Registry Bureau was set up. The long and often heartbreaking task of identifying the dead and tracing the missing began.

Spreckels, Downey Harvey, de Young, and all the others in Franklin Hall felt that the spirit of the city was the most valuable asset at their disposal. All agreed that the soldiers needed watching. Spreckels and James Phelan had given them a brief résumé of the senseless dynamiting and military brutality they had witnessed. Brigadier General Funston's "consultations" had never really materialized. Until now, there had been military dictatorship and lapdog civil acquiescence. That, Eugene Schmitz assured them, would cease.

At 4:00 Fire Chief Dougherty—looking like an aging chimney-sweep—brought word that the wind was turning, blowing the inferno back over the devastated area, and that the water mains from Lake Honda, fractured by the great rip, had been repaired.

"There'll be water now to fight," he shouted to a cheering group.

There were further cheers when a young couple walked in and said they wanted to get married. They were the first of two hundred and twenty couples to be married in the city in the coming days.

At 4:30, Abe Ruef appeared.

There was almost total silence in the hall as Ruef walked slowly between the desks to where Eugene Schmitz sat. He had come, he told the Mayor, to do what he could to help.

Rudolph Spreckels and James Phelan were both on their feet, white-faced with anger.

"Glad to see you, Abe," said Schmitz. "We need all the help we can get!"

Ruef smiled. Svengali was back in the wings.

The return of Abe Ruef as civic string-puller continues to be one of the mysteries surrounding the wheeling and dealing that went on in the days immediately following the earthquake.

His whereabouts since he watched the Palace Hotel burn remain uncertain. Reports have placed him at various points—Van Ness Avenue, North Beach, and even in the Mission Hills—and they convey his expressions of genuine grief over the destruction all around.

Certainly Ruef's own losses were considerable; nearly $750,000 of his real estate holdings were destroyed.

But that does not satisfactorily explain his sudden civic-mindedness; nor does it explain Eugene Schmitz's acceptance of his offer to help.

Was it all planned at that brief meeting in the Hall of Justice the previous day? Did Ruef himself decide to wait until the committee began work before he arrived on the scene? Certainly it would have been difficult even for Rudolph Spreckels and James Phelan to walk out in the middle of the crisis. Or is it possible that Eugene Schmitz was so caught up in the role of "man of the hour" that he believed he could cope with anything—that Spreckels, Phelan, even Ruef, could not now challenge his position in his hour of glory?

If that was the explanation for Schmitz's behavior, events proved him wrong. Whatever lay behind Abe Ruef's decision to make an entrance so late in the game, he wasted no time in establishing himself in a position from which he could plunder in safety.

But at that moment in the afternoon, Schmitz and Ruef had a more immediate problem. There wasn't a desk in the hall for Ruef. He accepted an offer to share a corner of the Mayor's desk.

On Russian Hill, Edward Dakin stood alone in the shingled house at 1654 Taylor Street. Everybody else had gone, leaving the buckets and pans of water untouched. Nobody believed the house could be saved.

The old Civil War veteran insisted that he remain a little longer. He told the neighbors he had something special to do.

Now, with the heat warming the paintwork inside the house, Dakin walked slowly around the drawing room, where his historic collection of naval flags hung. He stopped before each one and saluted.

Finally he reached the Stars and Stripes. He lifted the great banner off the wall and carefully furled the cloth. Then he turned and, holding the long pole like a knight entering a jousting tournament, marched proudly from his museum and climbed out onto the flat roof.

Below him smoke and flame advanced on Russian Hill.

Dakin hoisted the pole and fixed it in a stout holder he had prepared for this moment. Then he unfurled the flag. For a second it hung limp. Then the wind caught it, and Old Glory stiffened in the rush of hot air.

Slowly the old man lowered the flag, then raised it again. Twice more he dipped the emblem in salute. Then, after fastening the halyards, he left the roof, locked the front door behind him, and walked away from the house.

Half a mile away, at the corner of Vallejo and Montgomery, Lieutenant Christopher Evans halted his company of the 20th United States Infantry.

The company, part of the military buildup that Brigadier General Funston had called for, had just arrived on a ferry from Oakland.

They watched Dakin raise and lower the flag. Then the solitary figure disappeared from the roof.

"Boys," shouted Evans, "a house that flies a flag like that is **worth saving! Let's go!"**

Holding their muskets loosely, the company charged up Russian Hill. They reached No. 1654 Taylor Street, dashing through flames that licked at their boots.

"On the double now!" shouted Evans.

Soldiers leaped forward and tore at the smoldering woodwork of the verandah. A trooper smashed open the front door with a musket butt. The men poured inside and found the filled bathtubs and the row of soda siphons that had been bought for the emergency.

"Get earth from the garden!" Evans ordered.

His men carried the soil into the house, where it was mixed with water to the consistency of wet plaster. The remainder of the company stationed themselves at windows and on the roof. From these positions they bombarded with mud any spot that caught fire.

One by one the surrounding houses burned to the ground. In the end, No. 1654 stood alone.

Evans spotted a fire burning fiercely beneath one corner of the eaves.

"Get the siphons," he ordered.

A squad carried them to the roof. One of the men lay over the edge, while four others held him fast by the legs. A soda siphon was passed to him. He squirted its contents on the fire. He used up all but two of the soda jets before the flames were finally subdued.

On Van Ness Avenue, Brigadier General Funston gave the order to commence destruction of the houses across the street.

At 5:00 the first house, on the corner of Golden Gate Avenue and Van Ness, was successfully dynamited.

Turning to Captain Coleman, whose plan to dynamite a deep fire break around the city he had approved, Funston asked: "How long will it take to accomplish this first part?"

"An hour or so, sir."

Funston looked toward the approaching fire.

"It must be faster."

"Then we should use the cannon," urged Coleman.

"Very well. Give the order."

Funston turned back to watch the three-man naval demolition squad demonstrate again how successful properly placed high explosives could be in blasting a gap. In twenty minutes the squad razed three blocks of houses.

Car dealer Alan Clayton wondered how much longer his runabout would hold up under the rough handling it had had for twenty-four hours. The car had been commandeered to transport dynamite. Flying a red flag, it raced from one building to another, carrying boxes of explosives and a group of armed soldiers. The car's wheels were beginning to buckle under the jolting they had endured; treads were wearing thin.

Now, as 6:00 approached, another trooper jumped up in the passenger seat and ordered Clayton to carry a fresh supply of dynamite from Fort Mason. The car, its back seat piled high with the lethal cargo, lurched down Van Ness Avenue.

At the corner of Golden Gate it swerved sharply to avoid a wagon and team of horses galloping full tilt toward Market Street.

Clayton caught a glimpse of the group of people in the back of the wagon. One was holding some sort of picture above his head. After the wagon disappeared it occurred to Alan Clayton that he recognized the man clutching the photo.

"Hey! I know him," he cried. "It's Caruso!"

"Caruso who?" asked the soldier.

In the back of the wagon, Enrico Caruso, Martino, and Antonio Scotti held on for dear life as it swayed onto Market Street.

"Slow down!" screamed Scotti.

"No, sir!" bellowed the teamster. "Slow down, and they'll stop us. Go like this, and they'll think we're on official business!"

"He's mad," groaned Scotti as the wagon bounced along Market Street, forcing people to scatter in all directions.

It had taken Martino the entire afternoon to find a driver and bring him back to Golden Gate Park. There the valet found that Scotti had joined Caruso. The other members of the touring opera company, Scotti reported, had crossed the Bay hours earlier.

The driver had demanded fifty dollars for the journey to Golden Gate Park; now he insisted on three hundred dollars, in advance, for the trip to the Ferry Building. Among them the three men raised the fare for what was ordinarily a ten-cent ride. Climbing into the wagon, they set out for the terminal.

At the sight of the building and the ferry boats beyond, Caruso's spirits rose.

He marched up to one of the railroad officials on duty.

"I am Enrico Caruso," he announced. "The singer."

"Gotta wait your turn like everybody else, mister," said the railroad man.

"I am a friend of President Roosevelt," repeated Caruso. "See! He gave me this!"

The singer thrust the signed portrait of Theodore Roosevelt at the nonplussed official. "He is expecting me in Washington!"

Another official came over.

"Ever heard of Caruso?" asked the first man.

"The singer? Sure."

"That is me," said Caruso.

"Says he's got important business with the President in Washington. Wants to line-jump."

The second man nodded thoughtfully.

"You Enrico Caruso? Then sing!"

"Sing! I want to leave here!" spluttered Caruso.

"Sure. But you sing first!"

For the third time in two days the tenor gave a free public performance, singing a few bars from *Carmen*.

The second railroad official nodded. Then he indicated to Caruso, Scotti, and Martino that they were to follow him.

In minutes the three men had boarded a ferry headed for Oakland. As the boat nosed away from the pier, Caruso turned to Scotti and Martino and said, waving the portrait in their faces, "You see—it *was* my passport!"

6 P.M. to Midnight

Union Square, rallying point for those fleeing from south of the Slot (*Fireman's Fund American Insurance Companies*)

21. The Last Defense Breached

HUDDLED IN THE PROW of the ferry boat, widow Hazel Yardley also clutched a photograph—an oval-framed sepia picture of her two-year-old daughter Annie.

She had last seen the child alive nearly two days earlier.

At 5:00 on the morning of the earthquake, Mrs. Yardley slipped out of her apartment south of Market Street to go bargain hunting at the fruit and vegetable stalls of the produce district. Her husband had worked there as a drayman until his death a year earlier.

The rip caught her on Market Street. In terror she rushed back to the flat and found it had collapsed. A passing rescue team told her nobody could be alive beneath the wreckage.

Mrs. Yardley clawed at the rubble. The only trace of Annie she found was the oval-framed photograph, still intact.

Gently, neighbors led her away from the rubble, unable to convince her that Annie lay dead beneath the ruins.

"No!" Mrs. Yardley screamed. "She is alive. I know it."

Half crazed with grief, she stumbled from one group of refugees to another, asking the same question of each group: had anybody seen the little girl in the photograph?

Late in the afternoon a policeman led the distraught woman into the Ferry Building. Officials there put her, dazed and exhausted, on the ferry to Oakland. One of them said that if her daughter were alive, Oakland was the place to look for her; all day large numbers of unaccompanied children had been sent across the Bay.

Now, as the ferry chugged toward Oakland Pier, Mrs. Yardley

scanned the shore eagerly for a glimpse of the child she refused to give up for dead.

In two days Oakland had been transformed into a huge transit camp. Fifty thousand refugees were quartered in and around the town. Another fifty thousand had already been shipped out by train.

Neither martial law nor the military was allowed to take over the town. By swift and firm action, Mayor Frank Mott and his police force, reinforced by a small army of "specials," ensured that Oakland would not repeat the San Francisco experience.

For two days John Keenan kept vigil at the end of Oakland Pier. He scanned every boat arriving from across the Bay, looking for his girl friend, Bessie Stone.

Late in the evening he spotted her on the deck of a ferry. A cry of welcome froze on his lips. Bessie came off the boat, her arm tightly linked through that of a dark-haired man.

Numbly John Keenan walked toward her. Bessie explained to him that she and her companion had fallen "instantly in love," and planned to marry as soon as possible.

Stunned, the rejected suitor could utter only two words, as generous as they were banal: "Good luck."

Enrico Caruso, safely seated on a New York-bound train with the rest of the touring opera company, had no inhibitions about a public display of his emotions. Alternately close to tears and laughter, the tenor was explaining to his fellow artists the trauma he had survived.

Looking for sympathy, he found indifference. Each, if asked, could have told of an equally traumatic experience.

Desperate to create some rapport, the tenor shouted: "On the boat I saw this woman with a picture of a dead child. She had lost everything, but like me, she had faith in a picture!"

At about that time Mrs. Hazel Yardley was walking through a refugee camp outside Oakland. At each group of refugees she asked the question she had repeated so many times during the past two days, each time without success.

As darkness fell over the Berkeley hills she reached a tent housing the Adams family, whose home on Howard Street had been destroyed by one of the first fires following the earthquake.

Harry Adams and his wife Angela squatted on the ground outside their shelter, and broke chunks of bread into a stew pot. Mrs. Yardley stopped beside them and asked her question once again.

Mr. Adams rose and went into the tent. In a moment he returned with a sleepy-eyed child in his arms.

It was Annie Yardley.

Harry Adams had rescued the little girl from the wreckage of her home and brought her with his wife and their own two children to the refugee camp in Oakland.

Cuddling her daughter, Mrs. Yardley, a devout Catholic, knelt before the young Jewish family and recited prayers of deliverance.

Father Peter Yorke stood on the deck of the paddle steamer *Medoc,* which had been moored at Oakland after its hurried conversion into a floating hospital the previous evening. As far as Father Yorke was concerned, the sight of the burning city across the Bay also called for prayers.

All afternoon the Roman Catholic priest moved among the refugees in Oakland, urging them to give thanks for their salvation. More than one exhausted group had been pressed by the enthusiastic Father to repeat the words of Job: "The Lord gave; the Lord has taken away; blessed be the name of the Lord."

Father Yorke was one of those who firmly believed that the destruction of San Francisco was a deliberate act of God.

He pointed dramatically across the Bay and thundered: "There has been no town in the world, in modern times or ancient, in which vice has been so naked and unashamed. Its people made it a merit when a stranger came to show them how wicked they could be. The town turned its face away from God. San Francisco has received her warning. Let us hope it has received purification."

All along the path of the earthquake, priests seized upon this act of nature to warn that damnation was at hand. Frequently bigotry crept into the sermonizing. "The pygmy ministers of Chicago" were warned that their "vapid and to some extent blasphemous behavior" could send an earthquake to pull down their Protestant churches.

The Bible Belt preachers of America also seized upon the disaster with something close to righteous glee. In Georgia, the Reverend

Ian Upjohn gave positive thanks for the earthquake; two more dis-asters of a similar nature, he announced, and the world would return to his version of Christianity.

In Benton Harbor, Michigan, Miss Mary McDermitt, who barely a week earlier had damned San Francisco to destruction by earth-quake, fire, and pestilence within a month, was venerated by her disciples in the Flying Rollers of the House of David. Hundreds of people enrolled in the sect in two days.

Still more joined when Miss McDermitt announced that God was going to end the world at "around ten past three" on Christmas Eve, 1916.

He had asked her to select 144,000 "all Americans" worthy of survival. Immigrants with less than a year's residency, Miss Mc-Dermitt regretted, could not be included. She urged the rest to sell their possessions, give the money to the Flying Rollers, and start assembling an Ark. In the end only the keel was laid.

In London, Paris, Berlin, and even Moscow, religious leaders saw the earthquake as an omen; while urging their flocks to con-tribute to the relief of San Francisco, they warned that help might soon be needed closer to home. In cathedrals and churches more than one minister built a sermon around the words of St. Luke: "And great earthquakes shall be in divers places, and famines, and pestilences; and fearful sights and great signs shall there be from heaven."

Secular seers were also having their finest hour.

In Brighton, Sussex, England, clairvoyant Edna Savage announced from her booth on the Palace Pier that the tremor had been caused by an "airquake"—a great "rush of air had sucked all the moisture out of the earth, and it had cracked open." In Nantes, France, Madame Simone Porodi—"the well-known astrologer who predicted the Boer War"—was of the considered opinion that the whole prob-lem was simply that "there is too much earth on the world." She saw the day coming when whole land areas would "crack open" and fall into the sea. Pressed for specifics, she predicted the Canary Islands, Sardinia, and Corsica might well vanish.

William Randolph Hearst instructed his newspapers to find a more scientific cause for the earthquake.

Professor Simon Newcomb of the United States Geological Survey had been in the middle of trying to establish the weight of the earth when he was asked for his opinion. Peevishly, the Professor explained to a reporter that the great tremor had upset his calculations.

To weigh the earth, Professor Newcomb hoped to use a tremendous pendulum, about a quarter of a mile long, suspended on a great cable between two peaks in the Rocky Mountains.

What, asked the reporter, would he learn from the swinging pendulum? The calculations, the Professor replied, would be incomprehensible to the layman. As for the cause of the earthquake, the nearest lay interpretation he could give was that it had resulted from "a gradual lessening of the earth's surface."

Professor J. A. Branhome of Allegheny, Pennsylvania—"one of the best-known astronomers in America"—believed that the earthquake was the result of the North Pole's wobbling up to fifty feet out of line. Professor James Kemp of Columbia University proclaimed that the earth was spinning a little slower each day, and as it slowed down, chunks were flaking off.

Professor Paul Grant of Northwestern University said: "We don't really know except that it was a little slip of a few feet in the rocks, a slight twitching of the earth."

Proportionately, he added, it was less violent than the act of a horse flicking his tail to drive off a fly.

That flick of nature's tail set in motion the largest financial rescue operation the American government had ever mounted.

By late afternoon, in Washington, President Roosevelt had at last received a balanced picture of the scope of the disaster. The report, which came via Admiral Goodrich's flagship, confirmed many of the wildest rumors.

Roosevelt acted swiftly. He sent a message to Brigadier General Frederick Funston authorizing him to take all steps necessary to control the situation, and assuring him of presidential support in his actions. To Mayor Eugene Schmitz he sent a message informing him that Dr. Edward Devine had been personally appointed by the President to handle relief operations in the city.

In the meantime Congress—within ten minutes—voted $2,500,000 for the stricken city. Secretary of War Taft reported that he had "authorized the expenditure of money to provide 900,000 rations.

Express trains are already on their way with tents for 100,000 people. One hundred thousand blankets, 7500 mattresses, 11,500 bedsocks, and 8000 cots are also on their way."

Back in San Francisco's Franklin Hall, Mayor Schmitz and his Committee of Fifty temporarily suspended all relief work to debate the presidential proclamation officially appointing Edward Devine as relief administrator for the city.

The mood was belligerent. James Phelan voiced the opinion of many of those present when he growled, "It's an insult. We don't need outsiders telling us how to put our house in order."

Surprisingly, Abe Ruef disagreed. He argued that an outsider would bring a clearer perspective.

To Rudolph Spreckels, Ruef's statement "smelled of some scheming." Was it possible, wondered Spreckels, that Ruef thought he could manipulate Edward Devine and siphon off some of the relief funds on their way to the city?

"Who is this Dr. Devine?" rumbled Spreckels.

Nobody knew.

At that moment, from his reserved compartment, Edward Devine was watching representatives of the Chicago City Council saying goodbye to Ernest Bicknell, the city's Director of the Bureau of Charities. Bicknell was to supervise the distribution of $275,000 that Chicago had subscribed for San Francisco relief. The city fathers distrusted the fledgling Red Cross and Dr. Devine. Bicknell was to travel with him to the devastated Western city.

The two men knew, liked, and respected each other. As the train began its long journey to San Francisco, they watched the throng of people streaming along its corridors.

In his book *Pioneering with the Red Cross* Bicknell wrote, "Scarcely any of those on board who were residents of the devastated region knew whether the members of his family were killed, safe, or injured; whether his home was destroyed or his business in ruins."

What little news they had been able to gather so far was far from reassuring. The flames were advancing uncontrolled; districts and streets were being razed by the acre.

"Our passengers were wrought up to an intense degree of suspense," Bicknell recalled. "Exclamations of horror or despair were heard. 'If the fire has reached *that* part of Geary Street, my home is gone! And my family!'

" 'What are our people going to do? What can they do? Golden Gate Park? Our women and children can't live under the trees.'

" 'Market Street, the Mission, Nob Hill, Russian Hill—all gone. Good old San Francisco is finished.' Many persons sat hour after hour with tense faces and tight lips, or strode restlessly back and forth through the crowded aisles."

A group of travelers latched on to the idea that the earthquake could not be blamed for the disaster.

"Earthquake talk is bad talk. It's the fire that did all the damage," one businessman insisted. "Fires can happen in the most well-ordered city."

His confused argument overlooked the simple fact that if there had been no tremor to break the water mains, there would probably have been no conflagration. Besides, few "well-ordered" cities could have matched San Francisco's record as a fire risk.

But the idea that the earthquake was not at fault spread. Many passengers felt it would create obstacles to the city's recovery if the notion that San Francisco was subject to destructive earthquakes were given credence.

The "minimize the earthquake" lobby gained such support that a mass meeting was called in a sleeping car to take action against all those rumors. In the end, the lobbyists unanimously adopted a resolution that the disaster in San Francisco was due solely to fire. "The slight tremor which preceded the fire had nothing to do with the tragedy, beyond, perhaps, breaking gas mains or water pipes here and there."

The "slight tremor" had felled an estimated five thousand buildings, twisted roads, sidewalks, gas, water, and electricity pipes into useless shapes, and paralyzed the transportation and communications systems. And all this before a single fire started.

The attitude on the train persisted wherever two or more San Franciscans met. It was, and still is, all part of a psychological block the city has about the San Andreas Fault.

When the train stopped at Cheyenne, Wyoming, the resolution was solemnly handed to the local newspaperman as an authoritative pronouncement.

As the train resumed its journey, Bicknell and Devine sat down to draw up a scheme that would later become an internationally accepted model for disaster relief.

Food, they decided, would have to be the first consideration. Shelter came next; then medical supplies. Under this last item Devine penciled: "Need for adequate number of surgeons, physicians, pharmacists, nurses, attendants."

None of this would work, Devine warned, unless there was a competent relief committee in San Francisco. Millions of dollars were on the way, and he was determined that every cent would be properly used.

The two men retired to sleep. Late in the evening Bicknell was awakened by excited cries. The train had stopped beside a string of freight cars carrying refugees from San Francisco.

To Bicknell they were "as forlorn a mass of human beings as one could imagine. Many lacked coats or wraps of any sort; some were barefoot, half were hatless, all were dirty, bedraggled, hungry, half-dead from loss of sleep."

Nearly a thousand miles from where the train stopped, the fight to save Van Ness Avenue was in full swing. Civil War veteran Edward Dakin was reminded of the battlefields of Georgia. Cannon were firing at houses one hundred and fifty feet away on the other side of Van Ness. Mingling with their thunder, the deeper boom of dynamiting came from farther down Van Ness.

Behind the firing lines, Brigadier General Frederick Funston and a group of staff officers watched the destruction in silence. Not far away another group, the Committee of Fifty and Mayor Eugene Schmitz, also stood in silence.

Down the Avenue, outside St. Mary's Cathedral, which was so far untouched by the fire, Father Charles Ramm watched a firefighting crew pour water onto a house burning furiously a few hundred yards away.

The priest started to walk toward them. He had only gone a short distance when he heard an anguished cry from behind him. "It's across! It's across!"

Father Ramm didn't have to turn around to know that his worst fears had been realized.

In moments the cry echoed the whole length of Van Ness. A terror-stricken throng poured from the Cathedral.

Quickly the fire crew shifted its attention from the burning house. Desperately they manhandled their steamer pump toward Father Ramm. As they passed him, the priest saw that more than one had tears in his eyes.

"Have faith," he cried, thinking as he said the words how inadequate they must seem to these men. "There's still a chance!"

"We need more than a chance, Father!" shouted a fireman. "We need the luck of the Devil!"

Exactly at midnight the inferno had leaped Van Ness Avenue. The last line of defense had been breached.

FRIDAY
APRIL 20, 1906

Midnight to 6 A.M.

Claus Spreckels' mansion completely gutted by fire
(*Southern Pacific Railroad*)

22. Rising Wind

THE CLAMOR FROM THE far end of Van Ness Avenue barely registered with actor John Barrymore. He was drunk.

The star of *The Dictator,* the idol of a thousand matinee performances, the darling of San Francisco morning-coffee society, had been drinking steadily for forty hours.

In this first hour of Friday morning it is doubtful whether any of his admirers would have recognized the actor. His air of cultivated sophistication was completely gone. Larry Lewis, the waiter at the St. Francis Hotel, still remembers Barrymore leaving the hotel after the earthquake alone, in search of a drink. At the Bohemian Club, the actor found a bottle of brandy, poured himself a stiff drink, and walked out into the street nonchalantly, playing the part of a man nothing could shake. That was Wednesday morning. A few hours later the façade started to crumble. "Troops had closed the liquor shops; the smell of burning was everywhere, and with it was fear," Lewis recalled.

Barrymore, as frightened as anybody else, knew that a drink—or better still, several drinks—was one way to fight that fear.

He headed for the home of some friends who lived on Van Ness. On the way he came to a decision. Somehow he would capitalize on the earthquake, though he did not yet know exactly how he would do so.

The tremor also provided the perfect solution to a nagging problem. He was booked to sail to Australia to tour with *The Dictator.* He loathed the prospect. In the confusion and panic, he could deliberately disappear. By the time he re-emerged, the touring company would be on its way to Sydney.

The actor found it no problem to vanish. His willing host on Van Ness promised a safe hiding place. So from Wednesday through Friday, he drank continuously, interrupting his binge only for an occasional nap. The marathon seemed to confirm the legend that his alcoholic intake was matched only by his success with women.

After forty hours, the normally fastidious actor looked like a derelict. His hair was matted; his unshaven face was streaked with sweat and dirt. Unaccountably, he was still wearing evening dress, but his bow tie hung slack at the neck, his dress shirt was filthy, and his suit was wrinkled beyond recognition.

If Barrymore was aware of the change in his appearance, it did not upset him. During his drinking jag, he had worked out a plan to exploit the earthquake for his own ends. He decided to present himself to the world as an on-the-scene "reporter" of what had really happened in San Francisco. The one discrepancy between John Barrymore's "report" and those written by others involved in the disaster was that the actor made up virtually all he claimed to have seen. Twenty years later Barrymore finally confessed to his deception. But by then he was so famous that the world merely smiled indulgently at his admission.

Fortified by brandy, he sat at a table and began setting down the story of "what I had seen in those harrowing days and what I myself had been through—people shot in the street, spiked on bayonets, and other horrors so great that the imagination was almost blunt from contemplating them."

He had already decided to release this piece of fiction to the world in the form of a letter to his sister, actress Ethel Barrymore. He was sure the letter would be "worth at least a hundred dollars." In terms of publicity it earned Barrymore a thousand times that amount.

A. P. Giannini, for vastly different reasons, had been preoccupied by worries about money for many hours.

The banker had arrived at his brother's home early the previous afternoon. Dr. Atillio Giannini's house at 2745 Van Ness had for all intents and purposes become the center of banking operations in the city.

Other bankers, their money sealed in vaults too dangerous to open or buried beneath tons of rubble, adopted the attitude of F. L. Lipman of the Wells Fargo Bank. After watching his bank burn to the ground, Lipman said simply, "There was nothing to do but go home." While Lipman, Crocker, and a score of other influential bankers decided to sit it out and send reassuring telegrams to the Stock Exchanges in New York, London, Paris, and Berlin, Giannini —the man they had dismissed as an upstart—was planning a financial coup.

During the previous afternoon a steady stream of information poured into the house on Van Ness. Giannini, seated at a large wooden kitchen table, fortified with endless mugs of coffee, sorted the pieces and put together an astonishingly accurate picture of the city in terms of hard-cash losses. Giannini calculated that at least four hundred blocks of real estate, representing nearly one third of the developed area of the city, had been destroyed. Within this two thousand acres lay the financial district, the retail district, the Washington Street commission district, Chinatown, and the slopes of Nob, Telegraph, and Russian Hills. The property loss could be as high as $350,000,000, according to his figures.

He had $80,000 in cash to set against the estimated losses—the only money the Bank of Italy had available to cover deposits of $846,000. If there were a "run"—if depositors, on learning of the bank's $80,000 cache of gold and silver buried in Giannini's living-room fireplace, demanded that the money be used to cover their losses in full—the Bank of Italy would face a crisis from which it could probably never recover.

In spite of this grim possibility, Giannini decided to stake the $80,000 in a gigantic gamble. The money would be used to encourage people to rebuild their businesses and homes. The bank would lend at a fair interest; by doing so, Giannini hoped to attract enough new customers to ensure a prosperous future.

The decision involved many risks. The loans would have to be carefully parceled out. He could not be sure they would be repaid. He could not know whether the venture would attract business.

Giannini summoned his brother and a handful of Italian small-business men, all of whom were depositors. To them he expressed a confident sentiment he used repeatedly in the coming days. "This is a great town, boys. We've been burned out before and have come up fighting. How about getting together and building again?"

There was silence in the kitchen. Then Attillio asked nervously whether the Bank of Italy could afford to go it alone.

"Yes," insisted Giannini. "To wait for other bankers would be a fatal mistake. We've got to fight our way out of this spot alone."

During the evening rumors had filtered in that some of the major bankers wanted to remain closed until "at least November." During that period they would have time to rebuild their premises, consolidate, and reopen—in short, to behave in the traditional, conservative, and leisurely manner to which they were accustomed.

"If our banks are closed until November, they may as well stay closed. In November there will be no city or people left to serve. Today is the time they need a bank. The time for doing business is right now!"

His listeners nodded in agreement. The risks were high; but the rewards, if the plan worked, would be substantial.

Giannini's plans had the genius of simplicity. A letter was to be circulated to all depositors announcing that the bank was open for business. Attillio's house would be the main "branch"; a second branch would be opened on the waterfront once the flames were stopped.

"All I need are a couple of barrels and a long plank stretched between to act as a table. Over this I want a Bank of Italy sign. Any man who wants to rebuild can come and get money with no trouble," Giannini concluded.

Early Friday morning, the banker worked out the rest of his plan. To the men seated around the kitchen table, Giannini explained: "If a customer wants $5000, he gets half. He'll have to make do with that. If we give everybody all they want, there won't be enough to go around. Everybody needs a chance. People have got to work—and work hard."

Giannini didn't need to look at a man's bank balance to estimate his capacity for work. He knew every depositor intimately: "I know his credit rating, what sort of worker he is, how reliable, what property he had. I've got it here," said Giannini, tapping his head.

But even if every man got only half of what he asked for, ventured Attillio, the $80,000 would soon be used up.

Giannini already had an answer to that. The men around the table would be sent among the Italian community to convince those who had hoarded cash that "their money will be safer with us than in some refugee camp. They can bring it here at any time of the day or night."

At 2:00 in the morning, James B. Stetson sat in a window of his mansion at 1801 Van Ness, alternately watching the excitement down the Avenue and recording it in his makeshift diary. A pioneer of the Gold Rush, Stetson disapproved of the way the crisis was being handled and his disapproval increased steadily. The indiscriminate destruction of property by artillery fire and dynamite angered him particularly because the explosions set off the mansion's burglar alarm system. A squad of Funston's soldiers tried to evict him at bayonet point even when "it was clear that the fire was no danger to my property." He stood for a few moments on Van Ness, and then sneaked back into his home, confident he could meet any reasonable fire threat. "I had buckets of water in the front and rear rooms with an improvised swab ready to put out any small fire which would be within my reach."

Outside, the flames were shooting high into the air on both sides of Van Ness. Silhouetted against them were groups of soldiers and firemen, who were showing little more control than the frightened refugees.

As Stetson watched, a number of the soldiers stopped outside a neighboring mansion—the home of millionaire Claus Spreckels.

The soldiers were a dynamite squad, one of a dozen who had been roaming the length of Van Ness since midnight looking for likely targets to demolish. For the moment they had run out of supplies. Then car dealer Alan Clayton's runabout arrived with a load of explosives.

Clayton remembers his horror when he saw that the soldiers intended to demolish the Spreckels mansion, long regarded as one of the most elegant on Van Ness.

"As I started to unload the dynamite, a soldier suddenly said it wasn't needed. The mansion was on fire."

Just how the Spreckels mansion caught fire is a mystery. At that moment the wind was blowing the flames away from the house. William Bronson suggests in his description that "somehow falling sparks had set flame to a stable that stood on the grounds . . . and the fire had been missed until too late."

It was a neat theory in which no one is held responsible, but it overlooks one important piece of evidence: Stetson's diary. In it he recorded: "I saw smoke coming out of the *chimney* of the Spreckels mansion. Firemen had arrived and one of them said that the house was full of smoke and on fire." (A search of the Fire Department's records shows no evidence of the fire originating in a stable.) Stetson's diary continues: "The house was on fire in the upper rooms, blazing out of the upper windows." How had the fire—which ostensibly began in a stable—leaped to an upper story before attacking the mansion's ground floor? According to the 1970 Fire Chief of San Francisco, such a pattern would be "most unlikely, even allowing for the odd way things happened in '06."

There is another theory to set against the one offered by William Bronson: the fire was deliberately started, either by a member of the dynamite squad impatient for the arrival of Clayton's buggy full of explosives, or more likely, by an unknown arsonist. There had been cases of arson since Wednesday morning.

But why, of all the mansions along Van Ness, was the home of Claus Spreckels—who like his son was a deep-rooted opponent of City Hall graft—selected for destruction? And why was absolutely no attempt made to stop the blaze? Stetson, who saw how slowly the fire had started, said that "a bucket of water" could have put it out. By midnight there was an adequate supply of water available at points along Van Ness. Not a drop was used on the Spreckels mansion.

There are some people who still believe that the responsibility for the burning of the Claus Spreckels mansion can be traced to Abe Ruef; that in the time he effectively "disappeared" from public view he secretly briefed, and paid, an arsonist to strike at the *Rudolph* Spreckels mansion farther down on Van Ness. Ruef may have believed —correctly, as it turned out—that Rudolph Spreckels had a number of incriminating documents in the house—documents which provided evidence of widespread graft in the city's administration. But the fire raiser, confused by the panic along Van Ness, attacked the wrong Spreckels mansion.

Whatever started the blaze, the Claus Spreckels mansion was soon beyond help.

At the northern end of the Avenue, near its intersection with Lombard Street, Henry Anderson Lafler watched another squad of soldiers preparing to clear the area before it was dynamited.

Lafler later testified that during the operation he saw soldiers looting newly vacated premises. It was not an isolated instance; in other parts of the city other troops plundered what they were supposed to protect.

Outside St. Mary's Cathedral a group of men, including Mayor Schmitz and Brigadier General Funston, stood around Fire Chief John Dougherty. In the confusion that had followed the cannon fire across Van Ness, both the Committee of Fifty and Funston's staff had been scattered. The remnants of the two "ruling cliques" gathered around the old Fire Chief.

The only record of what followed comes from reporter Paul Ditzel. As far as Ditzel was concerned, Dougherty, who was on the verge of collapse, was a Homeric figure. Fifty years later the reporter recalled that moment, around 3:00 in the morning, when "San Francisco's darkest hour had arrived. Dougherty's men had fought their hearts out and all they had to show for it were a few buildings—islands in a sea of ashes. The fight was gone from them."

Even Schmitz and Funston appeared defeated. Having crossed Van Ness, the fire could now devour the rest of the city at its leisure.

"The city tottered on the edge of complete disaster. The conflagration was inches short of total victory," Ditzel wrote.

Then a remarkable change came over Dougherty. Normally a gentle man, he seemed transformed with the fury of a general in battle. Turning away from the group, he leaped into his buggy.

His "whiplash voice infuriated the men as the fire never could. They had done their best and he wasn't satisfied. Their hatred focussed upon the erect figure of Dougherty, proudly dashing up and down Van Ness. The firemen swore they would make Dougherty eat his words. They took a new grip on the hoses and drove their streams hard into the flames. This was just what Dougherty hoped for. He browbeat the exhausted firemen into an angry fury, until they hated him so much they would rather take a bellyful of smoke and flame than admit to the old man that he could stand the punishment longer than they could."

Firemen who shortly before seemed on the verge of collapse somehow found fresh energy to renew their assault on the burning buildings. Where they had no hoses, they attacked the flames with sacks and horse blankets. Burned and blistered hands tore at blazing woodwork.

By 4:00 firemen had reached the Claus Spreckels mansion. A hose company doused the surrounding property and left the mansion to burn.

On other parts of Van Ness the firefighting teams were meeting, with success. Reporter James Hopper of the *Call* recalled the sight as "the most heroic a man could watch. The future of the city—or rather what was left of San Francisco—was being decided here and now."

On the steps of St. Mary's Cathedral, another momentous issue was being resolved. Mayor Schmitz demanded that the artillery bombardment and dynamiting by Funston and his troops must cease.

Exact details of the confrontation between Schmitz and Funston have never been recorded, and those who witnessed it are all dead. But photographer Moshe Cohen recalled Funston stalking off toward Fort Mason "as black as thunder, like he had lost one hell of an argument."

Shortly after 5:00 in the morning, an order was passed down the fire lines that the use of explosives was to be stopped until further notice.

The order came a few minutes too late to stop the destruction of the Viavi Building on Green Street—and the by now predictable result. The force of the explosion catapulted burning rafters over a wide area previously untouched by the fire. William Bronson describes it as the work of a "zealous crew" being "careless." O. D. Baldwin, whose house stood only blocks away from the Viavi Building, saw the explosion as a monumental act of sheer stupidity, difficult to explain under *any* circumstances.

The fire raged along the north side of Green Street. By 6:00 it was being speeded along by a gale-force wind.

6 A.M. to Noon

The post office sent out messages written on anything, and without stamps (*Metropolitan Life*)

23. Fulfilling a Vow

SHORTLY AFTER 7:00, Leonard Ingham, the police patrolman whose nightmares had predicted the disaster, returned to his home. The wood-frame building on Dolores Street was still intact. Ingham had gone back to salvage the insurance policy he had taken out against the threat of fire. He found the policy where he had left it in the kitchen. Stuffing the precious document into his tunic pocket, Ingham left the house, carefully locking the door behind him.

In the street he stopped, mesmerized. "The air around me was still. Yet a few hundred yards away, a high wind appeared to be blowing. It was a terrible sound."

The policeman was witnessing a freak of nature common to the great fires that devastated ancient Rome, and Moscow in 1812. It did not occur again until the destruction of Hamburg and Dresden in World War II. After two days, the inferno in San Francisco had begun to create its own wind, pockets of superheated air that rushed through gigantic natural flues.

Ingham, terrified, recalled "that the vent a few hundred yards away seemed to have a giant bellows beneath it, sucking the flames upwards with new strength and purpose."

He turned and ran.

Arriving at the intersection of Dolores and Sixteenth Streets, he saw three figures running up Sixteenth. "They were about a hundred and fifty yards away when a tongue of flame came flashing along Sixteenth. It was low on the ground, and crackled like millions of fire crackers. It caught the three as they ran. The flame seemed to pass through them as it crossed Sixteenth. When it had gone there

were just balls of fire on the ground. Nobody could get near them.
The air was like a blast furnace. Anyway, there was nothing anybody
could do for them. They just lay there, frying."

Photographer Moshe Cohen, like all the other cameramen covering the inferno, had run out of film. Now, safe in the Mission Hills,
he sat down "and just looked, so that I would always remember."
Sixty-four years later he recalled: "It was early afternoon. But you
could only tell that with a timepiece. It could have been dawn, dusk,
anytime around then. Not that you worried about the light. The fire
took all your attention. There was just flame and noise and hell. The
whole city seemed to be drowning in flame. And not just ordinary
flames, but whole waves of orange and red and purple and yellow, all
mixed up together with a terrible dense smoke that seemed to boil up
inside the buildings and then spout upwards.

"Flame and smoke seemed to have a life of their own. Together
they seemed alive, writhing all over the place with a sound that
nobody had heard before. It wasn't normal fire sounds, for sure. No,
this was a *chattering,* yeah, chattering, like a billion monkeys were on
the run.

"Once in a while a building would collapse in a great rumble.
Now that was a sound you could get used to after a while; two days
of falling buildings, and you just don't notice any more.

"But that other sound—it don't belong on earth; it's from some-
place else."

The noise, in fact, was a combination of many things: the earth
itself igniting; firebrands whistling through the air, spreading the ocean
of flame until *everything was burning,* creating a giant kiln in which
lead bubbled, wood exploded, and glass melted, along with rubber and
tar and the corpses strewn in the fire's path.

At 9:00 in the morning, Bailey Millard, the artist, was watching
the inferno roll steadily up Russian Hill. The heat was so intense that
"it seemed as if the sky itself would evaporate."

The wooden buildings on the slopes of Russian Hill were particularly vulnerable to the inferno. "Softened up" by the great
draughts of hot air blown over them, they were defenseless against the
fiery onslaught.

As Millard watched, a group of men appeared beside a row of

houses a few hundred feet below him. They chopped and broke down fences and small outbuildings that could provide material for the fire. Then they picked up "blankets, rugs, and carpets, sprinkled them with water from buckets they brought out of the houses, and turned to meet the fire."

For a moment Bailey Millard watched them. Then he ran into the villa, picked up a canvas frame, and rushed to join the firefighters below. The artist wielded his canvas with almost maniacal fury for many hours. In the end this fire line held; the handful of houses were saved.

Their victory was recorded by Henry Anderson Lafler:

"It was the boys of the hill that saved the hill. It was Toby Irwin, the prizefighter, and Tim O'Brien, who works in the warehouse at the foot of the hill, and his brother, Joe, who works in a lumberyard, and the Dougherty boys, and the Volse boys, and Herman, the grocery clerk—it was they who saved the hill.

"It was the old Irish woman who had hoarded a few buckets of water through the long days of fear and rumor and who now came painfully toiling up the slopes with water for the fire—it was she who saved the hill.

"It was the poor peasant Italian with a barrel of cheap wine in his cellar who now rolled it out and broke its head in with an axe, and with dipper and bucket and mop and blanket and cast-off coat fought the fire till he dropped—it was he who saved the hill.

"It was Sadie who works in the box factory and Annie who is a coat finisher and Rose who is a chocolate dipper in a candy shop who carried water and cheered on the boys to the work—it was they who saved the hill.

"It was a great, brave, roistering fight of all the dwellers on the hill for their homes and their lives, and gloriously they won. Thank God, there were no soldiers there to drive these humble people from their homes, no soldiers with loot-stained fingers, clutching gun-butts to make there a desolation—to lay the feast upon which the flames might feed to gorging unmolested, unchecked, undisturbed."

Lafler observed that the soldiers "filled men with fear of violence, breeding deadly apathy and dumb despair." All morning he collected evidence of what he considered scandalous behavior; it became carefully documented proof of allegations that demanded serious investigation. Yet there was never an official inquiry into these allegations.

Brigadier General Frederick Funston rejected them as "mental gymnastics and fairy tales."

On Van Ness, the firemen refused to give up. Reporter Paul Ditzel recalls that their water streams "bored into the flames with renewed fury; nobody knew what kept the men on their feet, unless it was the haranguing of Dougherty."

At 11:00 the Fire Chief noticed that the wind had changed once more and was blowing the inferno back across ground it had already scorched.

At first the crowd didn't notice the change. When it did, it gave a rousing cheer.

But for those gathered around St. Mary's Cathedral, the jubilation was cut short when somebody shouted: "Look! The Cathedral's on fire!"

A tiny tongue of flame appeared at the top of the spire. In a moment the tower was blazing brightly.

Four miles from the Cathedral, Mrs. Marjorie Brown watched anxiously as the pall of fire and smoke rose over the city. Somewhere in that chaos was her husband, Hugh. Several hours before, after bringing her to the safety of a friend's house near the Presidio, he had insisted on returning to the city to try to cable reassuring news to his family in Ohio. He had not yet returned.

Mrs. Brown was also worried that the air temperature might injure her unborn baby. Already she had noticed that "the child was evidently feeling the effect of the shock. It lay still in my body for long periods of time, then trembled with a spasm far too violent, and lapsed again into quiet."

If only there had been a doctor to convince her that these symptoms were a normal stage of pregnancy.

In the emergency hospital in Golden Gate Park, Dr. Alfred Spalding, one of the surgeons on duty, wondered whether his call for a priest would be answered in time. For the third time in thirty-six hours of almost continuous surgery, he had summoned a priest to administer the last rites.

This time it was a dying middle-aged woman. She had already been on the point of death when she had been brought to the hospital earlier that morning. In a properly equipped hospital there might have been a chance to save her. But in the open air, in poor light, with limited surgical equipment, Dr. Spalding was forced to abandon her. The woman was laid on a litter beneath a tree to await the arrival of the priest—and death.

Death arrived first.

When the priest came, the woman was being carried away for burial. No one knew her name or background.

Dr. Spalding asked why the priest had taken so long. The cleric explained that he had been leading a group of communicants in prayers for the safety of St. Mary's Cathedral.

Around the Cathedral itself, prayers were being offered by the crowd for the safety of the cassocked figure climbing up its spire.

Father Charles Ramm was fulfilling the vow he had made to risk his life to save St. Mary's.

Shortly after midday he began the ascent.

Noon to 6 P.M.

Looking East on California Street from Stanford home with the Fairmont Hotel on the left (*Roy D. Graves Collection*)

24. The Blind Gunner

THE CRACKLE OF fire from the steeple tip eighty feet above carried down to the priest as he clung, spreadeagled, to the side of the wooden tower. Craning his neck, Father Ramm could see "wicked little tongues of red" flickering around the cross that surmounted the spire. That movement was the only one the priest had been capable of for some minutes. Vertigo had paralyzed him. Pressed against the wooden slatboards, he looked down onto Van Ness. A wave of dizziness overcame him. He closed his eyes and prayed.

Now he opened them again, and forced himself to look downward. He had a hazy impression of upturned faces, and beyond them, the inferno. Then he became aware of something else. A fire company seemed to be maneuvering a ladder against the side of the Cathedral.

It fell short of the spire.

Below, sixteen-year-old Joan Spiers watched as a fireman began to climb the ladder. "All those who had been praying got off their knees," she remembered. "As far as Father Ramm was concerned, the time for prayers was over. We could see he was stuck, and it was obvious that the fire ladder could not reach him. A fireman stood on the top rung and shouted something up to Father Ramm. We couldn't hear what it was."

Out of the corner of his eye, Father Ramm could see the fireman about twenty feet below. The man was shouting: "It's too late! Nothing's worth risking your life for!"

Father Ramm shook his head and looked upward. The fireman's shouted advice somehow broke through "the hold of fear" which

245

gripped him. "I was determined to save St. Mary's even at the expense of my own life."

Feeling for toeholds with his boots, he began to inch up the spire. He supported his body with fingerholds found between the planking. Once the cloth bag slung around his neck snagged on a piece of wood. He yanked it free.

Halfway up the steeple Father Ramm suddenly encountered a new danger. The heat rising from the inferno had created drafts, which threatened to pull him off the pinnacle. Hugging the woodwork, he paused to look out across the city. Afterward he spoke of "great sheets of fire spinning across the ground with a sound that stunned the mind. With it came the heat, so oppressive that it was almost impossible to breathe and think."

Eyes smarting from the smoke, he resumed his climb.

To Tom Bellow, a reporter on the *Call,* there was something "horrific as that black-robed figure pulled himself up. At times you couldn't really see him through the smoke.

"Then he was at the top, hanging on with one hand, while he used the other to beat out the fire with the gully bag.

"When he had won, he just clung there, supporting himself on the scorched spire tip.

"For a moment the crowd did nothing. Then somebody shouted that we had just witnessed a miracle. Everybody was cheering like crazy. It was incredible."

From his perch, Father Ramm had a panoramic view of the devastation. San Francisco looked like hell on earth.

Walter Courtney Bennett reached the Ferry Building with a feeling of relief: his wife and daughter had stood the long walk well. Now they waited patiently in line for the Oakland ferry.

Bennett passed the time by writing up what he regarded as a vital addendum to his report to the Foreign Office.

During the trek down Market Street he had met insurance agent Adam Gilliland, a man he knew slightly. Gilliland told him that insurance losses "stood at forty million sterling." Bennett jotted down the estimate along with some of Gilliland's other observations.

"In the hands of the insurance people lies the future of San Francisco. At law, they are, it is held in many quarters, not bound to pay a cent, as the damage was done by earthquake, and the fire was the direct result of the earthquake.

"It seems unreasonable to expect a company to pay full value for a building which was wrecked by earthquake (and most were) and which was subsequently destroyed by fire."

Gilliland told him that "most British policies have a special clause to the effect that the policy is void in the event of any portion of the building insured falling while the policy is in force."

Bennett added: "If the insurance is not paid the city is ruined. If it is paid, many of the insurance companies will break."

Albert Truelove, a twenty-year-old insurance clerk, spent the morning working, at bayonet point, in a burial gang. Over sixty years later the memory of the stench and sights remained fresh in his mind.

"Lots of the bodies had sort of melted. Eyes, hair, lips, ears, things like that, were gone—burned off. Most of the dead were old. I guess they were people who hadn't the strength in them to run. But there were some young ones and children.

"They were all burned, and some were little more than stumps. The bits of flesh that hadn't been scorched, looked waxy, the color of dummies in shop windows.

"In some of the buildings south of the Slot, the bodies had melted in with the general debris. You'd find a lump of fried flesh pitted with bits of iron, glass and other things. The smell was awful. You felt sick all the time."

There was no chlorinated lime available to sprinkle over the corpses, no disinfectant for the burial squads.

Shallow trenches were dug and the charred remains covered with earth. Sometimes the burial squads had barely patted the soil down before the first rats appeared.

Truelove remembers almost fainting when he saw a rat dragging an arm along the ground. "A soldier gutted the rat with his bayonet. He slit it right open, then spun it above his head on the steel before throwing it into a burning building."

By Friday afternoon, the rats were making a bid to take over the city. The ground shock had broken the sewers, many of which had never been very good, in hundreds of places. The fire had left the open stumps of sewer pipes on nearly every burned-over lot. The rats could use these holes to come and go as they pleased.

By Friday afternoon too, the first labor gangs had been conscripted. Supervised by the troops, they were employed to clear streets and excavate cellars. Many of them picked up fleas from the rats and carried them out into the suburbs.

"We got used to seeing hundreds of rats scampering across the ruins," Truelove recalled. "The place looked like a rat paradise. For a bit of amusement, the soldier in charge of our gang would take a pot shot at a really big one if it was a little way away. Those that came right close got speared. By the end of the afternoon he was a real expert at spiking them."

Elsewhere in the city, not only rats felt cold steel. The soldiers were behaving more and more senselessly, at times with terrifying viciousness. During the afternoon, more looters were shot on Market Street. Stevedore John Spencer later testified that in the case of one suspected looter, "a trio of Uncle Sam's soldiers raised their rifles to their shoulders and fired. The body was thrown into an alleyway for either the rats or flames to get it."

On Green Street, Mrs. Ida Dawbridge found a soldier looting her parlor. When she told him to get out, he threatened her with his gun; two days passed before she overcame her fear and reported the theft. By then the case was simply one of many the police would try to investigate. The growing list of crimes laid at the door of the military included one rape, a number of indecent assaults, and an indeterminate number of charges of grievous bodily harm.

Several times during the afternoon William Keller, owner of the Globe Flour Mill on Montgomery Street, had resisted threats from a company of soldiers.

The troops arrived at 4:00 and ordered Keller and his men to leave the mill. Keller refused. Later he testified: "We believed our building to be entirely fireproof. The roof was of iron, the walls of brick and the heavy window casings were also of metal. So were the doors. We had twelve fire extinguishers and a salt water tank of unlimited capacity connected to the Bay."

Keller was so sure his building was safe that only a few days before he had refused an offer from Adam Gilliland to insure it.

Keller boasted: "The whole city would have to burn first before this place went up."

For more than two days the mill owner and ten employees stood guard inside the building. Early Friday afternoon the inferno swept up to Telegraph Hill, at whose foot the building stood.

A few blocks ahead of the flames came the soldiers.

Keller recalled: "Their officer just said one word—'out.' I tried to show him the water tank. But he just repeated 'out.'

"By then his men were moving around jabbing at anybody who didn't move fast enough. I said a man had a right to die defending his property. The officer said that if I wanted to die he would oblige me there and now—by shooting me and any of my men on the spot. If we wanted to live, we had to get the hell out of the place."

Keller, a tough frontiersman, was not easily cowed. Finally, though, he ordered his men to withdraw.

To him the troops were "plumb crazy." When one of his men tried to close the heavy iron mill door in the last desperate hope to keep the fire from entering, a trooper jabbed him with a bayonet—and pushed open the door.

Keller recalled bitterly that even then the mill took hours to burn, "and there is of course no doubt whatsoever that one man could have saved the structure had he been permitted to remain. Our loss was $220,000."

At his temporary headquarters in Fort Mason, Brigadier General Frederick Funston had listened for an hour to Captain Coleman's passionate argument. At 4:00, Funston cut the discussion short: "All right. Do it."

Those four words were his authorization to resume the shelling along Van Ness. His order constituted a betrayal of his earlier promise to Schmitz to end what many later condemned as senseless destruction.

In retrospect, the decision to resume the bombardment late Friday afternoon is a baffling one. For the first time since the inferno had started, the firemen were holding a line along Van Ness. Water was available; the wind had turned the fire back on itself.

Yet Coleman was adamant. In effect, he said that it was essential for the shelling to resume. No record remains of the meetings Funston held throughout the day.

There are, however, clues from which some conclusions can be drawn. By midafternoon Funston was physically and mentally exhausted; he later admitted as much himself. His early-morning clash with Mayor Schmitz on the steps of St. Mary's Cathedral had stung him deeply. Funston was forced to recognize, possibly for the first time since Wednesday morning, that a civic administration really did exist.

His authority was shaken further. The special permits granting access to and from the city which had previously carried the words, "By authority of Brig. Gen. Funston," were now—by orders from Washington—to be issued "By order of Geo. C. Pardee, Governor of California." He received complaints from the Committee of Fifty that his troops were acting outrageously; Funston brushed them aside. But he could not ignore telegrams from Washington which demanded to know how far he proposed to extend his military domination of the situation.

Preoccupied with his role as the self-appointed savior of San Francisco, tired and hurt by the challenge to his supreme authority, Funston could well have seen Coleman's request to resume shelling as a chance to reassert his authority. It would certainly be consistent with his behavior until then. From the outset he had projected and interjected himself into the crisis.

Whatever the reason, at 5:00 the thunder of artillery fire boomed across Van Ness Avenue once more.

Along Van Ness the fire line still held, manned, reporter Ed Gleeson told us, "by pale, sleepless men who held their hoses until they dropped." When a fireman collapsed, a volunteer took over. When the supply of volunteers was exhausted, soldiers conscripted others into the line.

One of those pressed into service was a middle-aged Italian. The man was ordered by a trooper to "help pull hose." For some reason—a language difficulty, deafness, nobody will ever know—the Italian refused. The soldier promptly bayoneted him in the back. Seriously wounded, the man turned to ward off further attacks.

What happened then is related by John Castillo Kennedy: "Another man, one Ernest Denicke, who had volunteered for duty with the National Guard—although he was not actually a member of the Guard; he was wearing a uniform he had brought home from the

Philippines—shot and killed him. His body was carried out of the way and the fight went on."

At half past five, car dealer Alan Clayton made another run to Fort Mason.

"I was supposed to pick up more explosives. When I got there I was ordered to turn around and rush a doctor to Van Ness; one of the gunners had been injured."

When he reached Van Ness, Clayton found that the artilleryman had been badly burned by flashback that had seared his eyes. Virtually blind, the man was in no condition to continue firing. But he insisted on resuming his post. "He also made the perfectly valid point that he was the only soldier there trained in the use of artillery pieces."

As soon as the doctor patched up the gunner, Clayton was ordered to drive on to the Presidio. On Van Ness another driver, J. C. Cunningham, saw the gunner "carried to his gun. He was unable to walk. He aimed it and fired and then fell from a combination of concussion and exhaustion.

"The soldiers moved the gun to the next stand and then carried the brave fellow to it and stood him in position. He opened his eyes, surveyed the scene, sighted the gun, and gave the signal.

"Boom!

"A great sheet of flame belched forth. I could see a bunch of fire sailing towards the house. In it went; then there was a great explosion, and the house collapsed."

The virtually blind gunner moved on to the next target.

The booming of artillery fire brought a sudden silence to the Committee of Fifty, gathered in Franklin Hall. All eyes turned toward the Mayor. Schmitz took it as a personal insult. It was one more example of the Army's indifference to civic authority.

Schmitz wrote a strongly worded note of protest to Funston and had it dispatched to Fort Mason. The messenger took hours to complete the journey. Several times on his way he was drafted to help bury corpses or clear rubble.

Schmitz spent most of the day at his writing desk. Dozens of telegrams had been scribbled for transmission from Oakland. One to

New York requested all available information on Dr. Edward Devine, the man President Roosevelt had personally appointed to control relief operations in the city. The Mayor virtually asked the President to reconsider the appointment.

A succession of wires provided running situation reports to the outside world. Even allowing for the fluidity of the situation, they made somewhat curious reading. At 7:00 this Friday morning, with the fire raging along Van Ness, Eugene Schmitz telegraphed Washington that the "fire situation was getting better." Shortly afterward he drafted a wire canceling the optimistic report. Still later another wire reversed the mood again.

During the day Eugene Schmitz did some things that may have given an indication of his confused state of mind. He went into a rage when James Phelan opposed the suggestion of another armed force in the city. Schmitz ranted until he had his way. At midday, the Committee of Fifty approved the appointment of a "Protection Committee" under the chairmanship of Julian Sonntag. Sonntag was sent to Fort Mason with a request for rifles and ammunition for this small private army. He returned empty-handed. This provoked another explosion from Eugene Schmitz.

Early in the afternoon, Schmitz made—or was party to—a number of curious decisions. Without consulting his committee, he sent another telegram to President Roosevelt: "WE ARE DETERMINED TO RESTORE TO THE NATION ITS CHIEF PORT ON THE PACIFIC." Then he called the Committee of Fifty into session to read a special proclamation to be offered "as congratulation and encouragement to the public." The proclamation began: "To the Citizens of San Francisco. The fire is now under control and all danger is past. . . ."

From more than one quarter came astonished murmurs. Members of the committee knew that the inferno was still out of control. Schmitz, sensing the reaction, assured the committee that the proclamation would be held ready "for the right moment."

Shortly afterward he hurried from the hall and drove off toward Golden Gate Park. And late in the afternoon a couple of trumpet players marched through the park announcing, "on the Mayor's authority," that the fire was virtually over.

As 6:00 approached, the Mayor began a tour of the fire lines. Reporter Ed Gleeson recalled that "Schmitz was here, there, and everywhere. He was like a cheerleader, popping up in the most un-likely places. You'd find him with a fire crew one time; next he'd be out at North Beach encouraging people there. If he had been running for office, he could not have worked harder."

At 6:00 Schmitz told a group of newspapermen waiting outside Franklin Hall, "The fire is virtually under control."

But at that very moment the struggle on the waterfront had entered a new and dangerous phase. Had he been ill informed? Was he trying to boost the city's morale—or was it wish-fulfillment?

6 P.M. to Midnight

Carcasses of cattle killed by the earthquake
(*Metropolitan Life*)

25. Reunion

PHOTOGRAPHER ARNOLD GENTHE, standing at the corner of California and Dupont Streets, looked out across the rubble that had been Chinatown.

Nothing appeared to be moving. Then in the distance, he saw first one, then another, figure darting through the shells of buildings. The figures moved carefully, stooping from time to time to pick up something and put it in a sack each of them carried.

Crouching behind the remains of a wall, Genthe was at first puzzled by their movement. Unable to photograph the scene—like all the other photographers, he had run out of film—Genthe could only watch the men picking their way over the warm ashes.

As they came closer he recognized them as National Guardsmen. They were looting the ruins, "carrying off bushels of bronzes, brasses, and partly melted jewellery."

Sickened, and frightened for his own safety, Genthe turned and ran down California Street.

Shortly after 6:00 Eugene Schmitz—following another of his many extreme changes of mood—cornered James Phelan. The Mayor ordered him to count the number of Chinese encamped in Golden Gate Park.

Such sudden interest in the Chinese population was surprising. Schmitz's previous concern with the oriental community had been confined largely to collecting his percentage from at least one Chinese brothel.

In any event, his request to James Phelan—an impossible task—was not acted on. Phelan believed there were more "important things to do than worry about where the orientals have gone."

Phelan's attitude was shared by many others on the Committee of Fifty. Since settling on the slopes of Nob Hill, the Chinese had been the victims of widespread discrimination. They were denied education, harassed by the police, and exploited by the white business community wherever possible.

Many a Chinese child grew up with a constant reminder of his unworthiness scrawled repeatedly on building walls: "I hate the nigger 'cause he's a citizen, and I hate the yellow dog because he won't be one."

A number of factors led to the persecution of the Chinese. Until gold was discovered in California, there were fewer than *twenty* Chinese in all of the United States. By 1850, another thirty-five had been admitted. Three years later, with the gold boom in full swing, they numbered fifteen thousand. But it was the building of the railways that proved the biggest draw—Chinese labor was cheap and the workers more reliable than white men. In 1870, the Chinese population west of the Sierra Nevada mountains was one hundred thousand, thirty thousand of whom inhabited San Francisco's Chinatown.

Although not actually welcomed, they were tolerated at first, if only because they were willing to do jobs scorned by white men. After the railway boom, they made their way to San Francisco to work as cooks and houseboys; thousands made a living twisting cigars or manufacturing clothes.

By 1870, the threat of "yellow power" was such a source of fear for large segments of San Francisco's white population that petitions were presented to Congress to deport all Chinese from the city. One such petition declared the Chinese undesirable because "they eat rice, fish, and vegetables, and that otherwise their diet differs from that of the white man; not one virtuous Chinawoman exists in Chinatown; and the Chinese are of no benefit to the country."

These racist accusations were rejected by Congress. But the government did put a curb on immigration from the orient, and introduced other measures making it more difficult for the Chinese community to live comfortably.

Chingwah Lee, Chinatown's historian, recalls that "at that time there was no work for white men, never mind the Chinese. But the

Chinese would take *any* work, at *any* pay. This just increased their unpopularity."

Jealousy, contempt, and hatred led to persecution and ultimately even to murder. To rob a "yellow dog" was no crime. The burning of Chinatown offered many opportunists the perfect chance to do just that.

The looting went on with some official knowledge. The Chinese Consul General in San Francisco, Chiang Pao-hsi, made a series of formal protests, including one to Governor Pardee that "the National Guard was stripping everything of value in Chinatown."

The complaints were ignored. The ransacking continued for days.

Shortly after 8:00 in the evening, Abe Ruef took up again what he called "the Chinese question." He chaired the first meeting of the Subcommittee on Relocating the Chinese.

Ruef told the dozen men seated around him that it is "taken for granted from the first that the Chinese must not be allowed to return to the desirable area that Chinatown occupied."

Abe Ruef admitted later that he had earmarked the area for European development—presumably in order to control the various franchises for huge personal profits.

The subcommittee set about finding a "suitable" site for a new Chinatown. Hunter Point, an area well outside the city, was suggested. Ruef objected on the grounds that its location in neighboring San Mateo County would mean the city would lose the tax benefits of having the Chinese among them.

By May 10, twenty-five meetings later, the subcommittee had still not found a solution. By then the Chinese were beginning to return to Chinatown, a third of whose land they owned outright. The balance was owned by absentee landlords, who did not care who occupied it so long as the rents were paid.

James Phelan, recognizing that it would be difficult to keep the Chinese from returning to their lawful homes, suggested, "If they prove obnoxious to whites, they can gradually be driven to a certain section by strict enforcement of antigambling and other city laws."

All through the evening, Mrs. Marjorie Brown kept her vigil at the window of her friend's house near the Presidio. During her wait she witnessed an endless procession of misery.

"There were all the Chinese women who had walked miles over the terrible hills. By the time they passed me they were in a terrible state.

"They just inched along; it wasn't even hobbling, just a tiny movement, clinging to anything they could hold on to. Some wept from the pain of just moving. They were often in such agony that they couldn't talk. They just opened their mouths and shut them again against the pain. It was heartbreaking."

Suddenly a familiar voice shouted her name out of the darkness. It was Hugh Brown, her husband.

"We ran to meet each other in the center of the street and cried in each other's arms. Hugh was completely done in. He had been walking for hours and hours. I led him into the house and found him a couch. I kissed him gently and he was asleep as the last moments of Friday passed."

By Friday evening, Julian Sonntag, the head of the "Protection Committee"—the newest of a number of vigilante movements springing up all over the city—had finally succeeded in arming his little private army. Weapons were "acquired" from a number of sources.

The men who were to use them assembled at Sonntag's house on Scott Street to be sworn in by Judge Cool as "special deputies." Each man received a shotgun, rifle, or pistol, and a pocketful of cartridges or bullets, and instructions to "tolerate no nonsense."

By 10:00 this untrained, undisciplined band was roaming the fire lines, ready to blast anybody who looked troublesome.

On Post Street, carriage driver Frank Riordin was gunned down when he refused to allow his cart to be searched.

A couple of vigilantes riddled a tethered horse with shot. Later they pleaded, "We challenged it, and it didn't answer."

Insurance clerk Herbert Brown—who eventually became Assistant Treasurer of the Pacific Mutual Life Insurance Company—vividly remembered his fear at encountering a vigilante who "offered to shoot me then and there, and for absolutely no reason."

Brown talked his way out of trouble. Others were not so lucky. Regular Police Officer Donald Alpers was winged in the shoulder when he asked two of Sonntag's men to produce evidence of their authorization to carry pistols. Having shot him, the gunmen walked off with a parting remark: "Let that be a warning to you."

The man who might have stopped all these acts of terrorism was preoccupied with a problem that, for him, overrode all others. Brigadier General Frederick Funston was turning Fort Mason into his version of the Alamo.

Flushed and disheveled, Funston stomped around the fort checking and rechecking the defenses. A fire pump stood outside the main fort building. From it a line of hose ran down to the Bay. The outbuildings and fence around Fort Mason had been demolished; on the roof of the remaining building, squads of soldiers stood by with water buckets.

Even making allowances for the speed with which the fire spread, it is difficult to consider Funston's fears realistic. To threaten Fort Mason the fire would have had to travel an additional hundred blocks; with the prevailing wind blowing the flames away from Fort Mason, it is doubtful whether that would have happened.

The firefighters standing by at Fort Mason could have been more usefully deployed along the immediate fire lines. At 11:00 Funston himself seemed to have at last grasped this. He drafted a telegram to the War Department that Fort Mason was now "safe." The fire teams were then sent down to the waterfront.

SATURDAY
APRIL 21, 1906

Men begin to clear the wreckage outside the Orpheum Theater
(*Metropolitan Life*)

26. Flickering Flames

IN THE EARLY MORNING HOURS of Saturday Hannah Waldron was still waiting for her husband to return. Seated in the darkness of the tiny parlor of her home on Twenty-second Street, she struggled to stay awake. She had been without any food for two days. Refugees streamed past her modest home, but now they too were gone.

Robert Waldron had left the house on Wednesday morning, minutes after the earthquake. His last words to Hannah were: "They're going to need all the help possible."

She never saw him again. The fate of Robert Waldron has never been determined.

Was he trapped in a burning building, crushed by falling rubble, or the victim of a trigger-happy soldier?

At the age of eighty-seven, living in Chicago, Hannah Waldron still wondered.

At 1:00 Saturday morning, fifteen-year-old Celia Adamson had no doubt about the effect of the fire on her father.

Richard Adamson had just returned empty-handed from a foraging trip down Market Street. There wasn't even "a tin of corned beef to pick up."

For storekeeper Adamson the trip was a nightmare of avoiding General Funston's armed patrols and of trying to find his way home when many of the familiar landmarks had disappeared. He, like many others, found that distance had been distorted. The city appeared to have shriveled.

The scope of the destruction had a traumatic effect on Richard

Adamson. Years later, at the age of eighty, Celia Adamson recalled: "Like so many others, my father changed almost overnight with the shock. He took it as a personal tragedy the destruction of the Palace Hotel, which he had helped furnish. You see, he loved the city almost as much as he loved his family."

Richard Adamson went to his grave still haunted by his memories of the disaster.

There were happier moments that Saturday morning. Karl Schlaich spent the first hours of the day walking halfway across the still-burning city carrying a wedding cake. He and his bride, Louise, ate it later in the day at their marriage feast—one of the first to be held in the city after the earthquake.

That night, the Schlaichs spent their first hours together as man and wife in a tin shack, sharing it with three other homeless families.

On their sixty-fourth wedding anniversary Louise Schlaich remembered that "our best man had noplace to go, so we asked him to spend the night with us. When it came to sleeping arrangements, my mother, my husband, and myself shared the iron bed, while the best man slept across our feet."

As the morning wore on, photographer Moshe Cohen sensed steadily growing optimism; one had the feeling "that at last we were winning."

The feeling prevailed all along the fire lines. At 4 A.M., Fire Chief Dougherty arrived in his buggy at the Pacific Mail Dock Pier as its timbers began to smolder.

Dougherty thought of it as *"the* desperate moment. The crews were exhausted. Yet if that pier went, all the others would go. For the men a defeat would be the blow that might just make them throw in the sponge."

Dougherty changed the tactics he had used on Van Ness Avenue to encourage the firemen. Grabbing a hose from a fireman, he rushed toward the Mail Dock Pier.

"The sight of their aged fire chief refusing to give up acted as a powerful spur," James Hopper remembered. "The firemen moved with new life."

At 5:00 the Pacific Mail Dock Pier was safe.

It was the turning point. At 5:30 A.M., the firemen on Van Ness reported that the fire there was finally out. Thirty minutes later the Mission District was declared safe.

Now everything turned on the final battle for the waterfront.

Yard by yard the fire teams gained ground. They drove the flames away from the brick-built U. S. Customs warehouses and the grain sheds around the foot of Telegraph Hill. They forced the flames from the piers around East Street back over the burned area south of the Slot. There, where the fire had begun its destruction, it flickered and died.

At exactly 7:15—seventy-four hours after it had begun—the Great Fire of San Francisco was over.

Not long after, it began to rain.

AFTERMATH

A family poses in front of the ruins of City Hall
(*Metropolitan Life*)

27. An Inconvenient Interruption

MONTHS AFTER all danger had passed, refugees still refused to leave the safety of Golden Gate Park. They felt secure. They had made new friends, almost a new life.

In San Francisco, 4.7 square miles had been burned, more than twenty-eight thousand buildings destroyed. Many of those buildings were homes. Whole communities had been decimated. No wonder the park seemed so inviting, even with its bread lines and beans—beans mixed with sand, which made it impossible for some "to look a bean in the eye" for years.

Amid all the rubble, it was impossible for many San Franciscans to identify the lots their homes had stood on, not to mention the houses themselves. Lost or burned records, especially those in the County Court House, caused chaos and confusion that continues to this present day. (Even now citizens of San Francisco sometimes have to refer to pre-earthquake newspapers in order to secure birth certificates, establish proof of marriage or death, apply for visas, or prove social security status.)

In the end, over $9,000,000 in relief funds was received. Even this sum—enormous at the time—seemed small compared with the total loss of between $350,000,000 and $500,000,000. Insurance helped make up the difference; finally, after defaulting, about 80 percent of the $229,000,000 in insurance was paid. There was still, of course, a large deficit. Someone suggested that this and more could easily have been recovered by charging admission of the thousands of sightseers who invaded, and looted, San Francisco soon after the fire.

There had been no lessening of Henry Anderson Lafler's desire to focus public attention on the behavior of Brigadier General Funston's troops. By the end of May he had compiled a nine-thousand-word dossier cataloguing a series of serious misdemeanors. Lafler was no amateur journalist. Recognizing that it is easy to deface monuments, he wrote to Funston:

"It is not I who attack you; it is the facts which attack you. Because of the magnitude of the event with which you were concerned your every act will be the subject of the not indifferent scrutiny of future historians. Nothing that you can now say can alter or obscure the record of what you did or failed to do. While the judgment of history may be delayed, all in good time it will mete out to you either praise or blame.

"If in your secret heart you are conscious that in the time of peril which proves a man, your acts were such as become a man of wisdom and bravery; your conduct was such in its unerring judgment and wise discretion as befits one who wears the uniform of a general in the Army of the United States; and your manifest achievements such as in your declining years you may take a just and honest pride, then you may indeed wait in calm confidence, undisturbed by casual criticism, the verdict of the future.

"But if it should be, sir, that in your secret heart you are conscious that in the presence of an opportunity such as comes to few men in their lifetime, with under your control that tremendous engine—the army—for the accomplishment of any executive purpose, you yet failed to use your power with the energy and wisdom which befits your rank as general; if you are conscious that, with the best intentions in the world, you yet made, as generals have, such fatal errors in the exercise of your power as in a battle-at-arms would have spelled defeat and in this battle with fire did spell ruin and desolation; if you are conscious that to this fiery ordeal to which you were ordained and were after all inadequate, and were even as a man who puts his hand valiantly to the plow and then wavers and looks back, then indeed it may well behoove you to stand, while yet you may, full in the pleasant sunlight of deluded praise."

Funston did not reply.

Nor did he reply to the evidence submitted by the Southern Pacific Railroad which detailed acts of looting by his troops. The railroad did not pursue the matter. Lafler did. After his report was rejected by a local journal, *The Argonaut*, Lafler published his indictment at his own expense.

It fell for the most part on deaf ears.

On Monday, April 23, General Funston's immediate superior returned to the city and took over. General Adolphus W. Greely, a sixty-two-year-old career man with forty-five years' service in the Army, was as different from Funston as chalk from cheese. Tall, imposing, sensitive regarding his position, the Commander of the Pacific Division immediately took exception to much the exhausted Funston was doing. In particular, he objected to the near-martial law imposed by Funston. Immediately he made it clear to Schmitz that the Army was subordinate to the civil authorities. Nevertheless, in Greely's mind, this did not mean accepting orders from Schmitz. To begin with, he did not agree with Schmitz's projected role for the Army in the administering of relief. Dr. Devine had arrived and President Roosevelt had made it clear that relief funds were to be his and the Red Cross's responsibility. Later the President agreed that Devine could distribute funds with the assistance of the trusted ex-Mayor Phelan, thus keeping the money out of the hands of Ruef and Schmitz.

On April 27, the War Department in Washington finally sent a telegram authorizing and assigning U. S. Army troops to San Francisco. For the first time since the earthquake, the soldiers were there officially.

With this somewhat belated order in hand, General Greely eventually agreed that the Army could control the distribution of relief to some 350,000 people who badly needed food; but he refused to be responsible for the actions of the National Guard. The National Guard marched out of the city on May 31—to nearly everyone's relief.

In the meantime, Greely decided that the tremendous waste of government funds "threatened to exhaust the Treasury and deplete the storehouse." He saw to it that this waste would not continue. Relief administration improved almost immediately, though some of General Greely's views were thought a little unorthodox. "Those who won't work shouldn't eat." If Funston seemed iron-handed, Greely was even more so; but Greely's actions were authorized.

At the end of June, he decided the time had come for the Army to relinquish its responsibilities. In his words, their "free labor" was no longer required. After all, there were many unemployed in the city, "for instance the firemen." If they were not unemployed they were certainly underemployed. They could do the Army's work in the future. With that parting barb, General Greely and his soldiers withdrew from the scene.

Shortly afterward, General Greely retired, Brigadier General Frederick Funston took over as Commander of the Pacific Division. The "war games" scheduled for the end of April had been canceled. Funston remained remote from the city, from politics, and from Washington.

Later, unable to satisfy his craving for action, he substituted travel. Funston gave up his post and his Nob Hill house; he and Eda packed their belongings and moved, first to Hawaii and then to the Philippines.

In 1914, he became Military Governor of Vera Cruz—unlike his experience in San Francisco, the appointment was official—and was promoted to Major General.

His lifelong quest for action continued to dog him. The need was partially satisfied when he took charge of the manhunt for the Mexican bandit Pancho Villa. Then, finally, Frederick Funston died —sitting in an armchair in a San Antonio hotel, waiting for dinner.

The rebuilding of the city began almost as soon as the earthquake was over. San Francisco's population was somehow able to see a possible—even promising—future.

Nevertheless, real opportunities were missed. Few cities ever found themselves demolished, with a ready-made plan for a new and grander city already drawn up, awaiting implementation, and with money pouring in to help realize the plan. San Francisco chose to ignore its Burnham Plan, and decided instead to build at a rate and manner which made the city not only less beautiful than was possible, but more dangerous. The rubble of the 1906 disaster was pushed into the Bay; buildings were built on it. Those buildings will be among the most vulnerable when the next earthquake comes.

After a long wrangle, Chinatown remained where it was. The Chinese refugees had been herded like cattle from one area to another during the days of the fire. White citizens thought their smell offensive; perhaps the Chinese thought the same of the whites. But the moment

Los Angeles offered to house them, San Francisco suddenly had a change of heart.

One plan that was immediately revived after the earthquake was the 1905 plan to hold the World's Fair in the city in 1915. A lesser city, even without the tragedy of an earthquake, might have found the plan too ambitious. But the San Francisco Exposition went ahead as planned, as if the catastrophe had been only a momentary annoyance.

Abe Ruef and Eugene Schmitz also pursued their plans as if nothing had happened. Indeed, in some ways the earthquake had been a help to them. Certainly Schmitz's standing had never been higher, his authority never stronger.

Almost before the rubble was cleared, San Franciscans were astounded to see that what appeared to be perfectly satisfactory underground railway cables were being unearthed in the process of repairing the streets. On Monday, May 21, San Francisco's Board of Supervisors passed by unanimous vote an ordinance allowing United Railroads to convert the underground cable system to an overhead trolley system. Schmitz and Ruef could look forward to receiving the remainder of the $200,000 promised to them for their part in easing the ordinance's passage.

In June, Special Prosecutor Francis J. Heney and William J. Burns—on loan from the U.S. Secret Service—became available to take part in consultations about the forthcoming graft investigations in San Francisco. Rudolph Spreckels guaranteed the $100,000 in financial backing that was needed. The earthquake had not delayed the investigation, nor had it reduced Fremont Older's determination to see it through.

The cast was assembled for the final scene of the drama.

28. *Trials and Tribulations*

On October 1, 1906, Mayor Schmitz left San Francisco for a trip to Europe with the admirable intention of persuading certain defaulting German insurance companies to pay up. He did not succeed, nor did he succeed in his ambition to dine with the Kaiser. The Kaiser, it appeared, could not find the time—even for the hero of the great San Francisco quake. Schmitz would have been better advised to follow Ruef's advice and stay at home. There, it is just conceivable that his popularity might have altered the future course of events. Certainly Ruef thought that success had gone to the Mayor's head, that the trip to Europe was a luxury Schmitz could ill afford at such a time. But not for lack of money.

Just five days after the earthquake, Ruef arranged that a small notice be pinned on the ruins of the City Hall stating that bids for the telephone franchise would be received at 3 P.M. by the Board of Supervisors. The Home Company—the company that had promised Ruef $125,000 as "attorney's fee"—was the only bidder. The Pacific States Telephone and Telegraph Company was not aware that the notice had been posted. They lost out, even though they in turn bribed eleven out of the eighteen supervisors with $5000 each to look after their interest. The same supervisors received a share of the $125,000 Ruef got as a result of the successful opposing bid.

By mid-October Burns and Heney had collected enough evidence for the San Francisco graft prosecutions to begin. The crimes unearthed fell into three main categories:

276

Police graft—money received for protection of illicit enterprises (e.g., the French Restaurants);

Franchise graft—money received for obtaining franchises or special privileges (e.g., the Home Telephone franchise, the United Railroad's overhead trolley franchise, the prize fight monopoly, in which money was paid to ensure that a certain body of promoters would receive the rights to stage lucrative boxing matches);

Rate graft—money received for procuring advantageous rates for quasi-public corporations (e.g., the gas, water, and electricity rates).

On October 24, Francis Heney took the oath of Assistant District Attorney in front of William Langdon, the District Attorney. Choosing a jury took weeks, but it was eventually sworn in on November 9. By November 15, five joint indictments on extortion charges were filed against Ruef and Schmitz. Ruef immediately surrendered himself to Sheriff O'Neal. By this time Schmitz was on his way home from his unsuccessful trip to Europe; as soon as he crossed the California state line, he was arrested.

The two men were arraigned in court on December 6, 1906. As the indictments were read out by the clerk, Ruef made clear his disdain for the proceedings by standing with his back to the judge.

Over Christmas and into the New Year, the attorneys for the two men took every opportunity to try to delay the trial; at times they even attempted to have it called off. They also insisted that Schmitz and Ruef be tried separately.

In February, Schmitz (throughout the trial he continued to act as Mayor) was allowed a leave of absence to visit President Roosevelt in Washington to discuss the continuing problem of the Japanese and Chinese schools in San Francisco. While he was away, Abe Ruef pleaded "not guilty" and on March 4, in front of Judge Hebbard, who was quite drunk, Ruef was allowed bail, whereupon he promptly disappeared. When he failed to appear in court on March 5, a search was initiated. After three days, his good friends the sheriff, the coroner, and the police had still not located his hiding place, a comfortable roadhouse, the Trocadero, some six miles from the center of the city. The court then appointed a special officer, William J. Biggy, to conduct the search. With the help of William J. Burns, Ruef was found within two hours.

Burns was also busy with other preparations. To break the deadlock that seemed likely in court—witnesses were reluctant to speak

out for fear of the repercussions on themselves and their families—
he and Heney agreed that somehow the supervisors must be made
to confess. After Burns's "persuasion," they all did confess before
the grand jury on March 18, 1907. In exchange, for turning state's
evidence and confessing to receiving money from Ruef in connection
with the Home Telephone, overhead trolley, prize fight monopoly,
and gas rates deals, they were promised complete immunity and
would not be forced to resign their offices.

The grand jury then returned sixty-five indictments against Ruef
for bribery of the supervisors. Subsequently, Ruef himself offered
to confess in return for the same terms the supervisors had received.
Heney was willing to offer only partial immunity, and negotiations
for the terms of Ruef's confession began at 2849 Fillmore Street,
where Ruef was being held—in the same house Schmitz and his
family had occupied as their family home until two years before.

Finally, according to Heney, an agreement was reached between
Ruef and his two "advisors"—Rabbi Jacob Nieto and Rabbi Bernard
M. Kaplan—and the prosecution, according to which if Ruef's testimony were of enough value, Ruef would receive leniency, and perhaps even immunity. Nevertheless, on May 8, a "contract" was
signed by Heney, Ruef, and District Attorney William H. Langdon,
stipulating that Ruef should give a "full and fair disclosure" of
"the truth, the whole truth, and nothing but the truth." In return,
he would be granted full and complete immunity, apart from indictment No. 305 in connection with the French Restuarants case.

On May 15, 1907, the court convened and anxiously awaited
Ruef's confession. Instead of confessing, he dramatically fired two
of his four attorneys. He then proceeded, with tears pouring down
his cheeks, to state that although he was "not guilty of the offense
charged" in indictment 305, in the interests of expediency he wished
to withdraw his plea of not guilty "and to enter the contrary plea."

The next day, before the Oliver grand jury (so called because of
jury foreman B. P. Oliver), Ruef began his confession, which was
to incriminate Schmitz, among others. Their long friendship was
over.

After just eight days, on June 13, 1907, Eugene Schmitz was
found guilty of extortion in the matter of the French Restaurants.
The office of Mayor was declared vacant, and one by one the super-

visors resigned. Schmitz was sent to jail to await sentence. Shortly thereafter, he was sentenced to five years at San Quentin, the maximum sentence the law allowed. He immediately appealed. While awaiting the outcome of the appeal, Schmitz was kept in a cell in the county jail, where he claimed that his six-foot-two-inch frame was not only longer than his bed, but longer than his cell. On January 9, 1908, the District Court of Appeals nullified Schmitz's conviction; two months later the State Supreme Court upheld the Court of Appeals' ruling, one of the reasons being that the original indictment had neglected to mention that Schmitz was Mayor of San Francisco. He was released on bail, pending the resolution of the outstanding bribery indictments.

Meanwhile, Ruef's trial continued, not without its full share of drama. On April 22, an attempt was made on the life of Chief Supervisor Gallagher—the man through whom Ruef had made most of his payments to the other supervisors. When his house was dynamited, Gallagher escaped with his life; the dynamiter escaped to Europe, and was never caught. The motive was not established. Gallagher continued to give evidence. A month later, three more buildings, all partly owned by Gallagher, were dynamited. Again the offender was not caught, nor the motive proved.

By this time, the jury was deadlocked six to six, and had to be discharged. A new jury was even more difficult to select than before—especially when one prospective juryman was found guilty of accepting a one-thousand-dollar bribe to vote for the acquittal of Ruef. He was promptly sentenced to four years' imprisonment. On November 6, a new jury was finally sworn in.

Just a week later, a man walked up to Assistant District Attorney Heney in the courtroom, drew a pistol, held it within inches of Heney's head, and pulled the trigger. The bullet tore through Heney's mouth and lodged in the muscles under his left ear. He survived, but it was some weeks before he could continue with the prosecution.

Heney's would-be assassin, Morris Haas, had been a prospective juror in April, but had been rejected by Heney on the ground that he was an ex-convict who had spent time in San Quentin and was therefore likely to accept a bribe. Haas had evidently harbored the grievance since then. He was immediately imprisoned.

The next day, William J. Burns tried unsuccessfully to wring a confession from Morris Haas. During the evening, a shot was heard in the jail, and Haas was found dead. Whether he had somehow concealed a pistol on his person and committed suicide or was murdered, was never established.

Burns blamed his former friend, the newly appointed Chief of Police, William J. Biggy, for Haas's death, and began to hound him. The *Call* joined in the criticism. Biggy decided to resign, but after visiting a colleague in Oakland was persuaded to remain at his post. On his return journey across the Bay, he mysteriously disappeared from his police launch; his body was found floating in the Bay a few weeks later. Whether it was an accident or suicide was of course never proved. The only other man on the launch was William Murphy, the pilot. Two years later Murphy went mad and was committed to an insane asylum, continuously muttering: "I don't know what happened."

In the midst of all the furor, the trial of Ruef continued. Finally, after the fifth ballot, on December 10, 1908, the jury returned a verdict of guilty. Abraham Ruef was given the maximum sentence for bribery—fourteen years in San Quentin.

He spent the next year in the county jail awaiting his appeal. In December 1909, he was released on bond of $600,000. Almost a year after that, in November, his conviction and sentence were upheld. On March 7, 1911, Abe Ruef at last entered San Quentin Penitentiary. Almost immediately there were petitions for his release; surprisingly, Fremont Older threw his considerable weight on the side of an early release. Older had concluded that a great part of San Francisco society was to blame, and that it was unfair that Ruef be the scapegoat.

Eugene Schmitz, who by now had been almost forgotten, was brought to trial once more early in 1912, on charges of bribery. Ruef was brought from San Quentin to testify, but he refused to give evidence unless all pending indictments against him were dismissed. It was one of the few deals of his lifetime that were unsuccessful. The judge refused.

The other key witness who could have sent Schmitz to prison— Chief Supervisor Gallagher—had disappeared without leave to Canada, and did not return. Schmitz was acquitted. Later he had the temerity to run once again for Mayor. Although he was unsuccessful, he was elected to San Francisco's Board of Supervisors for a two-year term—twice. He died, forgiven and much loved, on November 20, 1928.

Meanwhile, Abraham Ruef, in San Quentin, was writing his memoirs, and Fremont Older was preparing to publish them in the *Bulletin*. But there was a hitch. The *Bulletin* stated that no further memoirs would follow the first installment until all the indictments pending against Ruef were dismissed. In a flash, all the indictments against Ruef, as well as those against Schmitz, were waived. Ruef's memoirs were published as planned, almost daily, for months, until they petered out in the autumn of 1912, having stopped at the point where the graft investigation began. The agitation for Ruef's release continued, and on August 23, 1915, having served a little more than four and a half years of his fourteen-year sentence, he was released from San Quentin.

Abe Ruef was not allowed to return to the bar, but he still had extensive property interests to maintain. Before he went to prison he had been worth over a million dollars. Ten years after he came out, he was thought to be worth half a million dollars. When he died, on February 29, 1936, in San Francisco, he was bankrupt.

TODAY

In February 1971 more than 1,000 were injured and some 60 died in a relatively minor earthquake in Los Angeles. Hardest hit: the Veterans Hospital in Sylmar (pictured here) (*Wide World Photos*)

29. Encore

Sixty-five years after the San Francisco disaster, Edgar Gleeson, the reporter, said to us: "It doesn't require an encore. One earthquake in a generation is enough."

The probability of an encore, as Ed Gleeson knows, is great. But it is likely to be more than an encore, more even than a repeat performance—it is likely to be a totally new and much bigger production.

In 1970, 50,000 died in one earthquake in Peru—a much less densely populated region than California. Peru is on the land belt that encircles the Pacific Ocean and on which most of the world's active volcanoes are situated and most earthquakes occur. So is Japan, where in 1923 an earthquake killed 156,000. So is Los Angeles, where in February, 1971 over 1,000 were injured and some 60 died in a relatively minor quake. And so is San Francisco.

More important to San Francisco, and California, is the present state of the great San Andreas Fault—the 650-mile-long and 30-mile-deep fracture in the earth's crust.

The San Andreas Fault is on the move, not through its whole length, but along a great portion of it. The ground on the east side of the Fault is moving southward in relation to that on the coastal side, at a rate of one to two inches a year.

There are two contrasting interpretations of this movement. The more comforting one is that as the Fault moves, the strain is released slowly, instead of in one great shudder. Some believe that the 1957 and 1971 earthquakes have released the strain. They are wrong. It would take fifty thousand earthquakes of the 1957 magnitude to equal the energy output of the 1906 quake. And the 1971 quake— which did not occur on the Fault—may have *increased* the strain.

A more realistic view is that the slipping is simply an indication of the enormous pressure which is building up and which must ultimately be released in a great earthquake. Historically, the Fault has been characterized by infrequent major shocks rather than by many small ones, which lends weight to this interpretation.

There is, however, one other theory, a combination of these two, which holds the most ominous prospects. The part of the Fault nearest San Francisco, which broke in 1906, does not seem to be moving. Nor is that part nearest Los Angeles, which broke in 1856. Both of these sections, for some reason, seem to be locked. It is possible that because there is no movement in these segments, the pressure is building up for a "big one"—in *precisely these areas.*

To make matters worse, the Hayward Fault, just east of the San Andreas, is also looking dangerous. It runs across the campus and stadium of the University at Berkeley, where it is already causing damage. The San Francisco Bay Area Rapid Transit System— BART—has driven a tunnel right through this fault zone; a major earthquake can be expected to pass through the tunnel within its lifetime. The same earthquake will hit the hospital built on that part of the Fault which broke in the great earthquake of 1868.

One thing seems beyond dispute: the State of California can expect a devastating earthquake at any time. Here are some recently reported "educated guesses" from recognized authorities:

Dr. Bruce Bolt, Director of Seismology at the University of California, Berkeley: "It is highly likely in the next twenty to fifty years that there will be a major earthquake in the Bay area."

George Gates, former Deputy Director, U. S. Geological Survey: "The evidence that a strong earthquake is due in the Bay area is increasing."

Karl V. Steinbrugge, Past President, University of California Earthquake Engineering Research Center: "For planning purposes [as opposed to an outright prediction] it should be tacitly assumed that an earthquake will occur somewhere in California in the near future."

Stanley Scott, Assistant Director, Institute of Governmental Studies,

University of California, Berkeley: "We are virtually certain that this inevitability [of future big earthquakes] is measured only in months or years, or perhaps in decades if we are *very* lucky, but certainly not in centuries."

Louis C. Pakiser Jr., Chief, Office of Earthquake Research, U. S. Geological Survey: "In the next thirty years or so, it does seem reasonable to expect one that will be severe and possibly even great, comparable to the 1906 earthquake, near San Francisco. That is what I am willing to predict at the present time."

In July 1970, the California state legislature was presented with what the San Francisco *Examiner* called a "frightening report," prepared by the legislature's Joint Committee on Seismic Safety. It described the results of a hypothetical earthquake of 8.3 magnitude and forty seconds' duration: property damage would be more than thirty billion dollars, six-story buildings would collapse, water systems would be damaged, hundreds would die.

"Hypothetical," maybe, but perhaps because it erred on the conservative side. On presenting the report to the legislature, Senator Alfred E. Alquist of San Jose was quoted as saying: "We only hope that the plan and implementing action are completed before California's next great earthquake."

Insurance companies, which tend to hedge their bets, are playing it safe. Only 5 percent of the property in California that is insured against fire is also insured against earthquakes. Generally, clients are not encouraged by the companies to take out earthquake insurance, for if everyone did the companies would be forced to withdraw it from the market because of the risk of heavy losses concentrated at one time.

Lloyd's of London has reportedly attempted to reduce insurance in the San Francisco area, including policies for BART and the bridges. In 1966, after negotiating with Lloyd's, a spokesman for the East Bay Municipal Utility District was reported as saying, "We didn't get as much insurance as we wanted, but we're very happy to buy any kind of insurance at all." The spokesman for Lloyd's replied, "Some day you're going to have a big jolt and we'll have to pay. What I'm doing is playing dice with God."

San Francisco is making a major effort to prepare for the earth-quake. The public is being made aware of the danger—carefully, to avoid causing panic. Some continue to blame the fire for the 1906 disaster, ignoring the fact that without the earthquake there would have been no fire.

Still, fire is a real danger and San Francisco's Fire Chief is well aware of it. He is certainly better off today than Chief Sullivan was in 1906. He may, for instance, be able to direct operations from a helicopter. There are huge reservoirs in the hills capable of supply-ing water by gravity flow to most of the congested, high-value dis-tricts; there are 1400 hydrants; there are pumping stations built on bedrock to pump salt water from the Bay into the mains; there are more than 150 underground reinforced-concrete cisterns scattered throughout the city as an emergency supply, if all else fails. Fail it may, for the pipes carrying the water can buckle and break again—despite their improved flexible joints.

In spite of the extra precautions (most of which were completed soon after 1906, when the danger was fresh in people's minds), in 1970, San Francisco was still rated Class II because it lacked a second fireboat. In 1909, San Francisco *had* two fireboats, each capable of delivering ten thousand gallons of water a minute. But in 1954, these two fireboats were "retired from service due to pro-hibitive maintenance costs," and replaced by one fireboat with less capacity than either of its ancient predecessors.

The master plan—the Emergency Operations Plan—for fighting disaster in San Francisco was issued in 1970 by Mayor Joseph Alioto. This impressive document has attempted to prepare for every possi-bility—even to providing plastic body bags for the coroner. There are plans for mass burials to be supervised by the Engineering Divi-sion in order to avoid a repetition of 1906, when bodies had to be removed from temporary burial grounds.

The Emergency Operations Plan covers man-made and natural disasters. At the top on the list of man-made disasters is nuclear war. On the natural-disasters table, earthquake occupies first place.

In times of disaster, the Mayor will assume overall direction of the emergency organization set up in the "operations room"—the specially reinforced Youth Guidance Center in the hills four miles from the Hall of Justice. Its coordinator of operations will be the Disaster Corps Director. In 1970 he was Edward Joyce.

Joyce's relationship with the city has been unusual. During World War II, he was a pilot. In 1942, while Joyce was flying over San Francisco, the tail of his plane was sheared off by the propeller of another aircraft. He was carrying a one-hundred-pound bomb, a full load of gas, and as much ammunition as was allowed. As his aircraft spun down toward San Francisco he ordered his crew to bail out. "We finally came out of the spin at eight hundred feet . . . I made a slow turn and landed in the Bay. Now, here I am the Civil Defense Director of San Francisco—the city I almost destroyed myself. It's fate."

In 1970, the director's budget was $160,000, sixth among big American cities. It is not enough, but as Joyce says, "Today there is a great stress on the taxpayer, and the Board of Supervisors is looking for every possible opportunity to save a tax dollar."

Stretching his budget by buying federal surplus goods, Joyce— known locally as the Junk Dealer—is quite properly proud of acquiring two jeeps and a quantity of stretchers for the Police Department, a truck for the Water Department, and a tractor for pulling damaged cable cars—all at minimum cost.

Joyce is also appropriately realistic. He knows that when the earthquake comes, the loss of life could be terrible. If the quake's magnitude is near the 8.25 level of the 1906 disaster, Joyce believes there could be casualties of up to 350,000 dead and injured. He thinks the main danger area is downtown in the shopping district, where, if the earthquake occurred during a busy day, thousands would be killed by falling glass, debris, and parapets. He also believes that since "we are literally on wheels here," traffic jams could occur, effectively blocking the way out of the city, and at the same time increasing the danger of panic.

Although some believe San Francisco's famous bridges might withstand the shock, others do not. Peter Franken, Professor of Physics at the University of Michigan, is reported to have said that a major earthquake could bring down both bridges, cause the city's overpasses to collapse, and crack the airport runways. The city would be largely cut off from outside help.

Dams and reservoirs also present a hazard only recently appreciated. A failure of any one of the two hundred small dams in the Bay Area would cause loss of life and property. Joyce expects that "one or two" of the reservoirs above the city could go. If the Mount Sutro reservoir broke, millions of gallons would probably pour down into the heavily populated Sunset area. If the reservoir north of Twin Peaks went, the water might sweep down into the Mission District, risking the lives of perhaps eighty thousand people. Dams and reservoirs are being rechecked. A 1964 examination of the forty-seven-year-old San Pablo dam resulted in the expenditure of $350,000 to reinforce it against the earthquake hazard.

Mud and earth landslides and avalanches, which rarely happened in 1906, and then only in sparsely populated areas, will be a real possibility if the earthquake takes place after or during a heavy rain. Even now, during a wet winter, slides are quite common. Joyce believes that on Telegraph Hill houses could topple one against another, producing a "domino effect."

But of all the dangers, fire remains the greatest. Chinatown is built to burn, as it was in 1906. So are the older downtown hotels—especially those buildings with light wells in the middle that are open to the top, a design ideal for creating a fire draft. Water can be drawn from the Bay and fed directly into the mains, but what if the mains break? The half mile of five-inch pipe standing by for emergency use is hardly enough.

However well Joyce prepares himself and his city, he cannot be held responsible for badly constructed buildings, buildings which are firetraps, buildings built on the rubble of the 1906 earthquake.

Above all, he cannot be expected to arrange to replace or repair the schools that are considered unsafe. In 1968, an estimated two thirds of the Bay Area school districts still had one or more school buildings that were legally considered dangerous. But, as Joyce points out: "The American public today is so crisis-ridden that one more is just one more."

The possibility of being able to predict earthquakes seems good. There is a growing body of opinion that believes research funds for this purpose should be earmarked immediately. However, if qualified scientists predict an earthquake on a certain day, the result of that prediction—chaos on the roads, financial confusion, disruption of public services, not to mention the damage to California's prestige and its reputation as a holiday haven—may be worse even than the effects of the earthquake itself—especially if the earthquake does not happen.

If the prediction is not so precise but instead places the likelihood of the earthquake between two dates—say a year apart—the nerves of the population would be sorely tried if they decided to stay within the city and see what happened. If they moved out for a year, it would be the end of San Francisco as it is today.

Nevertheless, if it can be positively established that the earthquake will not occur for one hundred years—or ever—it will be worth all the effort and research money put into discovering this.

Earthquake researchers have made some other interesting discoveries. They have found, for example, that the strain building up along the Fault could be intentionally released by nuclear explosions.

In fact, earthquakes *have* been sparked off by nuclear explosions. In April 1968, the so-called Boxcar blast triggered thousands of mini-earthquakes. In December 1968, the 1.1-megaton underground nuclear explosion Benham in the Nevada test site initiated a sequence of earthquakes lasting several months. For the first two days after the "event," earthquakes were occurring at the rate of one a minute. Even forty days after the explosion, about five earthquakes were occurring each day. This led some observers to the dubious conclusion that in the future, "large explosions may be used for the safe release of tectonic strain energy."

The nagging doubt remains that instead of releasing the strain, the explosions might trigger off a big earthquake—perhaps in a most inconvenient or faraway place, like Russia. The men in the Kremlin would not be pleased if an earthquake struck their country as a result of man's meddling with nature in another. Indeed, questions are already being asked about the virtual coincidence of the recent Peruvian earthquakes with French nuclear tests.

Another recent discovery suggests an alternative to the easing of tectonic strain through controlled nuclear explosions. Waste fluids injected into rocks near Denver, Colorado, were found to have triggered off small earthquakes. Why not deliberately inject fluid into certain fault zones to produce moderate earthquakes? Conversely, why not strengthen a fault zone by withdrawing fluid, thereby delaying the possibility of an earthquake?

Large questions still remain as to whether the use of nuclear weapons or waste fluids seems a suitable answer to the earthquake problem, or whether public money should be spent on research into earthquake prediction.

It is easy to be critical; there will never be sufficient precautions. It is probably impossible, in any case, for man to thwart an act of God. But if the experience of 1906 can be taken as a guide, then when the next earthquake comes, the ordinary people of San Francisco will be the real heroes. San Francisco's civic leaders have the highest respect for their citizens. They believe that the spirit of '06 will be enough to pull them through. They may be right.

In the end, it's likely that San Franciscans, if they choose to remain in their beautiful city, will simply have to live with the threat, having prepared themselves as best they can. Citizens should make certain that their houses are built as safely as possible. If they are not—if they are not earthquake-resistant, if they are fire hazards— whatever the cost, they should be put right. The same holds true for the buildings in which they work, public buildings—and above all, the schools.

San Franciscans must be prepared to pay a great deal to enable the authorities to safeguard their city. They should continuously agitate for and take an interest in improvements. For the privilege of living in one of the loveliest, most sophisticated cities in America, its citizens must spend, for their own good, literally tens, if not hundreds, of billions of dollars.

We love San Francisco. We will return. For a visit.

APPENDIXES

Special Thanks

Individuals

Barbara Adams
Ross Adey
Stephen Agrell
William Ashton
Quintin Aune
Derek Barnard
Betty Bell
Alma K. Bine
Rene Bine
Monroe A. Bloom
Robert L. Boardman
Andrea Boggs
Bruce A. Bolt
Marge Booker
Herbert Buel
John Burlingame
Arnold Butler
Frances Chin
Sandra Choy
Dan Chu
Ronald Deutsch
H. J. Degenkolb
Jeannette Dere
Patrick A. Devine
Rodney J. Diridon
Margot Doss

Tom Earnfred
Charles Edwards
Richard Raoul Emparan
Peter A. Evans
Eddie Faulkner
Jeanine Fitschen
Julia Fogherty
Bryan Folley
G. R. Gould
Roy D. Graves
Hubert W. Gropp
Gladys Hanson
Philip E. Hiaring
Mrs. William Hilbert
Clare Giannini Hoffman
George W. Housner
John Hughes
Richard H. Jahns
Sister Mary Joanna
Benjamin Jordan
Frank Jordan
Kee June
Paul Kauffman
Doris Keebler
Andrew Keitley
Elizabeth Keitley
George Kraus
Wayne Krebsach

Frederick Kroll
Sarah Lai
Walter Landor
Louise L. Larson
L. M. Lee
James Lessley
Herbert Lieb
George Lindsay
Putnam Livermore
Samuel Logan
Dan E. London
Maggie Macdonald
Ray Margulas
C. W. Mason
Estelle Bouman Matthews
Charles McCabes
Frank E. McClure
Mary McDonald
Kevin McGettigan
Sheila L. McGough
Mary McLoud
Patricia Meredity
William J. Mitchell
B. E. Miller
William Miller
Augusta E. Moullen
Stephen Narian
Arthur Newman
Susan Nutter
William O'Brien
Jim Oliverson
Paul Olney
Edna Olney
Victor Page
Louis C. Pakiser, Jr.
Helen Park
Sister Mary Patrick
Patricia Pauley
Jonathan Pearce
Patricia Percival
Patrick Percival
Bernard Peters

Jan Petitte
William L. Petrie
David Plant
George Provoo
William G. Quinn
Jack Redenger
Wendy Regalia
Ian Revell
Hal Richardson
Millie Robbins
Frank Robertson
Peter Roebeck
Charles Rotblat
Peter Roy
Amos Rubenstein
Thomas W. Ryan
Albert George Schadel
Edward O. Scharetg
Ian Seeley
Albert Shumate
Dr. Peter Simmonds
Irene Simpson-Neasham
Dick Skuse
L. Wood M. Slee
Gary Smart
Karl V. Steinbrugge
Susie Strauss
Thomas Thomasser
Don Tocher
John Barr Tompkins
Charles Tomkinson
Virginia Trodden
Peter Upton
Napoleon P. Vallejo
Paul Verity
Murdoch Wagstaffe
Olive M. Wallace
Monseigneur Donald Walsh
Earl Wedertz
Michael Weill
Bronnie Williams
Randolph Williamson

O. R. Wilson
Paul J. Wimmer
H. K. Wong
Roger Yates
Howard Young

Oganizations, Societies, and Institutions

American Geographical Union
American National Red Cross, S.F. and Washington
American Society of Civil Engineers
Automobile Manufacturers Association, Inc.
Bancroft Library, Berkeley
Bank of America
British Consulate General, S.F.
British Embassy, Washington
California Historical Society
California Legislature Joint Committee on Seismic Safety
California State Library
Carnegie Institution of Washington
Chamber of Commerce, S.F.
Chinese American Citizens Alliance
Chinese Historical Society
Crocker-Citizens National Bank, S.F.
Department of the Army, S.F.
Fairmont Hotel, S.F.
Fire Department, S.F.
Fireman's Fund Ins., S.F.
Foreign Office, London
Garrison Troys
Hartford Insurance Group

Hoover Institution, East Asian Collection
Huntingdon Library, San Marino
Letterman General Hospital
Metropolitan Life Insurance Society
National Research Council, Washington
Oakland Public Library
Oakland Tribune
Office of the Mayor, S.F.
Office of Science and Technology
Pacific Fire Rating Bureau
Police Department, S.F.
Redwood City Public Library
St. Francis Hotel, S.F.
St. Mary's Hospital, S.F.
San Francisco Chronicle
San Francisco Examiner
San Francisco General Hospital
San Francisco Public Library
San Francisco Theological Seminary Library
San Mateo County Library
Seismological Society of America
Sheraton-Palace Hotel, S.F.
Sixth U. S. Army Library, Presidio, S.F.
Society of California Pioneers
Southern Pacific Railway
Trans World Airlines
U. S. Department of Commerce, Washington
U. S. Department of Justice, Washington
U. S. Embassy, London
U. S. Travel Service, London
U. S. Geological Survey
University of California, Berkeley
R. J. Walters & Co., S.F.
Wells Fargo History Room

Correspondents

As well as those eyewitnesses whom we were able to meet, we should also like to thank all those who communicated with us by letter.

Grace M. Aitchison
Helen James Anderson
Vivian Batman
Joseph J. Bliss
Chesley Bonestell
Bettina Bruckman
Alice Clark
Mrs. T. E. Claxton
Mrs. George Clemens
Mrs. J. S. Conrado
Sister M. Cyril
Ethel G. Daly
Miriam A. De Ford
Patrick A. Devine
Charlotte I. Eder
Colin D. Edwards
Alba W. Eldridge
Rita Feldhaus
Dorothy Forde
Viola Freitas
H. J. Friedman
Noel Gaubert
Alma S. Goodman
Gordon R. Gould
Ione C. Graff
Ralph W. Henn
Charles A. James Hoe
Edwin M. Hoss

Leonie C. Hudson
Mrs. R. Johnson
Gladys H. Larkin
Louise Larson
Adele Lewis
Mrs. G. Lowry
William A. Marcus
Herbert Mason
Jeannie Mason
Mrs. B. E. Matthews
Francis E. McClenegan
Dorothy McGinnis
Nellie C. McNickle
Mrs. George McNulty
Emma E. Milestone
Mrs. B. Miller
Augusta Moullen
Stephen Narinian
James J. O'Brien
Ralph E. Peters
Dr. T. K. Peters
Julia Scharlach
Jacob Stadtfeld
Gladys B. Stallard
Dr. Leo L. Stanley
Mrs. E. J. Vaccari
Mrs. Robert B. Weaver

Bibliography

Note: Apart from individuals and organizations, written evidence of many kinds from a multitude of sources was consulted. We believe the facts stated in this book to be correct, but time has created some differences of opinion with regard to fact, sometimes reflected in the books and other principal sources consulted that follow.

Books

Aitken, Frank, and Hilton, Edward, *A History of the Earthquake and Fire,* San Francisco, E. Hilton Co., 1906.

Andrews, Allen, *Earthquake,* London, Angus & Robertson Ltd., 1963.

Atherton, Gertrude (ed. Erskine Caldwell), *Golden Gate Country,* New York, Duell, Sloane & Pearce, 1945.

Banks, Charles E., and Read, O., *The History of the San Francisco Disaster and Mount Vesuvius Horror,* San Francisco, C. E. Thomas Co., 1906.

Barrymore, John, *Confessions of an Actor,* London, Robert Holden & Co. Ltd., 1926.

Bean, Walton, *Boss Ruef's San Francisco,* London, Cambridge University Press, 1952.

Berry, James, *The Earthquake of 1906,* privately printed, 1907.

Bicknell, Ernest P., *Pioneering with the Red Cross,* New York, the Macmillan Co., 1935.

Boardman, Mabel T., *Under the Red Cross Flag at Home and Abroad,* Philadelphia, J. B. Lippincott Co., 1915.

Bronson, William, *The Earth Shook, the Sky Burned,* New York, Doubleday, 1959.

————, *Still Flying and Nailed to the Mast,* New York, Doubleday, 1963.

Brown, Mrs. Hugh, *Lady in Boomtown,* Palo Alto, American West Publishing Co., 1968.

Bruce, J. C., *Escape from Alcatraz,* London, Hammond, Hammond & Co., 1963.

Buckingham, Clyde E., *Red Cross Disaster Relief: Its Origin and Development,* Washington, Public Affairs Press, 1956.

Burns, William J., *The Masked War,* 1913.

Caidin, Martin, *The Night Hamburg Died,* London, New English Library, 1966.

Caruso, Dorothy, *Enrico Caruso: His Life and Death,* London, J. Werner Laurie Ltd., 1946.

Chambliss, William H., *Chambliss' Diary,* New York, Chambliss & Co., 1895.

Cleland, Robert Glass, *A History of California,* New York, the Macmillan Co., 1923.

Deacon, J. Byron, *Disasters and the American Red Cross in Disaster Relief,* New York, Russell Sage Foundation, 1918.

Dickelmann, William, *San Francisco Earthquake Fire, April 18, 1906,* San Francisco, 1906.

Downey, Fairfax, *Disaster Fighters,* New York, G. P. Putnam's Sons, 1938.

Dulles, Foster R., *The American Red Cross: A History,* New York, Harper & Bros., 1950.

Farago, Ladislas, *The Broken Seal,* London, Arthur Barker Ltd., 1967.

Faulkner, Georgene, *Red Cross Stories for Children,* Chicago, Daughaday & Co., 1917.

Froude, James Anthony, *Oceana, or England and Her Colonies,* New York, Charles Scribner's Sons, 1886.

Funston, Frederick, *Memories of Two Wars,* London, Constable and Co., 1912.

Genthe, Arnold, *As I Remember,* New York, Reynal & Hitchcock.

————, and Irwin, Will, *Pictures of Old Chinatown,* New York, Moffat, Yard & Co., 1909.

Gentry, Curt, *The Last Days of the Late, Great State of California,* New York, G. P. Putnam's Sons, 1969.

Gillis, Mabel R., *California: A Guide to the Golden State,* New York, Hastings House, 1939.

Glassock, C. B., *The Big Bonanza,* Indianapolis, the Bobbs-Merrill Co., 1931.

Grant, Jesse R., *In the Days of My Father, General Grant,* New York, Harper & Bros., 1925.

Greely, Adolphus W., *Earthquake in California, April 18, 1906*, Washington, U.S. Government Printing Office, 1906.

Goodwin, John, *Alcatraz: 1868–1963*, New York, Doubleday & Co., 1963.

Hammerton, J. A., *Stevensoniana*, Edinburgh, John Grant, 1910.

Heck, Nicholas Hunter, *Earthquakes*, Princeton, N.J., Princeton University Press, 1936.

Henry, Neil (pseudonym of Marshall Everett), *Complete Story of the San Francisco Earthquake*, Chicago, the Bible House, 1906.

Hewitt, R., *From Earthquake, Fire and Flood*, New York, Charles Scribner's Sons, 1957.

Himmelwright, A. L. A., *The San Francisco Earthquake and Fire, 1906*, New York, the Roebling Construction Co., 1906.

Hittell, John S., *A History of the City of San Francisco*, San Francisco, H. L. Bancroft & Co., 1878.

Hittell, Theodore H., *History of California*, San Francisco, N. J. Stone & Co., 1898.

Hurd, Charles, *The Compact History of the American Red Cross*, New York, Hawthorn Books, Inc., 1959.

Iacopi, Robert, *Earthquake Country*, Menlo Park, Calif., Lane Books, 1964.

Irving, Robert, *Volcanoes and Earthquakes*, New York, Alfred A. Knopf, 1962.

James, Marquis and Bessie R., *Biography of a Bank*, New York, Harper & Bros., 1954.

Jordan, David Storr, *The California Earthquake of 1906*, San Francisco, A. M. Robertson, 1906.

———, *The Days of a Man*, 1922.

Kartman, B., and Brown, L., *Disaster!*, New York, Pellegrini and Cudahy, 1948.

Keeler, Charles A., *San Francisco Through Earthquake and Fire*, San Francisco, P. Elder & Co., 1906.

Kennedy, John Castillo, *The Great Earthquake and Fire, San Francisco, 1906*, New York, Wm. Morrow & Co., 1963.

Key, Pierre V. R., *Enrico Caruso: A Biography*, Boston, Little, Brown & Co., 1922.

Kraus, George, *High Road to Promontory*, Palo Alto, American West Publishing Co., 1969.

Lafler, Henry A., *How the Army Worked to Save San Francisco*, San Francisco, Calkins Newspaper Syndicate, 1906.

Langley, Henry G., *The San Francisco Director*, San Francisco, Henry G. Langley, 1906.

Lawson, Andrew, *The California Earthquake of April 18, 1906* (2 vols.), Carnegie Institution of Washington, reprinted 1969.

Leet, L. Don, *Disasters and Disaster Relief,* Vol. 309, Philadelphia, American Academy of Political and Social Science, 1957.

————, *Causes of Catastrophe,* New York, McGraw-Hill Book Co., 1948.

Leng, John, *America in 1876,* Dundee, Dundee Advertiser Office, 1877.

Lewis, Oscar, *The Big Four,* New York, Alfred A. Knopf, 1938.

Lewis, Oscar, and Hall, Carroll D., *Bonanza Inn,* New York, Alfred A. Knopf, 1939.

Linthicum, Richard, *Complete Story of the San Francisco Horror,* Chicago, Trumbull White, 1906.

Livingstone, Alexander P., *Complete Story of San Francisco's Terrible Calamity,* San Francisco, Continental Publishing House, 1907.

Lloyd, B. E., *Lights and Shades in San Francisco,* San Francisco, A. L. Bancroft & Co., 1876.

Longstreet, Stephen, *The Wilder Shore,* London, W. H. Allen & Co., 1969.

Marcus, Rebecca B., *The First Book of Volcanoes and Earthquakes,* New York, Franklin Watts Inc., 1963.

Neville, Amelia Ransome, *The Fantastic City,* Boston, Houghton Mifflin Co., 1932.

Older, Fremont, *My Own Story,* New York, the Macmillan Co., 1926.

Olivier, Daria, *The Burning of Moscow, 1812,* London, George Allen & Unwin, 1966.

Palmer, P., and Walls, J., *Chinatown, San Francisco,* Berkeley, Howell & North, 1960.

Parsons, Geneve Shaffer, *Geneve,* New York, Vantage Press Inc., 1969.

Pough, Frederick H., *All About Volcanoes and Earthquakes,* New York, Random House, 1953.

Rae, W. F., *Westward by Rail,* London, Longman's, Green and Co., 1871.

Rink, Paul, *A. P. Giannini,* Chicago, Encyclopaedia Britannica Press, 1963.

Rodriguez, Mary Louis Bine, *The Earthquake of 1906,* San Francisco, privately printed, 1951.

Searight, Frank T., *The Doomed City,* Chicago, Laird & Lee, 1906.

Sherwood, Robert Emmett, *Roosevelt and Hopkins: An Intimate History,* New York, Doubleday & Co., 1948.

Smith, A. Howden, *Commodore Vanderbilt,* London, Philip Allan & Co., 1928.

Starr, John W., Jr., *Lincoln and the Railroads,* New York, Dodd, Mead, & Co., 1927.

Steinbrugge, Karl V., *Earthquake Hazard in the San Francisco Bay Area,* Berkeley, Institute of Governmental Studies, University of California, 1968.

Stetson, James B., *San Francisco During the Eventful Days of 1906,* San Francisco, Murdock Press, 1906.

Stover, John F., *American Railroads,* University of Chicago Press, 1961.

Sutherland, Monica, *The San Francisco Disaster,* London, Barrie & Rockliffe, 1959.

Swanberg, W. A., *Citizen Hearst,* London, Longmans, 1962.

Tebbel, John, *The Life and Good Times of William Randolph Hearst,* London, Victor Gollancz Ltd., 1953.

Thomas, Lately, *A Debonair Scoundrel,* New York, Holt, Rinehart & Winston.

Todd, Frank Morton, *Eradicating Plague from San Francisco,* San Francisco, C.H.C., 1909.

Tyler, Sydney, *San Francisco's Great Disaster,* Philadelphia, P. W. Ziegler Co., 1906.

Weatherred, Edith Tozier, *San Francisco on the Night of April 18, 1906,* San Francisco, Bachrach & Co., 1906.

Wilson, James Russel, *San Francisco's Horror of Earthquake and Fire,* Philadelphia, National Publishing Co., 1906.

Yardley, Herb, *The American Black Chamber,* Indianapolis, the Bobbs-Merrill Co., 1931.

Ybarra, T. R., *Caruso,* London, the Crescent Press, 1954.

Young, John P., *San Francisco: A History,* Vol. II, Chicago, J. J. Clarke Publishing Co., 1928.

Yun, Leong Gor, *Chinatown Inside Out,* New York, Barrows Mussey, 1936.

Periodicals, Pamphlets, Reports, etc.

Reports, Letterman General Hospital, 1899–1960.

Directory, California State Board of Medical Examiners, 1900–1909.

Report, St. Mary's Hospital and the Sisters of Mercy, 1903–1949.

Report, Sisters of Mercy in San Francisco, 1904–1954.

Bulletins, San Francisco County Medical Society, 1905–1907.

Bulletins, University of California Medical School, 1905–1907.

Reports, American Waterworks Association, 1905–1907.

Report, A Plan for San Francisco by D. H. Burnham assisted by E. H. Bennett, 1905.

Report, History of Journalism in San Francisco, 1906.

Letter, by Charles Page, 1906.

Letter, by T. T. Taylor, Metropolitan Life Insurance Co., 1906.

Letter, by Joseph Prince Tracey, 1906.

Report, Surgeon-General of the Army, 1906.

Letter, by Elmer E. Enewold, 1906.

Circulars, Nos. 1–30, Headquarters Department of California, Presidio, San Francisco, 1906.

Report, by E. H. Harriman, Southern Pacific Co., 1906.

Report, U.S. Mint, 1906.

Report, Pacific Medicine Journal, 1906.

Report, by P. J. Kindelon to Chief Superintendent, Buildings, Southern Pacific, 1906.

Report, Two Days in San Francisco by Lawrence M. Klauber, 1906.

Letter, Relief Committee, San Jose, 1906.

Report, The Story of the Bulletins, Postal Telegraph Cable Co., 1906.

Report, San Francisco, Official Memorial Souvenir, April 18, 1906, the Radical Co., Los Angeles, 1906.

Records, Document No. 714 29–29 House of Representatives 59th Congress, 1st Session, 1906.

Documents, Military Secretary's Office, National Archives, Washington, 1906.

Reports, Secretary of the Navy, Washington, 1906.

Report, Chicago Relief and Aid Society, 1906.

Reports, War Records Office, National Archives, Washington, 1906.

Report, Mayor and Committee on Reconstruction: section dealing with Burnham Plan, 1906.

Report, The Water Supply of San Francisco Before, During and After the Earthquake, and the Subsequent Conflagration, 1906.

Reports, 1–12, Foreign Office, London, 1906.

Menu, Jacks Restaurant, April 17, 1906.

Report, Southern Pacific Co., June 1906.

Historical File, San Francisco Department, 1906–1907.

Proceedings, San Francisco Board of Health, 1906–1907.

Municipal Records, San Francisco City and County, 1906–1909.

Report, Journal of Commerce, San Francisco, January 4, 1907.

Report, National Library of Medicine, 1907.

Records, San Francisco Polyclinic, 1907.

Report, Sub-Committee on Statistics, San Francisco, 1907.

Report, American Red Cross, 1907–1913.

Report, San Francisco Municipal Reports. Published by order of the Board of Supervisors, Neal Publishing Co., San Francisco, 1908.

Reports, Emergency Relief Board, 1908.

Report, Bank Commissioners of California, 1908.

Proceedings, Fourteenth Annual Convention of the California Bankers Assn., 1908.

Proceedings, Thirty-fourth Annual Convention of the American Banker's Assn., 1908.

Report, Eradicating Plague from San Francisco. Report of Citizens Health Committee, San Francisco, March 31, 1909.

Report, Best's Report Upon the San Francisco's Losses and Settlements, Alfred M. Best Co., New York, 1909.

Report, Report on the Causes of Municipal Corruption in San Francisco, as Disclosed by the Investigations of the Oliver Grand Jury, and the Prosecution of Certain Persons for Bribery and Other Offences Against the State, Published by order of the Board of Supervisors, City and County of San Francisco, January 15, 1910.

Report, San Francisco Relief Survey, 1913.

Report, Financial California, 1916.

Letters, By F. L. Lane, edited by Anna W. Lane and Louise Wall, 1922.

Report, Military Hospitals in the U. S. Medical Department, U. S. Army, 1923.

Documents, Documents of American History, edited by H. S. Commager, 1934.

Report, San Francisco Cisterns, 1937.

Report, Pacific Mutual Life Insurance Co., 1944.

Paper, Alcatraz, February 1945.

Transcript, Interview with F. L. Lipman, Wells Fargo Bank, 1946.

Letter, by A. P. Giannini, 1947.

Letter, by C. Grandona, 1947.

Aide-Mémoire, by Clarence Cuneo, 1947.

Aide-Mémoire, by John F. Burns, 1948.

Reports, Crocker First National Bank, 1949.

Report, Board Lines, Fire Underwriters of the Pacific, Vol. 10, No. 1, 1951.

Document, American Trust Co., 1953.

Report, San Francisco Chamber of Commerce, Board of Fire Underwriters of the Pacific, San Francisco Commercial Club, 1959.

Report, untitled, National Library of Medicine, 1960.

Report, by Herbert D. Crall, M.D., Medical School, University of California, 1961.

Report, 1899–1960, Letterman General Hospital, Presidio, San Francisco, 1962.

Paper, A Brief History of Letterman General Hospital, 1962.

Periodical, Our Earthquake Risk—Facts and Non-Facts, by Charles F. Richter, California Institute of Technology Quarterly, January 1964.

Report, National Guardsmen Do What Needs to Be Done, by Captain D. A. Anderson, 1964.

Reports, Science Newsletter, Earthquake "Rings" Earth: Earthquake Resistant Buildings: Earthquakes from Explosions, 1964.

Report, *Saturday Review,* Research, Science and Humanity Section, May 1964.

Documents, Hartford Insurance Group, 1965.

Reports, Nos. 135–778. U. S. Government Printing Office, 1965.

Transcript, talk by J. J. Conlon, 1966.

Reports, The Metropolitan Insurance Company, September/October 1966.

Letter, By L. S. F. Kindelon, 1967.

Proceedings, Proceedings of Conference on Geologic Problems of the San Andreas Fault System, Stanford University, Publication XI, 1968.

Report, San Francisco Fire Department, Historical Review, privately printed, San Francisco, 1968.

Pamphlet, History of the San Francisco Police Department, Planning and Research Bureau, San Francisco Police Department, 1968.

Report, Public Affairs Report, Vol. 9, No. 6, University of California, Berkeley, December 1968.

Syllabus, A History of the Chinese in San Francisco, 1969.

Records, Bank of America, 1969.

Pamphlet, Toward Reducation of Losses From Earthquakes, National Academy of Sciences, Washington, D.C., 1969.

Report, Geologic Hazards and Public Problems. Conference Report May 27/28, 1969, sponsored by Region 7, Office of Emergency Preparedness, Santa Rosa, California, 1969.

Report, Earthquake Hazard in the San Francisco Bay Area, Institute of Governmental Studies, University of California, Berkeley, March 1969.

Pamphlet, Mineral Information Service, Vol. 22, No. 4, California Division of Mines and Geology, April 1969.

Pamphlet, as above, Vol. 22, No. 5, May 1969.

Periodical, Bulletin of the Seismological Society of America, Vol. 54, No. 6, December 1969.

Reports, San Francisco Police Department, 1848–1970, 1970.

Paper, Responding to and Fighting Fires with Horse Drawn Apparatus, by J. J. Conlon, Wells Fargo Bank, 1970.

Plan, Emergency Operations Plan, City and County of San Francisco, 1970.

Periodical, Effects of Local Geology on Ground Motion Near San Francisco Bay, Bulletin of the Seismological Society of America, 1970.

Report, Progress Report to the Legislature of the State of California from the Joint Committee on Seismic Safety, June 30, 1970.

Newspapers and Magazines

Harper's Weekly, Vol. 50, "The Destruction of San Francisco," 1906.
Everybody's magazine, Vol. 14, "Our San Francisco," 1906.
Harper's Weekly, Vol. 50, "San Francisco Tragic Dawn," 1906.
Pacific Monthly, Portland, Oregon, "Story of the California Disaster," 1906.
Sunset magazine, Vol. XVII, 1906.
Collier's magazine, March 30, 1906.
New York *Sun,* "The City That Was," April 1906.
Harper's Weekly, "The Human Drama of San Francisco," April 1906.
Presidio Weekly Clarion, Vol. IV, No. XLIV, April 1906.
New San Francisco magazine, Vol. 1, No. 1, May 1906.
Sunset magazine, "The Valley of the Shadow," June 1906.
Journal of the Military Institute, No. 142, "An Earthquake Chronicle," July 1906.
Sunset magazine, "The Scientific Side of It," July 1906.
Sunset magazine, "San Francisco's Plight and Prospect," July 1906.
New San Francisco magazine, Vol. 1, No. 11, July 1906.
Cosmopolitan magazine, Vol. XLI, No. 3, "How the Army Worked to Save San Francisco," July 1906.
Sunset magazine, "How the Mint Was Saved," August 1906.
Sunset magazine, "Handling a Crisis," August 1906.
Journal of the Military Institute, No. 143, "An Earthquake Chronicle," September 1906.
Harper's Weekly, "The Long Day," November 1906.
Nurses Journal of the Pacific Coast, "San Francisco Hospitals After the Earthquake and Fire," January 1907.
Daily Express, London, "San Francisco in Ruins," April 1907.
Overland Monthly, "Confessions of a Stenographer," August 1907.
Overland Monthly, No. 2, Vol. 7, August 1907.
Sunset magazine, "The Man Who Saved San Francisco," May 1928.
New York *Evening Journal,* "Where Are They Now?," April 1935.
Oakland *Tribune,* "Land of the Pioneers," November 1940.
San Francisco *News,* "In the Grip of Disaster," April 1942.
Oakland *Tribune,* "Architecture of Yesterday," August 1942.

Christian Science Monitor, "This Is the City," May 1945.

Sunday Express, London, "The City They Rebuilt in a Year," April 1946.

The Listener, London, "Country of the Golden West," June 1946.

Western Wrestling, "When San Francisco Rocked and Rolled," November 1946.

Life magazine, "San Francisco Houses," October 1949.

The Observer, London, "Meeting Place of Nations," September 1951.

San Francisco *News,* "First Editor of the News," May 1953.

London Calling, "Portrait of San Francisco," August 1955.

San Francisco *Call-Bulletin,* "Rock and Roll in San Francisco, '06 Version," October 1955.

Collier's magazine, "San Francisco," March 1956.

American Weekly, "Those of Us Who Didn't Flee," April 1956.

Saturday Evening Post, "The Wonderful World of Fisherman's Wharf," May 1956.

True Stories magazine, "The Man Who Saved San Francisco," May 1956.

Engineering and Science magazine, "The San Andreas Fault," May 1957.

San Francisco *News,* "San Franciscans Day of Travail," April 1958.

The Tatler, London, "San Francisco," April 1959.

San Francisco *Chronicle,* "San Francisco's Presidio," November 1959.

The Guardian, London, "Calculating the Risk of Earthquakes," May 1960.

Northern Whig and Belfast Post, "Thirteen Minutes Past Five in the Morning," May 1961.

Engineering and Science magazine, "Earthquakes and Mountains Around the Pacific," January 1963.

The Illustrated London News, "A Panorama of San Francisco," March 1963.

Financial Times, London, "Rebuilding San Francisco," October 1964.

Oakland *Tribune,* "The Devastating Shake of 1906 Wrecked More Than San Francisco," April 1967.

San Francisco magazine, "Caruso's Plight at the Palace," April 1967.

The Times, London, "Battle to Safeguard San Francisco Bay," September 1967.

New York *Herald Tribune,* " 'Quake Zone Shows Slippage," April 1968.

Daily Mirror, London, "Countdown to a Crack-Up," January 1969.

Sunday Times, London, "The Earthquake That San Francisco Is Sure Will Come," February 1969.

The Economist, London, "San Francisco's New Golden Coast," April 1969.

San Francisco *Examiner,* " '06 Quake: A Great City in Rubble," April 1969.

New Scientist magazine, London, " 'Quake Worries in San Francisco,"
     April 17, 1969.
Daily Telegraph, London, "The Quaking City," June 1969.
San Francisco magazine, "City's Schools on Shaky Ground," October
     1969.
Science magazine, Vol. 166, "Earthquake Prediction and Control," De-
     cember 19, 1969.
Atchison Daily, Kansas, "The Cobbles Were Burnt," April 1970.
San Francisco *Examiner and Chronicle,* "More Quakes Likely," April 19,
     1970.
San Francisco magazine, "Chinatown," June 1970.
San Francisco *Examiner,* "Grim Earthquake Forecast," July 16, 1970.

     Plus many editions of *McClure's* magazine of 1905/1906, *Collier's*
magazine of 1906/1907, and San Francisco's daily newspapers of the
times: *Bulletin, Call, Chronicle, Daily News, Evening Post, Examiner,
Globe.*

Index